W9-CNM-659

CAMBRIDGE TEXTS IN THE
HISTORY OF PHILOSOPHY

———

IMMANUEL KANT
Religion within the Boundaries of Mere Reason

CAMBRIDGE TEXTS IN THE
HISTORY OF PHILOSOPHY

Series editors
KARL AMERIKS
Professor of Philosophy at the University of Notre Dame

DESMOND M. CLARKE
Professor of Philosophy at University College Cork

The main objective of Cambridge Texts in the History of Philosophy is to expand the range, variety and quality of texts in the history of philosophy which are available in English. The series includes texts by familiar names (such as Descartes and Kant) and also by less well-known authors. Wherever possible, texts are published in complete and unabridged form, and translations are specially commissioned for the series. Each volume contains a critical introduction together with a guide to further reading and any necessary glossaries and textual apparatus. The volumes are designed for student use at undergraduate and postgraduate level and will be of interest not only to students of philosophy, but also to a wider audience of readers in the history of science, the history of theology and the history of ideas.

For a list of titles published in the series, please see end of book.

IMMANUEL KANT

Religion within the Boundaries of Mere Reason
And Other Writings

TRANSLATED AND EDITED BY
ALLEN WOOD
Yale University
GEORGE DI GIOVANNI
McGill University

WITH AN INTRODUCTION BY
ROBERT MERRIHEW ADAMS
Yale University

CAMBRIDGE
UNIVERSITY PRESS

CAMBRIDGE
UNIVERSITY PRESS

University Printing House, Cambridge CB2 8BS, United Kingdom

Cambridge University Press is part of the University of Cambridge.

It furthers the University's mission by disseminating knowledge in the pursuit of
education, learning and research at the highest international levels of excellence.

www.cambridge.org
Information on this title: www.cambridge.org/9780521599641

First published 1998
16th printing 2015

Printed in the United States of America by Sheridan Books, Inc.

A catalogue record for this publication is available from the British Library

Library of Congress Cataloguing in Publication data
Kant, Immanuel, 1724–1804.
[Selections. English. 1998]
Religion within the boundaries of mere reason and other writings /
Immanuel Kant; translated and edited by Allen Wood, George Di
Giovanni; with an introduction by Robert Merrihew Adams.
p.   cm. – (Cambridge texts in the history of philosophy)
Includes bibliographical references and index.
ISBN 0 521 59049 3 (hardback) – ISBN 0 521 59964 4 (paperback)
1. Good and evil – Early works to 1800.   2. Religion – Early works
to 1800.   3. Ethics – works to 1800.   4. Free will and
determination – Early works to 1800.   5. Reason – Early works to 1800.
I. Wood, Allen W.   II. Di Giovanni, George, 1935–   .   III. Title.
IV. Series
B2758.W66 1998
210–dc21 97–52668 CIP

ISBN 978-0-521-59964-1 Paperback

Contents

Introduction

As the title, *Religion within the Boundaries of Mere Reason*, rightly suggests, Immanuel Kant's religious thought is strongly rationalistic. In this Kant belongs to an important current of eighteenth-century thought – but with a difference. Rationalistic religious thought of the period, in Germany as in Britain, typically proposed to base religious belief on metaphysical proofs of the existence of God. Kant himself propounded and defended such a demonstration of divine existence in *The Only Possible Ground of Proof for a Demonstration of God's Existence* (1763), a work of his earlier, "precritical" period. In the *Critique of Pure Reason* (1781), however, which inaugurated the "critical" period to which all the works collected in the present volume belong, Kant criticized traditional attempts at metaphysical demonstration of the existence of God, and argued that the nature and intrinsic limits of human thought and knowledge preclude any such demonstration. Such a critique might be expected to support atheism, but that was not Kant's intent. On the contrary, he argued that any metaphysical demonstration of the *non*-existence of God is equally precluded by the limits of reason. In a famous phrase, he declared that he "had to deny *knowledge*, in order to make room for *faith*" (B xxx).[1]

The faith Kant has in mind is a purely rational faith, but it is grounded in practical (action-guiding, moral) reason rather than in theoretical reason. In Kant's view the inability of our theoretical

[1] Immanuel Kant, *Critique of Pure Reason*, translated and edited by Paul Guyer and Allen W. Wood (Cambridge: Cambridge University Press, 1998). This, Kant's "First critique," is customarily cited by pages of the first (A) and second (B) German editions of 1781 and 1787; this pagination is normally given in the margins of translations, including that in the Cambridge Edition of the Works of Immanuel Kant, which I follow.

faculties to prove the truth or falsity of religious claims leaves room for our practical reason to determine our religious stance. He welcomes this because he thinks it crucial for religion to be controlled by moral considerations.

Both in the *Critique of Pure Reason* and more fully in the *Critique of Practical Reason* (1788), Kant argues that the needs of morality demand and justify a sort of faith in the existence of God; he gives related arguments for believing in human immortality and affirming the freedom of the human will. We will touch on Kant's views on free will below; the arguments for belief in God and immortality both turn on claims that morality demands that we set ourselves certain ends, and that we therefore need, morally, to believe in the possible attainment of those ends. One such end is the perfection of our own virtue. Kant argues that we cannot reasonably hope to reach perfect virtue in any finite period of time, and that the only reasonable way in which we can seriously take perfect virtue as an end, as morality demands, is by believing in an immortality which makes possible an infinite approximation to perfect virtue. More comprehensively, Kant holds that morality demands that we take as an ultimate end the highest good that is possible in the world. The perfection of our own virtue is only a part of this highest good. Other parts, which according to Kant include the eventual happiness of moral agents in strict proportion to their virtue, are beyond our power to achieve, and also beyond anything we can reasonably expect from the ordinary course of nature. Therefore, Kant argues, we can reasonably believe the highest good possible, and seriously take it as our end, only if we believe there is a God who can and will supplement our contribution to the achievement of the highest good with whatever divine assistance may be required.

This is not the place for a thorough interpretive and critical examination of these arguments. They are developed primarily in Kant's three *Critiques*, and are largely presupposed in the writings collected in the present volume, though the latter do contain occasional passages that add substantially to the arguments.[2] What calls for more

---

[2] Notably the long note (AK 6:6ff.) in the Preface to the first edition of *Religion within the Boundaries of Mere Reason*. Kant's works, other than the *Critique of Pure Reason*, are cited here by volume and page of the German Academy edition, which are given in the margins of the Cambridge edition of Kant's works, and of the present collection.

discussion here is the metaphysical framework established by the *Critique of Pure Reason*, which conditions everything said in Kant's critical writings on religion.

Phenomena and noumena

Kant's exclusion of theology from the realm of theoretical knowledge is an example of a larger program for establishing the boundaries of reason that lies at the heart of his "critical" philosophy. The *Critique of Pure Reason* claims to establish mathematics and physical science on a sure foundation, but only at the price of restricting their scope to mere appearances (phenomena). Things as they are (or may be) in themselves (noumena) are inaccessible to our theoretical knowledge. Kant's reasons for this limitation of theoretical reason spring from a central feature of his grounding of mathematics and physics. He argues that any experience that is possible for us must be structured by certain fundamental concepts such as those of substance and cause, and by space and time as "forms of intuition" within which objects of sensation can be represented. On this basis he argues, on the one hand, that we can know that any world that we can experience must necessarily conform to certain principles of mathematics and natural philosophy, connected with these forms and concepts; and on the other hand, that since our knowledge of the experienced world is so profoundly shaped by the needs of our cognitive faculties, we cannot reasonably take it as knowledge of things as they are in themselves, but only of things as they must and do appear to us.[3] Specifically, Kant argues, rightly or wrongly, that space and time definitely do not characterize things as they are in themselves. As we shall see, this conclusion generates both resources and problems for the argument of *Religion within the Boundaries of Mere Reason*.

This sharp divide between phenomena and noumena had a major attraction for Kant in the solution it made possible to the problem of free will. One of the main principles about objects of experience that Kant claimed to prove in the *Critique of Pure Reason* is that they are all subject to a complete causal determinism. At the same time he maintained that morality requires free will in such a way that its

---

[3] This is a gross oversimplification of a famously complex argument, but I think it will do for present purposes.

commands can be addressed only to wills whose choices are not causally determined. How then can the demands of empirical knowledge be reconciled with the demands of morality? Kant's answer, in a nutshell, is that both can be satisfied if we are subject to causal determinism as phenomena (as we appear to ourselves and to each other) but free from causal determination as noumena (as we are in ourselves). We cannot be experienced (not even by ourselves) except as subject to a thoroughgoing causal determinism; but since objects of experience as such are only phenomena, it does not follow that we are causally determined as we are in ourselves. As a phenomenon the self is causally determined, but as a noumenon the self of the same person can still be the free agent that morality requires.

The theoretical part of Kant's philosophy thus leaves open at least a formal possibility that we are indeterministically free as we are in ourselves. And since morality requires such noumenal freedom, he argues, our moral, practical reason (though not our theoretical reason) warrants us in believing in it. Indeed, Kant even makes the noumenal, morally competent will an object of cognition, saying that in its acknowledgement of the moral law "our reason itself . . . cognizes [*erkennt*] itself and the being that is conscious of this law (our own person) as belonging to the pure world of the understanding."[4]

Like our free will, God is conceived by Kant as a thing in itself (a noumenon). In a way this is religiously unsurprising; one might think that a God that is merely an appearance would be no God at all. More controversial religiously is a consequence that Kant draws from the noumenal status of the deity: that we cannot experience God at all – since all our experience is necessarily structured by the forms of space and time, and hence is only of appearances. This thesis is applied to the critique of types of religious piety in *Religion within the Boundaries of Mere Reason*. Of course the controversial thesis will not follow if God can be, like human selves, a noumenon that is *also* experienced as a phenomenon.

---

[4] *Critique of Practical Reason* (AK 5:105f.) I use the translation of this work in Immanuel Kant, *Practical Philosophy*, translated and edited by Mary J. Gregor (Cambridge: Cambridge University Press, 1996).

Original sin and the good will

Religion within the Boundaries of Mere Reason (hereafter, *Religion*) is he largest of Kant's works focused mainly on religion. Its principal subject is not the nature of the moral grounds of religious belief, but, more concretely, the sort of religion that morality does and does not commend. The thematic question of religious belief, Kant once suggested, is "What may I hope?" (A 805 = B 833) As this suggests, Kant espouses a religion of aspiration, of deeply moral aspiration, and to that extent a religion of salvation. In this Kant's rational religion has obvious points of contact with Christianity; and his *Religion* is a product of intense engagement with the Protestant Christianity in which he was raised, and which was the established religion of the Prussian state of which he was a subject. The book is in part an investigation into whether there is a form of Christianity that can at the same time be a form of the rational religion demanded by morality. Kant is sharply critical of traditional theology and church practice on a number of points, but he is also quite sympathetic with some of the Christian views in which he is most interested.[5] On some points indeed he shows a depth of engagement with theological tradition that is quite uncommon in modern philosophical writing.[6]

This is particularly true of his treatment of the issues of sin and salvation from sin that are central to the whole of his *Religion* book, but especially to the first two Parts of it. His concerns and views on these issues may seem surprising to some students of Kantian ethics, but I will try to show how they are motivated (and in part, perhaps, frustrated) by a main starting point of his moral philosophy, the doctrine of the good will. I will then take up, more briefly, issues about church and revelation that dominate the third and fourth Parts of the *Religion*.

Nothing in the *Religion* is likelier to surprise than Kant's endorsement of a form of the doctrine of original sin. What could be more

[5] As the reader will see, the same cannot be said for Kant's attitude toward other historic religions (especially Judaism), which may well be found offensively dismissive. In this way Kant is less suited than other German thinkers such as Gottfried Wilhelm Leibniz (1646–1716) and Gotthold Ephraim Lessing (1729–81) to serve as a model for the use of religious rationalism to promote interreligious harmony.

[6] He grapples much more seriously with Luther's central theological concerns (and seems to understand them better) than Leibniz, for example, despite the latter's vast theological erudition and ostensibly more orthodox Lutheranism.

out of tune with Kant's emphasis on individual moral responsibility and its implication of free will? And what is there in his Enlightenment rationalism that could ground such a gloomy view of the human moral condition? Yet Kant's conception of original sin or, as he calls it, "the radical evil in human nature" is in fact well connected with his moral theory.

In traditional forms of the doctrine of original sin, human beings are said to have inherited two moral liabilities from their first ancestors, Adam and Eve. One is guilt: we are said to share in the guilt of the first sin that our ancestors committed. The other is corruption, a perversion of motivation that is itself evil and makes people likelier to do wrong deeds. Kant has no use at all for the first of these; his conception of moral responsibility cannot allow guilt to be imputed to one person for another's sin. In his version of original sin, therefore, corruption is fundamental; if guilt too is innate, it is guilt for one's own corruption and not for another person's misdeed. This is a departure, but not a radical one, from theological tradition; for in the history of the doctrine the idea of an inborn morally corrupt condition has probably been more important than that of inherited guilt.[7]

Kant departs more radically from tradition in denying that even the corruption is inherited from our ancestors, in the sense of having been caused by their sin. Nothing is to be charged against us as sin, in Kant's view, unless it is the product of our own free will (*Religion* AK 6:40–41). It follows that the biblical story of Adam and Eve cannot explain our corrupt condition; its value for Kant was merely illustrative, providing a model for understanding our own sin (*Religion* AK 6:41–43).[8] For this reason it is appropriate that in stating his own position Kant does not use the usual German term for original sin, *Erbsünde*, which means literally "hereditary sin," though he does use the Latin *peccatum originarium* (*Religion* AK 6:31), which does not imply heredity.

How then can moral evil be innate in us, as Kant is prepared to say (*Religion* AK 6:21,38,43) that it is? The only sense in which good or

[7] Cf. John Calvin, *Institutes of the Christian Religion*, edited by J. T. McNeill, translated by F. L. Battles (Philadelphia: Westminster Press, 1960), p. 251 (II,i,8).
[8] Much of subsequent Protestant theology has followed Kant's example on this point. The biblical Fall narrative is allowed only illustrative or symbolic value, for example in the twentieth century's most noted defense of the doctrine of original sin, Reinhold Niebuhr's *The Nature and Destiny of Man* (New York: Scribners, 1949), vol. 1, p. 269.

evil can be innate in us, Kant says, is "that it is posited as the ground antecedent to every use of freedom given in experience (from the earliest youth as far back as birth) and is thus represented as present in the human being at the moment of birth – not that birth itself is its cause" (*Religion* AK 6:22). Evil deeds as experienced in time proceed from immoral or amoral dispositions – from a propensity to evil, as Kant calls it. One's propensity to evil cannot have originated in any evil deed one performed in time, for all such deeds presuppose the propensity to evil.

"This propensity [to evil] must itself be considered morally evil" (*Religion* AK 6:32). But how can it be morally evil, since it did not originate in any free act in time? Kant's answer is that it originated in a free and voluntary act that was not in time. Appealing to the timeless character that he ascribes to moral freedom as a noumenon, he distinguishes two senses of the word "deed" [*Tat*]: an empirical sense in which it applies to acts in time, and a noumenal sense in which it applies to acts of a free will that transcends time. Our most fundamental ethical dispositions originate in the second sort of deed, according to Kant. Indeed "the propensity to evil is a deed in the [noumenal] meaning" (*Religion* AK 6:31).

Suppose this appeal to the difference between phenomena and noumena is successful in preserving the consistency of Kant's conception of original sin with the rest of his system. What leads him to believe that we actually have this propensity to evil, and that it is universal among human beings? *Experience* establishes this conclusion, Kant says (*Religion* AK 6:32–35). Some may find this claim of empirical grounding plausible enough without further argument, but its appeal may be also strengthened if it is viewed in relation to Kant's standard of moral goodness.

Moral aspiration is central to Kant's religion, as was noted above; it is also central to his ethics. His *Groundwork of the Metaphysics of Morals* begins with a thesis, not about the criterion of right action, but about the proper object of aspiration for a rational agent: "It is impossible to think of anything at all in the world, or indeed even beyond it, that could be considered good without limitation except a *good will*" (AK 4:393).[9] It may be thought odd that an argument so

---

[9] I quote from the translation of the *Groundwork* in Immanuel Kant, *Practical Philosophy*, translated and edited by Mary J. Gregor (Cambridge: Cambridge University Press, 1996).

resolutely anticonsequentialist in its aims and conclusions should begin with a thesis about the good rather than the right; but so it does begin. Kant's ethics is anticonsequentialist, not because there is no object of aspiration at its heart, but because its object of aspiration is not one that Kant thinks can be pursued as a goal by extrinsic means.

Kant's aspiration for the good will is in important ways religious. The religious character of the aspiration does not impress itself upon the average reader of the *Groundwork*. That is in part because the good will can sound quite ordinary, in its initial introduction, although it is in fact rather transcendent for Kant. He indicates that he is looking for something that would be good without limitation, something unqualifiedly good. Will we find empirically, in ourselves or in our neighbors, any will that is good without limitation? Kant (plausibly enough) thinks not.[10] The good will is therefore for Kant a *transcendent* object of aspiration, in the sense that it transcends any empirically available realization of it, though he does *not* think of it as transcending the human as such.

Kant's perception of evil is rooted thus in the absolute, unqualified character of the goodness he requires of a good will. This unqualified goodness is demanded of our moral disposition [*Gesinnung*] and not just of observable behavior. For Kant as for Luther a disposition incorporating and ordering ends in a morally deficient way is already sin. That is why the "propensity [to evil] must itself be considered morally evil" (*Religion* AK 6:32). Like the propensity to evil, the good will must be a noumenal deed in order to be imputed to us; it is not an empirical deed but something deeper that orients a whole life and grounds empirical deeds.

This motivational orientation is characterized by Kant in terms of the adoption of maxims, or principles of action. The human being in whom radical evil dwells is one who "has incorporated into his maxim the (occasional) deviation from" the moral law (*Religion* AK 6:32). When we think of someone as a good person, we normally make light of occasional deviations; but then we are not talking about

---

[10] I take here (as suggested, in my opinion, by the argument of the *Religion*) a more rigorous view of the requirements of a Kantian good will than some interpreters would accept. For canvassing and discussion of some of the views in this area, see Karl Ameriks, "Kant on the Good Will," in Otfried Höffe, ed., *Grundlegung zur Metaphysik der Sitten: Ein kooperativer Kommentar* (Frankfurt am Main: Vittorio Klostermann, 1989), pp. 45–65, especially pp. 56–9.

absolute, unqualified goodness. The religious character of Kant's aspiration is revealed at this point. It is one of the points at which his thought about good and evil in human nature is deeply attuned to the dynamics of the Lutheran piety in which he was reared. That was a piety in which the absolute perfection of the divine ideal brings into strong relief, by contrast, the universality, subtlety, and depth of evil in human motivation, which in turn gives rise to a powerful need for salvation.

The justification of the sinner

Kant proposes what he calls a "deduction of the idea of a *justification* of a human being who is indeed guilty but has passed into a disposition well-pleasing to God" (*Religion* AK 6:76). Philosophers are familiar with the ideas of a justification of a belief and a justification of an action, but here the reference is to "a justification of a human being." And what is meant is *not* a person's being justified in believing or doing something. That would be merely another way of speaking of justification of a belief or an action. What is meant is something much closer to the forgiveness of sins. This use of the term "justification" is familiar only in theology. In this context the question of justification is the question, how a human being can be acceptable in the eyes of a holy judge. And the question is asked about a person "who is indeed guilty."

One of the most interesting things about Kant's treatment of the subject is that he sees a problem here at all. In most purely philosophical moral systems ideas of the removal of moral guilt have little or no role to play; and some might think that questions of the removal of moral guilt arise only in theology. A theologian who believes that God is committed to punishing sin faces the question, how the sinner can escape such punishment, or how, if the punishment cannot be escaped, the sinner can nonetheless attain salvation. But how does this problem arise if one does not believe on independent grounds that God is committed to punish sin?

Kant does think of God as committed to punish sin. But that is not the ground for his belief that there is a problem here. The reverse is much closer to the truth. It is only because Kant thinks there is a problem about the removal or requiting of moral guilt, that he believes in divine punishment. Kant's central religious problem is not, "How I can escape divine punishment and be happy?", but (as he regularly puts it) "How can I be *worthy* of happiness?" And when he asks, as he does, "How can I be well-pleasing to God?" the question is explicitly one that does not lose its interest for Kant if God is not there to do anything about it. Kant is prepared to rephrase it as the question, how he can be a person that would be well-pleasing in the sight of his own pure practical reason if he knew his own heart as God knows it. He talks about the verdict of "the judge within" oneself, about which he thinks one may well be anxious (*Religion* AK 6:77).

If the problem of guilt is not motivated by prior or independent beliefs about divine punishment, many philosophers will (or should) find it hard to see a problem. This is true particularly of utilitarianism, by which I here mean the classical, hedonistic utilitarianism (German as well as British) of the eighteenth and early nineteenth centuries, which forms part of the background of Kant's ethical thought. For the utilitarian, happiness is the intrinsic good, and morality is only an instrumental good. It follows that the utilitarian should be expected to see guilt as a problem, not in its own right, but only at a technical and instrumental level – a problem in moral education, we might say. The utilitarian's problem about guilt will be how to introduce, in moral education, just such patterns of guilt feelings as will produce directly much less unhappiness than they indirectly prevent by deterring wrongdoing – or something along those lines. But in and of itself, guilt does not seem to be a problem for a utilitarian. Once a wrong deed has been done, all it leaves behind that matters to the utilitarian are the extrinsic consequences of the deed for happiness, and possibly a dangerous continuing state that caused the misdeed. The state of having done a wrong action is in itself of no importance to someone whose outlook on these matters is thoroughly utilitarian.

Kant's regarding guilt as a problem in and of itself can be seen as an aspect of his self-conscious rejection of utilitarianism. His fundamental principle that nothing can be called good without qualification except a good will is an anti-utilitarian principle. For it says that morality is not merely an instrumental good but an intrinsic good. This anti-utilitarian principle generates a problematic of guilt. For if the one thing unqualifiedly good is a good will, we cannot say that it does not matter whether one's will is or has been good. On the contrary, that must be what matters most of all about one's life. But in fact, according to Kant's account of radical evil, our wills are not and have not been as good as they ought to be; we are guilty.

In theory, at least, one alternative at this point would be simply to pass a harsh judgment on ourselves and go on to some more attractive subject. This approach is not acceptable to Kant, however. It is an article of faith for him that moral worthiness is possible for us; and he believes that in order to make steady progress in goodness, it is necessary to have a certain favorable and hopeful (though not over-confident) attitude toward oneself as a moral being (*Religion* AK 6:68).

How can such a self-affirmation be justified? Given my guilt and given the dependence of moral worth on the goodness of one's will, how can I both be serious about morality and have the affirmative attitude toward myself and my life that is necessary, as Kant agrees, for moral health? Here, without any essential reference to punishment, is a problem of guilt that seems to flow very naturally out of Kant's conception of morality and his conception of the good. Some such problem of guilt should in general be expected to arise for non-utilitarian ethical systems that ascribe a non-instrumental value to morality. Not only is the problem not accidental in Kant; it is one of the expressions of his depth as a moralist that he does see a difficulty here.

How is the problem to be solved? Kant's fullest attempt at a solution involves the idea of punishment. Although, as I have argued, Kant's having the problem is not something that arises simply, or even primarily, out of his beliefs about divine punishment, nonetheless he does state the problem in a form that involves the notion of punishment, speaking of a "debt" that we have because of our past evil (*Religion* AK 6:72), and that must be discharged through punishment. There is much that is interesting in the solution that Kant tries to develop on this basis, but at bottom it seems to me unpromising because punishment really has little relevance to the problem that most concerns Kant here, which is "How can I be well-pleasing in the eyes of the moral judge?" or as I put it, "How can I, as a morally serious person, affirm my own life?" In relation to this question it is not clear why the occurrence of punishment in my life should serve to remove the blot on my pleasingness that is constituted by the evil in me. We will have to look elsewhere to see whether Kant has a more satisfactory solution to that problem.

If he does, I think, it will be in his beliefs about conversion, about which he says,

> that a human being should become . . . *morally* good (pleasing to God) . . . – that, so long as the foundation of the maxims of the human being remains impure, cannot be effected through gradual *reform* but must rather be effected through a *revolution* in the disposition of the human being. (*Religion* AK 6:47)

Like his Lutheran forebears, however, Kant does not interpret such a conversion as implying a time after which a person lives completely free from sin; for he believes that our action is defective, morally, at each instant of time (*Religion* AK 6:67). Kant actually extends this moral imperfection, as Christian tradition generally would not, to every instant of an endless life after death (a point that is important in his argument for immortality). He speaks of "the deficiency which is in principle inseparable from the existence of a temporal being, [namely] never to able to become quite fully what he has in mind" (*Religion* AK 6:67*n*), and offers an argument, which may or may not convince, for the everlastingness of moral imperfection:

> The distance between the goodness which we ought to effect in ourselves and the evil from which we start is . . . infinite, and, so far as the deed is concerned – i.e. the conformity of the conduct of one's life to the holiness of the law – it is not attainable in any time. (*Religion* AK 6:66)

As he thus rejects any sinless period of time for us, Kant can maintain that holiness is possible for us only by accepting something like Luther's doctrine that the regenerate person is *simul justus et peccator* (at the same time righteous and a sinner).

If we are, nevertheless, to be holy in such a way as to be "well-pleasing to God," Kant suggests, this holiness must be found in a "disposition" [*Gesinnung*] which "proceeds from a holy principle adopted by the human being in his supreme maxim" by a "change of heart" [*Sinnesänderung*] (*Religion* AK 6:66). But this leads to a further difficulty: "How can this disposition count for the deed itself, when this deed is *every time* (not generally,[11] but at each instant)

---

[11] *Überhaupt*. There is no perfect translation of this word in this context, nor is it unambiguous in the German. The solution toward which Kant is working involves ascribing holiness to the moral progress of the regenerate person considered as a whole, though not at any point in time.

defective?" (*Religion* AK 6:67) The question already signals Kant's solution, which borrows from the classic Protestant idea of the justification of the sinner by *imputed righteousness*. In the view of the Reformers, faith is imputed to the believer as righteousness. That is, God graciously counts faith as righteousness. In Kant's view a disposition is *counted for* the deed; or, more comprehensively, an endless progress toward true goodness is counted as achieved goodness.

[B]ecause of the *disposition* from which it derives and which transcends the senses, we can think of the infinite progression of the good toward conformity to the law as being judged by him who scrutinizes the heart (through his pure intellectual intuition) to be a perfected whole even with respect to the deed (the life conduct). And so notwithstanding his permanent deficiency, a human being can still expect to be *generally* [*überhaupt*] well-pleasing to God, at whatever point in time his existence be cut short. (*Religion* AK 6:67)

The following is one natural way of understanding Kant's solution. Drawing on his well-known belief in a distinction between the spatio-temporal world of experience as mere "phenomena," and "noumena" or things in themselves that are timeless and nonspatial, we may suppose that a temporally endless, and thus forever incomplete, progress in goodness is the appearance, or phenomenal expression, of a holiness which at the level of things as they are in themselves can be seen by God "as a completed whole." Since it is the self as it is in itself, and not as it appears in time, that is for Kant the free moral agent and the true subject of moral responsibility and moral worth, the true self can be seen as morally acceptable on the basis of this noumenal completed holiness. Is it then Kant's solution to the problem of justification that even though the appearance (in time) of our moral life is never completely holy, the (timeless) reality of our moral life is completely holy? Does he propose to solve the problem, in other words, by denying the reality of sin and classifying it as merely an appearance?

Certainly not. If our progress, in time, towards holiness has a timeless noumenal ground in a good disposition, our morally wrong acts in time, according to Kant, have equally their timeless noumenal ground in the adoption of an evil maxim. Both of these timeless facts are facts about our moral selfhood, and we are equally responsible for both of them. It is not, therefore, Kant's view that the noumenal reality of our lives, unlike its appearance in time, may turn out to be morally spotless. Whatever the timeless "completed whole" may be by virtue of which we can hope to be morally acceptable, it is not sinlessness, but something more dynamic that incorporates a tension between good and evil.

In this connection it is significant that the temporal expression of the timeless reality on which Kant pins his hope of justification is progress. "Progress" signifies a dynamism that incorporates the imperfection from which one starts as well as the goal toward which one progresses. The timeless, noumenal correlate and ground of progress toward holiness is what Kant calls "a *revolution* in the disposition of the human being (a transition to the maxim of holiness of disposition)" (*Religion* AK 6:47). He can describe it in the vocabulary of conflict, in terms of "a good disposition which has the upper hand over the evil principle formerly dominant in" the person (*Religion* AK 6:73). These images of revolution and conflict are, of course, no less temporal than the idea of progress. They must be taken to refer to a timeless condition of the self as it is in itself, in which both a good disposition and a morally defective disposition are present, and the good disposition is stronger. The only available measure of the good disposition's triumph is that while each moment of one's temporal existence is grounded in both timeless dispositions, the extent to which one's phenomenal course of life is shaped by the good as opposed to the bad disposition increases as time goes on, and eventually approaches (though it never reaches) one hundred percent.

Here it appears that the metaphysical ascent from the phenomenal to the noumenal, from the temporal to the timeless, while it may be required by Kant's system, and does help him in dealing, for example, with original sin, is not the crucial move in his solution of the problem of justification. Both moral evil and moral good are present at both the phenomenal and the noumenal level. At both levels the question arises, how Kant can escape the conclusion that the evil spoils the good. And at either level it seems that he can do this only by setting a sufficiently high value on something that is more dynamic and dialectical than having a will that is simply good. What moral acceptability will require, at either level, is rather a will in which good prevails over evil. What does the main work in his solution is not the contrast between phenomenal and noumenal or temporal and timeless, but a shift of focus from a pure and possibly unconflicted moral goodness that would be manifested in particular acts, to a moral victory that is manifested in progress.[12]

In this shift of focus Kant has departed significantly from his insistence on a good will as the criterion of moral worth, in a way that may be difficult to reconcile with the rest of his ethics. The moral imperative, as Kant understands it, does not demand that we live each day a little better than we lived before; it demands categorically that we embrace morally correct principles and act always in accordance with them. If we are to make progress, on such a view, it could not be by making progress our aim. It could only be by striving with all our might to *be* morally perfect. So if progress is the most we can ever attain, the progress will involve a frame of mind that must judge itself a failure; and that reinstates the problem of justification. This disappointment in oneself cannot be avoided by thinking of the underlying reality of the progress as a timeless whole; for the timeless whole, as we have seen, must include an analogue and ground of the evil that is involved in the temporal progress.

Grace

The tension at this point between Kant's doctrine of the good will and his solution of the problem of justification is marked by an introduction of the concept of *grace*. Kant has an uneasy relation to this central concept of Christian theology. He fears the concept of grace for the potential he sees in it for a corrupt relaxation of the stern demands of morality (cf. *Religion* AK 6:51–52); but he thinks that moral faith may have to acknowledge a need for certain types of grace.

There is no place in the Kantian scheme of things for *prevenient grace* – that is, for divine assistance that precedes our first turning toward the good and indeed causes, or contributes causally to, that turning, without our previously having done anything to deserve it. Kant's rejection of prevenient grace is quite explicit; he says:

[12] This is not to say that the ascent to the noumenal is totally irrelevant. Kant does not suppose that an adequate moral victory of the good can be found within our empirical horizon. Where else can it be? One Kantian location for it is the indefinite future of immortality. Another is the noumenal realm. The relation between these will be discussed below.

Granted that some supernatural cooperation is also needed to his becoming good or better, whether this cooperation only consist in the diminution of obstacles or be also a positive assistance, the human being must nonetheless make himself antecedently worthy of receiving it. (*Religion* AK 6:44)

As indicated in the statement just quoted, however, Kant is open to the possibility of what Protestant theology has called *sanctifying grace*, the grace that provides divine assistance to the regenerate in becoming actually holy. Sanctifying grace, as Kant is prepared, hypothetically at least, to embrace it, is grace that will help the good principle in us to vanquish the evil principle if we have really done all that we can to accomplish that goal. He holds that we cannot know that we cannot do absolutely all that is required, but he suspects that we cannot. What we need, morally, to believe, according to Kant, is that if we do all that we can do, then God is there and will supply whatever else is needed, which would be sanctifying grace.[13]

The very idea of the divine assistance involved in sanctifying grace is problematic for Kant, however, because of his insistence that anything by virtue of which our lives are to have moral worth must be the work of our own freedom. As he puts it,

The concept of a supernatural intervention into our moral though deficient faculty, and even into our not totally purified or at least weak disposition, to satisfy our duty in full . . . is very risky and hard to reconcile with reason; for what is to be accredited to us as morally good conduct must take place not through foreign influence but only through the use of our own powers. (*Religion* AK 6:191)

Kant goes on to offer an interesting solution to this problem:

Yet its impossibility (that the two may not occur side by side) cannot be proven either, since freedom itself, though not containing anything supernatural in its concept, remains just as incomprehensible to us according to its possibility as the supernatural [something] we might want to assume as surrogate for the independent yet deficient determination of freedom. (*Religion* AK 6:191)

In other words, we do not know how anything works at the noumenal level; therefore we cannot say that both of these things cannot happen together.

---

[13] Parts of this view, in less developed form, are found in Immanuel Kant, *Lectures on Ethics*, edited by Peter Heath and J. B. Schneewind and translated by Peter Heath (Cambridge: Cambridge University Press, 1997), AK 27:317. The lecture in question was given in 1784–85.

This solution is ingenious, and seems consistent at the metaphysical level, for at that level Kant professes not to understand much about the constitution of freedom. At the level of ethical analysis, however, we may wonder whether the individualism of Kant's conception of the good will and its moral worth is significantly compromised by permitting us to share with God the productive responsibility for what is accredited to us as morally good – though of course Kant does insist that we must have done all we can by our own power if we are to receive such grace.

There remains what Protestant theology has called *justifying grace*, the grace of God that consists in God's justifying the sinner; and it is Kant's cautious embrace of justifying grace that marks the tension I mentioned in his thought about justification. On the Protestant Reformers' view, God accounts us as righteous when, strictly speaking, in our own minds and deeds, we are not yet righteous; and this justifying grace consists in God's imputing to us the righteousness of Christ. A version of this is a part of Kant's theory, though of course not in the same form in which it is found in Luther or Calvin. Kant speaks of "a righteousness which is not our own," being that of an "ideal of humankind" which we know by reason, whether or not it was manifested historically in Jesus of Nazareth, and of "an appropriation of [that ideal righteousness] for the sake of our own"; but he acknowledges that "rendering this appropriation comprehensible to us is still fraught with great difficulties" (Religion AK 6:66). Kant holds that the basis in ourselves for the righteousness that God imputes to us in accepting us as persons well-pleasing in God's sight is, so far as we can see, insufficient for the righteousness that is imputed to us. In his explanation of justifying grace, however, the righteousness that is imputed to us is that toward which *we ourselves* are *progressing*, rather than another person's fully achieved righteousness as in the doctrine of the Reformers. Kant says,

Here, then, is that surplus over the merit from good works for which we felt the need earlier, one which is imputed to us *by grace*. For what in our earthly life (and perhaps even in all future times and in all worlds) is always only in mere *becoming* (namely, our being a human being well-pleasing to God) is imputed to us as if we already possessed it here in full. And to this we indeed have no rightful claim [*Rechtsanspruch*]. (*Religion* AK 6:75)

Having said that we have no claim of right to the imputation of the needed surplus of righteousness, Kant immediately adds a qualification: we do not have such a rightful claim "according to the empirical cognition we have of ourselves." And when he goes on to say that "it is always . . . only a decree of grace," he adds that nevertheless it is "fully in accord with eternal justice (because based on a satisfaction that for us consists only in the idea of an improved disposition of which, however, God alone has cognition)" (*Religion* AK 6:75–76). The suggestion at least is there that it is only from the empirical, time-bound point of view that this appears as grace – that from the timeless point of view, God is only doing the right thing, only doing what we deserve, in counting moral progress as perfected holiness.

I have argued, however, that Kant really has no explanation of how moral progress could deserve to be counted as perfected holiness, and that the ascent to the timeless point of view does not explain this. I have also argued that Kant's fundamental concern is not what God will say about our moral worth, but whether our wills really are good; and that poses a further problem for Kant's account of justifying grace. Why should a clear-sighted Kantian care whether anybody at all *counts* a perpetual moral progress *as if* it were perfected holiness? Why should that be any moral consolation at all? What's the point of imputed righteousness for a Kantian?

For Luther the point of imputed righteousness is that it is part of a certain kind of relationship with Christ, a relationship that is for him the goal of spiritual aspiration.[14] It is a goal in which perfected holiness is found only in the divine party to the relationship, though the justified sinner cannot enter into the relationship without striving to approximate that holiness. To the extent that unqualified value is seen in such a relationship, rather than in an internal or monadic property of the self, it may indeed make sense to seek a solution to the problem of the justification of a sinner in religious conceptions of atonement. What I do not see is how such solutions can make sense on a Kantian view of the good will, which does place unqualified value only in an internal or monadic property of the self. It may be that the Kantian doctrine of the good will allows no really adequate solution of the problem of justification to which it gives rise; Kant

[14] Martin Luther, *The Freedom of a Christian*, in *Martin Luther: A Selection from His Writings*, ed. by John Dillenberger (Garden City, NY: Doubleday Anchor, 1961), pp. 6of.

himself acknowledges that the solution remains, in a sense, a mystery to him (*Religion* AK 6:143).

This-worldly and other-worldly hopes

An important current in recent Kantian thought rightly stresses the importance that this-worldly hopes, particularly political hopes, had for Kant. There is no doubt that Kant's thought offers compelling grounds to maintain, as long as we can, a hopeful attitude toward empirical goals that we morally ought to try to achieve. It is also clear, however, that Kant includes other-worldly hopes in his religious faith, particularly in his postulate of immortality. I think it can be shown that a strictly this-worldly horizon of hope is not adequate from the point of view of Kant's aspiration for a good will.

The most obvious problem with hopes strictly bound to the empirical order is that they are too easily undermined or even refuted. Hope in the moral progress of human society looks a lot less plausible to many people now than it did to Kant, partly because civilization, in our century, has provided little assurance against the most horrible immorality, and partly because growing ecological and cross-cultural awareness has left us less confident that what seems to be progress really is. In any event it is depressingly easy to conceive of scenarios that would lead from our present situation to circumstances in which the empirical world would definitely not offer a hopeful future for finite rational agents. And many individual human agents will find themselves eventually in situations in which it would be absurd to suppose that anything *they* can do has any likelihood of producing much good in the empirical order. Thus can hope be snuffed out if it is strictly limited to the empirical world.

Surely, you may object, our actual empirical situation is not that desperate, even if truly desperate situations are possible. True, we may hope, for most of *us* most of the time, but that will not satisfy Kant, who insists that moral faith must be as unshakable as the firmest knowledge. Moral hope must be unconditional, not dependent on fortune or empirical evidence. This is part of the point of Kant's strategy of "deny[ing] *knowledge* in order to make room for *faith*" (B xxx). It is a main point of his Transcendental Dialectic to establish that theoretical reason is no more able to disprove than to prove the religious doctrines required by practical reason (A 640f./ B 668f.).

Kant's reason for insisting that moral faith be unshakable is clear (A 828f./B 856f.). He held that our commitment to living a moral life must be unshakable. So if moral faith, or hope, is a necessity for living a moral life, as he claims, our need for moral faith or hope is absolute and unconditional. It cannot be limited to hopes that are liable to empirical refutation.

A committed this-worlder and naturalist who has followed the argument to this point may be moved to ask whether the possible failure of all this-worldly hopes does not show that Kant should have said (as he didn't) that we must be able to live without hope. I will press the objection in what seems to me its strongest form. According to Kant's doctrine of the good will, as I have emphasized, a good will has supreme intrinsic value, and not merely instrumental value. Mustn't moral action therefore retain its most important point and motive, as something worth doing for its own sake, even if it holds no hope at all of producing good results?

One answer Kant would probably give to this objection would appeal to the place of ends in his theory of action. That line of argument would be difficult, however, and there is a Kantian alternative more closely connected with his *Religion* book's themes of sin and salvation. Kant simply did not believe that our wills as we know them empirically are good enough, or that the virtues that are empirically possible for any of us are sufficiently inspiring, to bear the weight that is placed on them in the heroic alternative proposed by the objector.

For that reason, and contrary to the objector's assumption, Kant's moral hope is not merely outward looking. It is not designed for moral saints, secure in their own righteousness, who must rely on hope only in trusting that their actions will not be fruitless in external consequences. Rather it is designed for repentant sinners, engaged in a struggle for moral regeneration for which the empirical order promises no really adequate consummation. It is therefore not just a hope for external results, but also, and no less important, for a perfection of the agent's own inner moral life. It is, in short, a form of the aspiration for a good will. The conviction that morality demands this latter, internal hope, and that it would be unreasonable to look to the empirical order for its fulfilment, is the very heart of Kant's argument for the postulation of immortality in the *Critique of Practical Reason*. More generally, it is a powerful reason for Kant to resist a thoroughgoing restriction of moral hope to an empirical or this-worldly horizon.

There are two different ways in which Kant's aspiration for an unqualifiedly good will may be seen as transcending the empirical horizon. The more clearly indicated in his works is the way of immortality, the way of a moral progress that is infinite or endless in the sense that it continues after death throughout an infinite time. Kant repeatedly maintains that moral hope requires this, and it is such an endless progress toward holiness that he typically proposes as *counting*, in God's sight, as perfected holiness. His thought suggests an alternative, however. I have quoted a text in which he says that a person's progress toward holiness can be counted as "a perfected whole . . . at whatever point in time his existence be cut short" (*Religion* AK 6:67). In this phrasing Kant seems to envisage an existence, and hence a moral progress, that comes to an end in time but still is counted, in God's sight, as perfected holiness.[15]

This alternative hope for the perfection of a good will surely does not remain within the empirical horizon, however. It is only because it is grounded in a disposition "which transcends the senses" that the moral progress, in the text I just quoted, can be counted as "a perfected whole" (*Religion* AK 6:67). Kant is not interested in merely finding a way in which he can think of his life as if it were a morally perfected whole. Rather he is postulating the real possibility of an ultimately real ground for his life's really having the value of such a whole. He does not expect to find any such ground within the empirical horizon. If he sought it only in a timeless noumenal realm, he would be following the path of an alternative tradition of religious thought on this subject, which conceives of eternal life in terms of timelessness, rather than an endless life, in time, after death; but that would still be a hope that transcends the empirical horizon, a broadly religious hope, rooted in Kant's aspiration for an unqualifiedly good will.

[15] The conception of the end or goal of moral and religious aspiration as timeless is also discussed by Kant in *The End of All Things* (AK 8:327–28 and 333–36).

Introduction

Organized religion

Kant is sharply, in places even bitterly, critical of much organized religion, but he is not opposed to organized religion as such. On the contrary, he thinks a church, as an ethical community, is required for flourishing moral life (*Religion* AK 6:93–102). The ethical purpose of a church, for Kant, is to provide a social structure in which people instruct, encourage, and support each other in virtue, instead of providing each other with temptations to vice. Church and state are parallel but distinct institutions, equally rooted in practical principles. The state rightly *enforces* laws of *justice* or right [*Recht*], whereas the church is to inculcate *voluntary* compliance with laws of *virtue*, which cannot properly be enforced by any human institution because they extend to motivation and govern the inner life. A good will must effactually embrace the laws of virtue as well as those of justice.

Historically it is doubtless true that churches or, more broadly, religious communities have been the institutions that have most seriously and persistently focused attention on moral aspiration; or at least this has been true (and probably still is) in Western civilization. And it is plausible to claim that it is important for moral life to have an institution that does this. What may be less clear is what place this institutional role can have in the Kantian scheme of things. Kant is a fervent believer in the value and importance of moral education.[16] At the same time one may wonder how Kant can believe even in the possibility of moral education, given his moral individualism and his views about free will. Unless it is purely self-education, moral education involves one person taking another person's moral perfection as an end; certainly that sort of project is involved in Kant's conception of a church. Yet Kant himself, in his *Metaphysics of Morals*, declares that

it is a contradiction for me to make another person's *perfection* my end and consider myself under obligation to promote this. For the *perfection* of another human being, as a person, consists just in this: that he *himself* is able to set his end in accordance with his own concepts of duty; and it is self-

---

[16] See, e.g., his *Lectures on Ethics* (AK 27:471), and the "ethical doctrine of method from the doctrine of virtue" in his *Metaphysics of Morals* (AK 6:477–485).

contradictory to require that I do (make it my duty to do) something that only the other himself can do. (AK 6:386)[17]

Various interpretations may be proposed to rescue Kant at this point. Can the distinction between phenomenal and noumenal do it? It is not clear that Kant should have any objection to one person taking the empirical manifestations of virtue in another person as an end. All empirical manifestations, as phenomena, are part of a single deterministic causal nexus, according to Kant. My own physical actions, which are objects of my moral choice, are also phenomena, and as such part of this same causal nexus. Why then should they not have a causal influence, at the phenomenal level, on the phenomenal manifestations of virtue and vice in other people? And if they do or can have such an influence, will it not be morally incumbent on me to try to make it a good influence? This line of thought could provide Kant with a rationale for his views about moral education, and it would leave him free to say that we cannot coherently take it as an end to promote another person's virtue at the *noumenal* level, since we cannot know of any way to influence another person's noumenal free will. But if this is Kant's view, it is misleading, at best, for him to say as flatly as he does that one is not obligated to take another person's perfection as one's end.

Kant's ideal church would limit itself strictly to its ethical function. Much of his reasoning on this point, in the fourth Part of his *Religion*, is based on the conception of religion as *service to God*. This conception has deep roots in the discourse of Christianity, particularly in language about *worship*. Christians routinely speak of a (public) "service" of worship, where what was originally meant was certainly that the worship is a service to God. The word, "liturgy," likewise, which is often used to signify a form or instance of ordered public worship, is derived from a Greek word meaning service.

This way of talking about worship sets up Kant's critique of it. He interprets service to God as an attempt to please God. What pleases God? Kant is surely not alone in thinking that supposing that public praise of God is of itself pleasing to God comes far too close to conceiving of God on the unflattering model of human vanity. On a

---

[17] Immanuel Kant, *The Metaphysics of Morals*, translated and edited by Mary J. Gregor, with an introduction by Roger J. Sullivan (Cambridge: Cambridge University Press, 1996).

suitably exalted conception of God, Kant thinks, nothing but a morally good will is by itself pleasing to God, as nothing else is unqualifiedly good. *"Apart from a good life-conduct, anything which the human being supposes that he can do to become well-pleasing to God is mere religious delusion and counterfeit service of God"* (*Religion* AK 6:170). In a pure Kantian religion, therefore, any worship will be planned solely with a view to the inculcation and exercise of moral virtue. This is one of Kant's major disagreements with prevalent religious practices; he himself avoided attending public worship.[18]

A less restrictive view than Kant's of the proper function of worship might be based on other conceptions besides that of service. Much religious worship may be based, not just on the question, "How can we serve or please God?" but more broadly on the question, "How can we relate ourselves most fully to the divine goodness?" Praise of the divine goodness, grounded in teaching and meditation about it, may be seen, in its own right, as an important way of relating positively to the divine goodness, and thus as a supplement to moral endeavor, though certainly not an acceptable substitute for it.

Such a view of the purpose and value of worship implies that morally good life-conduct, to the extent that it is possible for us, is not enough to relate us as fully as possible to the divine goodness, perhaps because the divine goodness infinitely outstrips any value that our wills could achieve in time or eternity. Kant would disagree. In his view nothing can be better than a good will (unless it would be a good will suitably rewarded). God's will is purer and better than our wills are when viewed from any vantage point in time, but it is not of greater worth than the moral perfection that can be imputed to human wills on the basis of an infinitely continued progress in virtue. There is no infinite chasm between divine and human goodness.[19] Many theists, of course, will take issue with Kant on this point.

---

[18] Allen W. Wood, General Introduction to Immanuel Kant, *Religion and Rational Theology*, edited and translated by Allen W. Wood and George di Giovanni (Cambridge: Cambridge University Press, 1996), p. xv.

[19] Cf. Allen Wood, "Self-love, self-benevolence, and self-conceit," in S. Engstrom and J. Whiting, eds., *Aristotle, Kant, and the Stoics: Rethinking Happiness and Duty* (Cambridge: Cambridge University Press, 1996), pp. 141–61, especially pp. 148–49.

Introduction

Reason and revelation

Kantian religion is to be grounded in reason – not, to be sure, in theoretical reason, but in practical reason, as explained above. Kant allows revelation a role – but a carefully circumscribed role – in religious life. "Revelation" signifies for Kant empirical, historical sources of religious belief and practice. The essential religious doctrines that constitute for him "pure religious faith" do not depend on experience or history, but have their source a priori in pure practical reason. Kant does not think, however, that these essential rational doctrines sufficiently determine the form of a church or ethical community. Such a "union in a moral community of many human beings of equally many dispositions needs a *public* form of obligation, some ecclesiastical form that depends on experiential conditions and is intrinsically contingent and manifold, hence cannot be recognized as duty" on a priori grounds alone (*Religion* AK 6:105). Among these empirical conditions will typically be religious leadership that possesses authority that "presupposes a [historical] fact and not just a concept of pure reason" (*Religion* AK 6:158). Faith that is grounded in empirical, historical conditions and shapes a church Kant calls "ecclesiastical faith."

We can discern in Kant's *Religion* at least three conditions that a church must satisfy if it is to be a "true" church. (1) Its doctrines and practices must not contradict the principles of rational morality; it must be in that sense "within the boundaries of mere reason." (2) It must assign the pure religious faith of reason *priority* over its own historically conditioned doctrines and practices, regarding the latter merely as a means or vehicle to the fostering and social embodiment of the former (*Religion* AK 6:178–82). (3) A "true" church must enshrine "a principle for continually coming closer to pure religious faith until finally we can dispense" with historical faith as a vehicle for religion (*Religion* AK 6:115). Whether Kant believes that an ethical community that would dispense with all commitment to historically conditioned doctrines and practices is a real historical possibility, or whether he regards it rather as an ideal to be approximated in an indefinitely continued progress of religious life, is a question of interpretation that may be left here to the reader.

The relation of religion to history has been one of the dominant

xxxi

themes of nineteenth and twentieth-century religious thought, and Kant has certainly not been the last to associate the concept of revelation with the historical element in religion. Such major religious thinkers as Friedrich Schleiermacher (1768–1834) and Søren Kierkegaard (1813–55) have claimed to find a more important and fundamental role for this historical element than Kant grants it. Their claims depend in general on assigning to religion a significance in human life that is wider, or at least other, than the strictly moral value that Kant's exclusive exaltation of the morally good will allows him to assign to it.

Religious liberty and the composition of these writings

One of the themes that runs through all Kant's writings collected in this volume is his fervent advocacy of freedom of belief and expression in matters of religion. For most of his life Kant had lived under the "enlightened despotism" (1740–86) of King Frederick II ("the Great") of Prussia. It was a regime that extended to its subjects a religious liberty exceptionally generous by the standards of the time. Frederick the Great's nephew and successor, King Frederick William II, was much more conservative in these matters, however, and instituted severe pressures aimed at suppressing or silencing religious heterodoxy. Censorship was a major tool of this repression. All the works collected here were written during the reign of Frederick William II (the first of them within a few months of the death of Frederick II in 1786); and their comments on religious liberty reflect Kant's grave concern about the direction of events in Prussia. Kant's outspokenness in these writings drew on him the official displeasure of the King, who in October 1794 extracted from Kant a commitment not to speak or write publicly on religion. It was only after the death of Frederick William II in 1797 that Kant felt free to publish on the subject again.[20]

---

[20] What is said here (and in the Note on the texts) about the circumstances of composition, including the religious repression under King Frederick William II, is drawn from the general and specific introductions in Immanuel Kant, *Religion and Rational Theology*, edited and translated by Allen W. Wood and George di Giovanni (Cambridge: Cambridge University Press, 1996), to which the reader is referred for much fuller discussion of these matters. I am indebted to Karl Ameriks and Allen W. Wood for helpful comments on previous versions of this introduction, and to Kelly Sorensen, my research assistant, for much help in checking the proofs and preparing the index of the present volume.

Chronology

1787 Kant publishes the second edition of the *Critique of Pure Reason*

1788 Kant publishes the *Critique of Practical Reason*

1788 J. C. Wöllner appointed Minister of Education and Religion, issues edicts for the enforcement of religious orthodoxy in Prussia and censorship of ethical and religious books published in Berlin

1790 Kant publishes the *Critique of Judgment*

1791 Kant publishes "On the miscarriage of all philosophical trials in theodicy" in the *Berlinische Monatsschrift*

1792 Part one of Kant's *Religion within the Boundaries of Mere Reason* published in the *Berlinische Monatsschrift*

1793 Kant publishes *Religion within the Boundaries of Mere Reason* as a whole

1794 Second edition of *Religion within the Boundaries of Mere Reason*. In June Kant publishes "The end of all things" in the *Berlinische Monatsschrift*. In October Kant receives a royal letter, signed by Wöllner for the King, objecting to Kant's writings on religion and ordering him to avoid offending in this area in the future; Kant replies, affirming the innocence of his writings, but promising "as your Majesty's most loyal subject" not to speak or write publicly on religion

1796 Kant retires from university lecturing

1797 Kant publishes the *Metaphysics of Morals*. Death of King Frederick William II; Wöllner dismissed

1798 Kant publishes *The Conflict of the Faculties*, discussing the relation of theology to other disciplines, with a preface arguing that his promise not to publish on religion bound him only during the life of Frederick William II

1804 Kant dies in Königsberg

Further reading

The standard, and most complete, German edition of Kant's writings is *Kants gesammelte Schriften* (Berlin, 1900–), sponsored by the German (formerly Prussian) Academy of Sciences. The most complete set of English translations will be the Cambridge Edition of the Works of Immanuel Kant, now being produced under the general editorship of Paul Guyer and Allen W. Wood. All Kant's writings that will be mentioned here will be found in both of these series. Kant treated arguments for the existence of God, and the nature and grounds of religious faith, in *The Only Possible Ground of Proof for a Demonstration of God's Existence* (1763), and in the *Critique of Pure Reason* (1781 and 1787), the *Critique of Practical Reason* (1788), and the *Critique of Judgment* (1790). God and religious faith are also among the themes of the notes published long after Kant's death as his *Opus postumum*. Most of Kant's other writings on religion, in which he discussed not only the grounds but also the content of religious belief and practice, are contained in the volume of the Cambridge Edition on *Religion and Rational Theology*, translated and edited by Allen W. Wood and George di Giovanni (Cambridge: Cambridge University Press, 1996). This volume is the source of all the translations used in the present text; in addition it contains *The Conflict of the Faculties* (1798), Kant's brief preface to a book about his own philosophy of religion by his student Reinhold Bernhard Jachmann (1800), and Kant's *Lectures on the Philosophical Doctrine of Religion*. The lectures were given in the first few years after the 1781 publication of the first *Critique*, and are known only from student notes. They contain Kant's fullest treatment of the concept of God.

Further reading

Kant's philosophy of religion has been, until recently, one of the less studied parts of his thought, having been treated dismissively by some critics from an early date. That has changed in the last thirty years, as both Kant studies and philosophy of religion have flourished. The new era in the study of the topic, at least in English, can be dated from the publication of Allen W. Wood's comprehensive study, *Kant's Moral Religion* (Ithaca: Cornell University Press, 1970). Wood's later book, *Kant's Rational Theology* (Ithaca: Cornell University Press, 1978), focuses on Kant's treatment of the idea of God and the theistic proofs in the first *Critique* and the *Lectures on the Philosophical Doctrine of Religion*, and is a particularly important discussion of the *Lectures*. Wood is also the author of the chapter on the philosophy of religion in *The Cambridge Companion to Kant*, edited by Paul Guyer (Cambridge: Cambridge University Press, 1992). The *Companion* offers a useful introduction to the study of Kant; it is both comprehensive and up to date.

An earlier period of thought about Kant is represented by C. C. J. Webb, *Kant's Philosophy of Religion* (Oxford: Clarendon Press, 1926), and by Theodore M. Green's original (1934) introduction to the old translation of Kant's *Religion* book. A reprinting of the translation carries an additional (and important) introduction by John R. Silber, which focuses on the book's contribution to Kant's moral psychology, rather than on Kant's religious thought as such [Kant, *Religion within the Limits of Reason Alone*, translated by Theodore M. Greene and Hoyt H. Hudson (New York: Harper, 1960), containing both introductions].

The growing interest in Kant's thought about religion is attested by valuable recent papers on various aspects of it by a number of philosophers. Two collections of such papers are Philip J. Rossi and Michael Wreen, editors, *Kant's Philosophy of Religion Reconsidered* (Bloomington and Indianapolis: Indiana University Press, 1991), and *Kant über Religion*, edited by Friedo Ricken and François Marty (Stuttgart: Kohlhammer, 1992), the latter with a valuable bibliography. Philip L. Quinn has written an important series of papers, including "Original sin, radical evil, and moral identity," "Christian atonement and Kantian justification," and "Saving faith from Kant's remarkable antinomy," all in *Faith and Philosophy*, 1 (1984): 188–202, 3 (1986): 440–62, and 7 (1990): 418–33; and "In Adam's fall, we sinned all,"

Philosophical Topics 16 (1988): 89–118. Onora O'Neill, "Kant on Reason and Religion," in Grethe B. Peterson, ed., *The Tanner Lectures on Human Values*, v. 18 (1997): 267–308, provides a comprehensive and illuminating interpretation and evaluation, emphasizing the *Religion* book. Stephen Engstrom, "The concept of the highest good in Kant's moral theory," *Philosophy and Phenomenological Research*, 52 (1992): 747–80, is an important study of a concept that is central to Kant's philosophy of religion. A self-consciously Kantian but contemporary theory of religion, applied to a wide variety of the world's religious traditions, is found in Ronald M. Green, *Religious Reason: The Rational and Moral Basis of Religious Belief* (New York: Oxford University Press, 1978), and *Religion and Moral Reason: A New Method for Comparative Study* (New York: Oxford University Press, 1988).

The relation of Kant's philosophy of religion to his philosophy of history has drawn much recent discussion, notably in Michel Despland, *Kant on History and Religion* (Montreal: McGill-Queen's University Press, 1973) and in chapter 5 of Yirmiyahu Yovel, *Kant and the Philosophy of History* (Princeton: Princeton University Press, 1980). Among the shorter works included in the present volume, the "Orientation" essay is particularly emphasized in the discussion of Kant's philosophy of religion in Susan Neiman, *The Unity of Reason: Rereading Kant* (New York: Oxford University Press, 1994); and "The end of all things",, in an essay by Anthony N. Perovich, Jr., in the Rossi and Wreen collection.

The sources used by Kant in his writings on religion are extensively discussed in Josef Bohatec, *Die Religionsphilosophie Kants in der "Religion innerhalb der Grenzen der bloßen Vernunft": Mit besonderer Berücksichtigung ihrer theologisch-dogmatischen Quellen* (1938; reprinted Hildesheim: Georg Olms Verlag, 1966). A more recent account of the sources by Aloysius Winter is included in the Ricken and Marty collection; and a short account, in English, by Walter Sparn, in the Rossi and Wreen collection.

Note on the texts

"What does it mean to orient oneself in thinking?" was first published in October 1786 in the *Berlinische Monatschrift*. It was occasioned by the famous "pantheism controversy" between F. H. Jacobi and Moses Mendelssohn. Jacobi claimed that the celebrated Enlightenment thinker Gotthold Ephraim Lessing, then recently dead, had confessed to him his adherence to the pantheism of Spinoza. Lessing's friend Mendelssohn sought to defend him against what was widely regarded at the time as a scandalous accusation. Jacobi's aim in the controversy was not to support pantheism, but to oppose Enlightenment rationalism, arguing that since it led, as Lessing's case suggests, to pantheism, an acceptable religious outlook must depend on a faith that goes beyond reason. Mendelssohn was defending rationalism as well as Lessing. After Mendelssohn's death in January 1786, Kant's intervention was sought by both parties. Jacobi hoped for Kant's support; the attack on theoretical proofs of God's existence in the *Critique of Pure Reason* suggested to Jacobi an antirationalist approach to religion. Jacobi was disappointed. As the reader can see (for instance, at AK 8:134), Kant weighed in decidedly on the rationalist side, taking up and reinterpreting an idea of Mendelssohn's about the "orientation" of speculative reason through common sense.

"On the miscarriage of all philosophical trials in theodicy" was first published in September 1791, and "The end of all things" was first published in June 1794, both in the *Berlinische Monatschrift*.

Part one of *Religion within the Boundaries of Mere Reason* was published before the rest, in the *Berlinische Monatschrift* in 1792, having been approved by the censor in Berlin. The second part, however, was rejected by the censor and, on appeal, by the royal cabinet, as King Frederick William II wished to enforce a stricter religious orthodoxy in Prussia. Kant then took advantage of a law allowing universities to grant approval for the publication of academic books, and got such approval for his *Religion* book from the philosophy faculty of the University of Jena, having first obtained a decision from the theology faculty at Königsberg to the effect that it belonged to a philosophy rather than a theology faculty to pass on this book. The book as a whole was published by Nicolovius in Königsberg in 1793, with a second edition in 1794.

The English translations used here are taken from the volume of *Religion and Rational Theology*, translated and edited by Allen W. Wood and George di Giovanni (Cambridge: Cambridge University Press, 1996) in the Cambridge Edition of the Works of Immanuel Kant. "What does it mean to orient oneself in thinking" and "The end of all things" were translated by Professor Wood, and "On the miscarriage of all philosophical trials in theodicy" and *Religion within the Boundaries of Mere Reason* by Professor di Giovanni. A few emendations have been made in the present reprinting. Kant's own notes, signed by asterisks and daggers, and some of the translators' notes, signed by letters, are found at the foot of the page; the translators' other notes, including information on the sources of Kant's numerous citations and allusions, are printed as endnotes. The pagination of the now standard German edition of the German (originally the Royal Prussian) Academy of Sciences, *Kants gesammelte Schriften* (Berlin, 1900–) is given in the margins of the present text.

What does it mean to orient oneself
in thinking?

What does it mean to orient oneself in thinking?

However exalted the application of our concepts, and however far up from sensibility we may abstract them, still they will always be appended to *image* representations,[a] whose proper function[b] is to make these concepts, which are not otherwise derived from experience, serviceable for *experiential use.* For how would we procure sense and significance for our concepts if we did not underpin them with some intuition (which ultimately must always be an example from some possible experience)? If from this concrete act of the understanding we leave out the association of the image – in the first place an accidental perception through the senses – then what is left over is the pure concept of understanding, whose range is now enlarged and contains a rule for thinking in general. It is in just such a way that general logic comes about; and many *heuristic* methods of thinking perhaps lie hidden in the experiential use of our understanding and reason; if we carefully extract these methods from that experience, they could well enrich philosophy with many useful maxims even in abstract thinking.

Of this kind is the principle to which the late Mendelssohn expressly subscribed for the first time, so far as I know, in his last writings (the *Morning Hours,* pp. 164–165 and the *Letters to Lessing's Friends,* pp. 33 and 67):[1] namely, the maxim that it is necessary to orient oneself in the speculative use of reason (which Mendelssohn otherwise trusted very much in respect of the cognition of supersensible objects, even so far as claiming for it the evidence of demonstration) by means of a certain guideline which he sometimes called *common sense* or *healthy reason* (in the *Morning Hours*), and sometimes *plain[c] understanding* (*To Lessing's Friends*). Who would have thought that this admission would not only have a destructive effect on his favorable opinion of the power of *speculative* reason when used in theological matters (which was in fact unavoidable), but that even common healthy reason, given the ambiguous position in which he left the employment of this faculty in contrast to speculation, would also fall into

[a] *bildliche Vorstellungen*
[b] *Bestimmung*
[c] *schlicht*

the danger of serving as a principle of enthusiasm in the dethroning of reason? And yet this happened in the controversy between Mendelssohn and Jacobi, chiefly through the not insignificant inferences of the acute author of the *Results;** even though I do not ascribe to either of the two the intention of bringing such a destructive way of thinking into currency; rather I prefer to regard the latter's*d* undertaking as an *argumentum ad hominem,*e* which one is justified in using merely as a defensive weapon, so as to use one's opponent's vulnerabilities to his disadvantage. On the other hand, I will show that it was in fact *only* reason – not any alleged sense of truth, not any transcendent intuition under the name of faith, on which tradition and revelation can be grafted without reason's consent – which Mendelssohn affirmed, staunchly and with justified zeal; it was only that genuine pure human reason which he found necessary and recommended as a means of orientation. Yet here the high claims of reason's speculative faculty, chiefly its commanding authority (through demonstration), obviously fall away, and what is left to it, insofar as it is speculative, is only the task of purifying the common concept of reason of its contradictions, and defending it against its *own* sophistical attacks on the maxims of healthy reason. – The extended and more precisely determined concept of *orienting oneself* can be helpful to us in presenting distinctly the maxims healthy reason uses in working on its cognitions of supersensible objects.

In the proper meaning*f* of the word, to *orient* oneself means to use a given direction*g* (when we divide the horizon into four of them) in order to find the others – literally, to find the *sunrise*. Now if I see the sun in the sky and know it is now midday, then I know how to find south, west, north, and east. For this, however, I also need the feeling of a difference in my own subject, namely, the difference between my right and left hands. I call this a *feeling* because these two sides outwardly display no designatable difference*h* in intuition. If I did not have this faculty of distinguishing, without the need of any difference in the objects, between moving from left to right and right to left and moving in the opposite direction and thereby determining *a priori* a difference in the position of the objects, then in describing a circle I would not know whether west was right or left

8:135

---

* Jacobi, *Letters on the Doctrine of Spinoza.* Breslau, 1785. – Jacobi, *Against Mendelssohn's Imputations Regarding the Letters on the Doctrine of Spinoza.* Leipzig, 1786. – *The Results of the Jacobian and Mendelssohnian Philosophy Critically Investigated by a Volunteer* (ibid.).²

d i.e. Wizenmann, who in the *Results* had accused Mendelssohn, in his appeal to "healthy reason," of relying as much as Jacobi on religious faith.

e argument directed to the man

f Bedeutung

g Gegend

h keinen merklichen Unterschied

of the southernmost point of the horizon, or whether I should complete the circle by moving north and east and thus back to south. Thus even with all the objective data of the sky, I orient myself *geographically* only through a *subjective* ground of differentiation; and if all the constellations, though keeping the same shape and position relative to one another, were one day by a miracle to be reversed in their direction, so that what was east now became west, no human eye would notice the slightest alteration on the next bright starlit night, and even the astronomer – if he pays attention only to what he sees and not at the same time to what he feels – would inevitably become *disoriented*. But in fact the faculty of making distinctions through the feeling of right and left comes naturally to his aid – it is a faculty implanted by nature but made habitual through frequent practice. If only he fixes his eye on the Pole Star, he will be able not only to notice the alteration which has taken place, but in spite of it he will also be able to *orient* himself.

Now I can extend this geographical concept of the procedure of orienting oneself, and understand by it orienting oneself in any given space in general, hence orienting oneself merely *mathematically*. In the dark I orient myself in a room that is familiar to me if I can take hold of even one single object whose position I remember. But it is plain that nothing helps me here except the faculty for determining position according to a *subjective* ground of differentiation: for I do not see at all the objects[i] whose place I am to find; and if someone as a joke had moved all the objects around so that what was previously on the right was now on the left, I would be quite unable to find anything in a room whose walls were otherwise wholly identical. But I can soon orient myself through the mere feeling of a difference between my two sides, the right and left. That is just what happens if I am to walk and take the correct turns on streets otherwise familiar to me when I cannot right now distinguish any of the houses.   8:136

Finally, I can extend this concept even further, since it could be taken as consisting in the faculty of orienting myself not merely in space, i.e. mathematically, but in *thinking* in general, i.e. *logically*. By analogy, one can easily guess that it will be a concern of pure reason to guide its use when it wants to leave familiar objects (of experience) behind, extending itself beyond all the bounds of experience and finding no object [j] of intuition at all, but merely space for intuition; for then it is no longer in a position to bring its judgments under a determinate maxim according to objective grounds of cognition, but solely to bring its judgments under a determinate maxim according to a subjective ground of differentiation in the

[i] *Objecte*
[j] *Object*

determination of its own faculty of judgment.* This subjective means still remaining is nothing other than reason's feeling of its own need. One can remain safe from all error if one does not undertake to judge where one does not know what is required for a determinate judgment. Thus ignorance is in itself the cause of the limitations of our cognition, but not of the errors in it. But where it is not arbitrary^m whether or not one will judge determinately, where there is some actual *need* – and moreover one attaching to reason in itself – which makes it necessary to judge, and yet we are limited by a lack of knowledge in respect of factors which are necessary for the judgment, there it is necessary to have a maxim according to which we may pass our judgment; for reason will be satisfied. For if it has been previously made out that here there can be no intuition of objectsⁿ or anything of the kind through which we can present a suitable object to our extended concepts and hence secure a real possibility for them, then there is nothing left for us to do except first to examine the concept with which we would venture to go beyond all possible experience to see if it is free of contradiction, and then at least to bring the *relation* of the object to objects of experience under pure concepts of the understanding – through which we still do not render it sensible, but we do at least think of something

8:137   supersensible in a way which is serviceable to the experiential use of our reason. For without this caution we would be unable to make any use at all of such concepts; instead of thinking we would indulge in enthusiasm.

Yet through this, namely through the mere concept, nothing is settled in respect of the existence of this object and its actual connection with the world (the sum total of all objects of possible experience). But now there enters *the right* of reason's *need*, as a subjective ground for presupposing and assuming something which reason may not presume to know through objective grounds; and consequently for *orienting* itself in thinking, solely through reason's own need, in that immeasurable space of the supersensible, which for us is filled with dark^o night.

Many supersensible things may be thought (for objects of sense do not fill up the whole field of possibility) to which, however, reason feels no need to extend itself, much less to assume their existence. In the causes of the world, reason finds enough to keep it busy with those which are revealed by sense (or at least are of the same kind as those which reveal themselves to it), without having any necessity to make use of the influence of pure

---

* Thus to *orient* oneself in thinking in general means: when objective principles^k of reason are insufficient for holding something true, to determine the matter according to a subjective principle.^l

^k *Principien*
^l *Princip*
^m *willkürlich*
ⁿ *Objecte*
^o *dicker*

spiritual beings in nature; the assumption of these spiritual beings would rather be disadvantageous to the use of reason. For since we know nothing of the laws according to which they would operate, whereas we know – or at least we can hope to find out – a lot about the others, namely the objects of the senses, presupposing them would rather violate the use of reason. Thus that is not a need at all, but merely impertinent inquisitiveness straying into empty dreaming to investigate them – or play with such figments of the brain. It is quite otherwise with the concept of a first *original being* as a supreme intelligence and at the same time as the highest good. For not only does our reason already feel a need to take the *concept* of the unlimited as the ground of the concepts of all limited beings – hence of all other things* – ,   8:138
but this need even goes as far as the presupposition of its *existence*, without which one can provide no satisfactory ground at all for the contingency of the existence of things in the world, let alone for the purposiveness and order which is encountered everywhere in such a wondrous degree (in the small, because it is close to us, even more than in the large). Without assuming an intelligent author we cannot give any *intelligible ground* of it

---

* Since reason needs to presuppose reality as given for the possibility of all things, and considers the differences between things only as limitations arising through the negations attaching to them, it sees itself necessitated to take as a ground one single possibility, namely that of an unlimited being, to consider it as original and all others as derived. Since also the thoroughgoing possibility of every thing must be encountered within existence as a whole – or at least since this is the only way in which the principle of thoroughgoing determination makes it possible for our reason to distinguish between the possible and the actual – we find a subjective ground of necessity, i.e. a need in our reason itself to take the existence of a most real (highest) being as the ground of all possibility. Now this is how the Cartesian proof of God's existence arises, since subjective grounds for presupposing something for the use of reason (which always remains a ground only within an experiential use) is taken to be objective – hence *need is taken for insight.* Just as it is here, so it is also with all the proofs of the worthy Mendelssohn in his *Morning Hours.* They accomplish nothing by way of demonstration. But they are not for that reason by any means useless. For not to mention the fine occasion which such acute developments of the subjective conditions of the use of our reason provides for the complete cognition of this faculty of ours, of which they are lasting examples, a holding of something true on subjective grounds of the use of reason – if we lack objective ones and are nevertheless necessitated to judge – is always of great importance; only we must not give out what is in fact only a necessary *presupposition* as if it were a *free insight;* otherwise we needlessly offer the opponent with whom we are *arguing dogmatically* weaknesses which he can use to our disadvantage. Mendelssohn probably did not think about the fact that *arguing dogmatically* with pure reason in the field of the supersensible is the direct path to philosophical enthusiasm, and that only a critique of this same faculty of reasons can fundamentally remedy this ill. Of course, the discipline of the scholastic method (the Wolffian, for example, which he recommended for this reason) can actually hold back this mischief for a long time, since all concepts must be determined through definitions and all steps must be justified through principles; but that will by no means wholly get rid of it. For with what right will anyone prohibit reason – once it has, by his own admission, achieved success in this field – from going still farther in it? And where then is the boundary at which it must stop?

without falling into plain absurdities; and although we cannot *prove* the impossibility of such a purposiveness apart from an *intelligent cause* (for then we would have sufficient objective grounds for asserting it and would not need to appeal to subjective ones), given our lack of insight there yet remains a sufficient ground for *assuming* such a cause in reason's *need* to presuppose something intelligible in order to explain this given appearance, since nothing else with which reason can combine any concept provides a remedy for this need.

But one can regard the need of reason as twofold: *first* in its *theoretical*, second in its *practical* use. The first need I have just mentioned; but one sees very well that it is only conditioned, i.e. we must assume the existence of God *if* we *want to judge* about the first causes of everything contingent, chiefly in the order of ends which is actually present in the world. Far more important is the need of reason in its practical use, because it is unconditioned, and we are necessitated to presuppose the existence of God not only if we *want* to judge, but because we *have to judge*. For the pure practical use of reason consists in the precepts of moral laws. They all lead, however, to the idea of the *highest good* possible in the world insofar as it is possible only through *freedom: morality;*[p] from the other side, these precepts lead to what depends not merely on human freedom but also on *nature*, which is the greatest *happiness*, insofar as it is apportioned according to the first. Now reason *needs* to assume, for the sake of such a *dependent* highest good, a supreme intelligence as the highest *independent* good; not, of course, to derive from this assumption the binding authority of moral precepts or the incentives to observe them (for they would have no moral worth if their motive were derived from anything but the law alone, which is of itself[q] apodictically certain), but rather only in order to give objective reality to the concept of the highest good, i.e. to prevent it, along with morality, from being taken merely as a mere ideal, as it would be if that whose idea inseparably accompanies morality[r] should not exist anywhere.

Thus it is not *cognition* but a felt* *need* of reason through which Mendelssohn (without knowing it) oriented himself in speculative thinking. And since this guiding thread is not an objective principle[s] of reason, a principle of insight, but a merely subjective one (i.e. a maxim) of the only use of reason allowed by its limits – a corollary of its need – and since *by*

---

* Reason does not feel; it has insight into its lack and through the *drive for cognition* it effects the feeling of a need. It is the same way with moral feeling, which does not cause any moral law, for this arises wholly from reason; rather, it is caused or effected by moral laws, hence by reason, because the active yet free will needs determinate grounds.

[p] *Sittlichkeit*

[q] *für sich*

[r] *Moralität*

[s] *Princip*

itself alone[^i] it constitutes the whole determining ground of our judgment about the existence of the highest being, and its use as a means of orientation in attempts to speculate on this same subject is only contingent, so Mendelssohn erred here in that he nevertheless trusted speculation to the extent of letting it alone settle everything on the path of demonstration. The necessity of the first means could be established only if the insufficiency of the latter is fully admitted: an admission to which his acuteness would ultimately have brought him if he had been granted, along with a longer life, also that application of mind, found more often in youth, which permits the alteration of old, habitual ways of thinking to accord with alterations in the state of the sciences. In any case, he retains the merit of insisting that the final touchstone of the reliability of judgment is to be sought in *reason alone*, whether in the choice of its propositions it is guided by insight or mere need and the maxim of what is advantageous to reason itself. He called reason in its latter use "common human reason"; for this always has its own interest before its eyes, whereas one must have left the course of nature behind if one is to forget this interest and look around idly among concepts from an objective viewpoint, merely so as to extend one's knowledge, whether or not it is necessary.

Since, however, in the question before us the expression: *pronouncement of healthy reason* always remains ambiguous and can always be taken either – as Mendelssohn himself misunderstood it – for a judgment of *rational insight* or – as the author of the *Results* appears to take it – for a judgment from *rational inspiration*, it will be necessary to give this source of judging another name, and none is more suitable than **rational belief or faith**.[^ii] Every belief, even the historical, must of course be *rational* (for the final touchstone of truth is always reason); only a rational belief or   8:141
faith is one grounded on no data other than those contained in *pure* reason. All believing is a holding true which is subjectively sufficient, but *consciously* regarded as objectively insufficient; thus it is contrasted with *knowing*. On the other hand, when something is held true on objective though consciously insufficient grounds, and hence is merely *opinion*, this *opining* can gradually be supplemented by the same kind of grounds and finally become a *knowing*. By contrast, if the grounds of holding true are of a kind that cannot be objectively valid at all, then the belief can never become a knowing through any use of reason. Historical belief, e.g., of the death of a great man, as reported in some letters, *can become a knowing* if his burial, testament, etc. are announced by the local authorities. Hence what is held true historically based on mere testimony – e.g. that somewhere in the world there is a city of Rome – can be believed, and yet someone who has never been there can say *I know* and not merely *I believe*

[^i]: *für sich allein*
[^ii]: *Vernunftglaubens*

9

that Rome exists – these can very well be compatible. By contrast, pure *rational faith* can never be transformed into knowledge by any natural data of reason and experience, because here the ground of holding true is merely subjective, namely a necessary need of reason (and as long as we are human beings it will always remain a need) to *presuppose* the existence of a highest being, but not to demonstrate it. A need of reason to be used in a way which satisfies it *theoretically* would be nothing other than a pure *rational hypothesis*, i.e. an opinion sufficient to hold something true on subjective grounds simply because one can never expect to find grounds other than these on which to *explain certain given effects*, and because reason needs a ground of explanation. By contrast, *rational faith*, which rests on a need of reason's use with a *practical* intent, could be called a *postulate* of reason – not as if it were an insight which did justice to all the logical demands for certainty, but because this holding true (if only the person is morally good) is not inferior* in degree to knowing, even though it is completely different from it in kind.

8:142

A pure rational faith is therefore the signpost or compass by means of which the speculative thinker orients himself in his rational excursions into the field of supersensible objects; but a human being who has common but (morally) healthy reason can mark out his path, in both a theoretical and a practical respect, in a way which is fully in accord with the whole end of his vocation; and it is this rational faith which must also be taken as the ground of every other faith, and even of every revelation.

The *concept* of God and even the conviction of his *existence* can be met with only in reason, and it cannot first come to us either through inspiration or through tidings communicated to us, however great the authority behind them. If I come across an immediate intuition of such a kind that nature, as I am acquainted with it, could not provide that intuition, then a concept of God must serve to gauge whether this appearance agrees with all the characteristics required for a Deity. Now even if I have no insight at all into how it is possible for any appearance to present, even as to quality, what can only be thought but never intuited, this much is still clear: that in order to judge whether what appears to me, what works internally or externally on my feelings, is God, I would have to hold it up to my rational concept of God and test it accordingly – not as to whether it is adequate to that concept, but merely whether it does not contradict it. In just the same way, even if nothing in what he discovered to me immediately contra-

---

* To the *firmness* of belief belongs the consciousness of its *unalterability*. Now I can be wholly certain that no one can ever refute the proposition *There is a God;* for where will he get this insight? Thus it is not the same with rational faith as with historical belief – where it is always possible that proofs of the contrary might be found out and where one must always harbor the reservation that one might alter one's opinion if our information about the matter should be extended.

dicted that concept, nevertheless this appearance, intuition, immediate revelation, or whatever else one wants to call such a presentation, never proves the existence of a being whose concept (if it is not to be vaguely^v determined and hence might be subject to association with every possible delusion) demands that it be of *infinite* magnitude as distinguished from everything created; but no experience or intuition at all can be adequate to that concept, hence none can unambiguously prove the existence of such a being. Thus no one can *first* be convinced of the existence of a highest being through any intuition; rational faith must come first, and then certain appearances or disclosures could at most provide the occasion for investigating whether we are warranted in taking what speaks or presents itself to us to be a Deity, and thus serve to confirm that faith according to these findings.

8:143

Thus if it is disputed that reason deserves the right to speak *first* in matters concerning supersensible objects such as the existence of God and the future world, then a wide gate is opened to all enthusiasm, superstition and even to atheism. And yet in the controversy between Jacobi and Mendelssohn, everything appears to overturn reason in just this way; I do not know whether it is directed only against *rational insight* and knowledge (through the supposed strength of speculation) or also against *rational faith*, so as to set up in opposition to it another faith which everyone can make up for himself as he likes. One would almost infer the latter intention when it is proposed that the Spinozist concept of God is the only one in agreement* with all the principles of reason and is never-

8:144

---

* It is hard to comprehend how the scholars just mentioned could find support for Spinozism in the *Critique of Pure Reason*.³ The *Critique* completely clips dogmatism's wings in respect of the cognition of supersensible objects, and Spinozism is so dogmatic in this respect that it even competes with the mathematicians in respect of the strictness of its proofs. The *Critique* proves that the table of the pure concepts of the understanding has to contain all the material for pure thinking; Spinozism speaks of thoughts which themselves think, and thus of an accident that simultaneously exists for itself as a subject:⁴ a concept that is not to be found in the human understanding and moreover cannot be brought into it. The *Critique* shows it does not suffice for the possibility even of a thought-entity that there is nothing self-contradictory in its concept (even though of course it then remains allowable, if necessary, to assume its possibility); but Spinozism alleges that it has insight into the impossibility of a being the idea of which consists solely of pure concepts of the understanding, which has been separated from all the conditions of sensibility, and in which a contradiction can never be met with;⁵ and yet it has nothing at all by means of which to support this presumption, which transgresses all boundaries. It is just for this reason that Spinozism leads directly to enthusiasm. By contrast, there is not a single means more certain to eliminate enthusiasm from the roots up than that determination of the bounds of the pure faculty of understanding. – Likewise another scholar⁶ finds *skepticism* in the *Critique*, even though precisely the starting point of the *Critique* is firmly to posit something certain and determinate in respect of the range of our cognition *a priori*. Similarly [he finds] a *dialectic* in the critical investigations, whereas the aim is to resolve and forever eliminate the unavoid-
^{v} *unsicher*

11

theless to be rejected.[8] For although it is wholly compatible with rational faith to concede that speculative reason itself is never in a position to have insight into the *possibility* of the being we must think of as God, it can't be reconciled with any faith, or with the holding true of any existence at all, to say that we could see clearly*ʷ* the *impossibility* of an object and nevertheless could have cognition of its actuality through other sources.

Men of intellectual ability and broadminded disposition! I honor your talents and love your feeling for humanity. But have you thought about what you are doing, and where your attacks on reason will lead? Without doubt you want to preserve inviolate the *freedom to think;* for without that even your own free flights of genius would soon come to an end. Let us see what would naturally become of this freedom of thought if a procedure such as you are adopting should get the upper hand.

The freedom to think is opposed **first** of all to *civil compulsion.* Of course it is said that the freedom to *speak* or to *write* could be taken from us by a superior power, but the freedom to *think* cannot be. Yet how much and how correctly would we *think* if we did not think as it were in community with others to whom we *communicate* our thoughts, and who communicate theirs with us! Thus one can very well say that this external power which wrenches away people's freedom publicly to *communicate* their thoughts also takes from them the freedom to *think* – that single gem remaining to us in the midst of all the burdens of civil life, through which alone we can devise means of overcoming all the evils of our condition.

8:145 **Second,** freedom to think is also taken in a sense*ˣ* in which it is opposed to *compulsion over conscience;* even without having external power some citizens set themselves up as having the custody of others in religious affairs, and instead of arguing they know how to ban every examination of reason by their early influence on people's minds, through prescribed formulas of belief accompanied by the anxious fear of *the dangers of one's own investigation.*

Third, freedom in thinking signifies the subjection of reason to no laws except *those which it gives itself;* and its opposite is the maxim of a **lawless use** of reason (in order, as genius supposes, to see further than one can under the limitation of laws). The natural consequence is that if reason will not subject itself to the laws it gives itself, it has to bow under the yoke of laws given by another; for without any law, nothing – not even nonsense – can play its game for long. Thus the unavoidable consequence

able dialectic in which pure reason becomes involved and entangled when it is employed dogmatically everywhere. The Neoplatonists, who called themselves "eclectics" because they knew how to find their own conceits all over the place in other authors – if they had previously put them in there – proceeded in just this way; hence nothing new happens under the sun.[7]

ʷ einsehen

ˣ Bedeutung

of *declared* lawlessness in thinking (of a liberation from the limitations of reason) is that the freedom to think will ultimately be forfeited and – because it is not misfortune but arrogance which is to blame for it – will be *trifled away*[y] in the proper sense of the word.

The course of things is roughly this. First *genius* is very pleased with its bold flights, since it has cast off the thread by which reason used to steer it. Soon it enchants others with its triumphant pronouncements and great expectations and now seems to have set itself on a throne which was so badly graced by slow and ponderous reason, whose language, however, it always employs. Then its maxim is that reason's superior lawgiving is invalid – we common human beings call this **enthusiasm**, while those favored by beneficent nature call its *illumination*. Since reason alone can command validly for everyone, a confusion of language must soon arise among them; each one now follows his own inspiration, and so inner inspirations must ultimately be seen to arise from the testimony of preserved facts, traditions which were chosen originally but with time become *intrusive* documents – in a word, what results is the complete subjection of reason to facts, i.e. **superstition,** because this at least has the *form of law* and so allows tranquility to be restored.

Because, however, human reason always strives for freedom, when it first breaks its fetters the first use it makes of its long unaccustomed freedom has to degenerate into a misuse and a presumptuous trust in the independence of its faculties from all limitations, leading to a persuasion of the sole authority of speculative reason which assumes nothing except what it can justify by *objective* grounds and dogmatic conviction; everything else it boldly repudiates. Now the maxim of reason's independence of its *own need* (of doing without rational faith) is **unbelief.** This is not a historical unbelief, for it is impossible to think of the latter as purposeful, hence it cannot be anything imputable (for everyone must believe a fact if it is sufficiently attested, just as he must believe a mathematical demonstration, whether he wants to or not). It is rather an *unbelief of reason,*[z] a precarious[a] state of the human mind, which first takes from moral laws all their force as incentives to the heart, and over time all their authority, and occasions the way of thinking one calls **libertinism,**[b] i.e. **the principle of recognizing no duty at all.** At this point the authorities get mixed up in the game, so that even civil arrangements may not fall into the greatest disorder; and since they regard the most efficient and emphatic means as the best, this does away with even the freedom to think, and subjects thinking,

8:146

---

[y] *verscherzt. Sich etwas verscherzen,* derived from *Scherz* = joke, means frivolously to lose or forfeit something.
[z] *Vernunftunglaube*
[a] *misslich*
[b] *Freigeisterei*

13

like other trades, to the country's rules and regulations. And so freedom in thinking finally destroys itself if it tries to proceed in independence of the laws of reason.

Friends of the human race and of what is holiest to it! Accept^c what appears to you most worthy of belief after careful and sincere examination, whether of facts or rational grounds; only do not dispute that prerogative of reason which makes it the highest good on earth, the prerogative of being the final touchstone of truth.* Failing here, you will become unworthy of this freedom, and you will surely forfeit it too; and besides that you will bring the same misfortune down on the heads of other, innocent parties who would otherwise have been well disposed and would have used their freedom *lawfully* and hence in a way which is conducive^d to what is best for the world!

---

* *Thinking for oneself* means seeking the supreme touchstone of truth in oneself (i.e. in one's own reason); and the maxim of always thinking for oneself is **enlightenment**. Now there is less to this than people imagine when they place enlightenment in the acquisition of *information;* for it is rather a negative principle in the use of one's faculty of cognition, and often he who is richest in information is the least enlightened in the use he makes of it. To make use of one's own reason means no more than to ask oneself, whenever one is supposed to assume something, whether one could find it feasible to make the ground or the rule on which one assumes it into a universal principle for the use of reason. This test is one that everyone can apply to himself; and with this examination he will see superstition and enthusiasm disappear, even if he falls far short of having the information to refute them on objective grounds. For he is using merely the maxim of reason's *self-preservation.* Thus it is quite easy to ground enlightenment in *individual subjects* through their education; one must only begin early to accustom young minds to this reflection. But to enlighten an *age* is very slow and arduous; for there are external obstacles which in part forbid this manner of education and in part make it more difficult.
^c *Nehme . . . an*
^d *zweckmässig*

On the miscarriage of all philosophical trials
in theodicy

On the miscarriage of all philosophical trials[a] in theodicy

By "theodicy" we understand the defense of the highest wisdom of the creator against the charge which reason brings against it for whatever is counterpurposive[b] in the world. – We call this "the defending of God's cause," even though the cause might be at bottom no more than that of our presumptuous reason failing to recognize its limitations. This is indeed not the best of causes, yet one that can be condoned insofar as (aside from that self-conceit) the human being is justified, as rational, in testing all claims, all doctrines which impose respect upon him, before he submits himself to them, so that this respect may be sincere and not feigned.

Now for this vindication it is required that the would-be advocate of God prove *either* that whatever in the world we judge counterpurposive[c] is not so; *or*, if there is any such thing, that it must be judged not at all as an intended effect[d] but as the unavoidable consequence of the nature of things; *or*, finally, that it must at least be considered not as an intended effect[e] of the creator of all things but, rather, merely of those beings in the world to whom something can be imputed, i.e. of human beings (higher spiritual beings as well, good or evil, as the case may be).

The author of a theodicy agrees, therefore, that this juridical process be instituted before the tribunal of reason; he further consents to represent the accused side as advocate through the formal refutation of all the plaintiff's complaints; he is not therefore allowed to dismiss the latter in the course of the process of law through a decree of incompetency of the tribunal of human reason (*exceptio fori*),[f] i.e. he cannot dismiss the complaints with a concession of the supreme wisdom of the author of the world, imposed upon the plaintiff, which would immediately explain away as groundless, even without examination, all doubts that might be raised against it; he must

---

[a] *Versuch:* a trial both in the sense of a scientific experiment and in the sense of putting somebody to the test.
[b] *das Zweckwidrige*
[c] *zweckwidrig*
[d] *Faktum.* The Latin *factum* literally means "something made or done."
[e] *Faktum*
[f] "An exception to the court," i.e., a challenge to the court's competence.

rather attend to the objections, and make comprehensible how they in no way derogate from the concept of the highest wisdom by clarifying and removing them.* – Yet there is one thing he need not attend to, namely a proof of God's wisdom from what the experience of this world teaches; for in this he would simply not succeed, since omniscience would be required to recognize in a given world (as gives itself to cognition in experience) that perfection of which we could say with certainty that absolutely none other is possible in creation and its government.

Now whatever is counterpurposive in the world, and may be opposed to the wisdom of its creator, is of a threefold kind:

I. The absolutely counterpurposive, or what cannot be condoned or desired either as end or means;

II. The conditionally counterpurposive, or what can indeed never co-exist with the wisdom of a will as end, yet can do so as means.

The *first* is the morally counterpurposive, evil proper[g] (sin); the *second*, the physically counterpurposive, ill[h] (pain). – But now, there still is a   8:257 purposiveness[i] in the proportion of ill to moral evil, if the latter is once there, and neither can nor should be prevented – namely in the conjunction of ills and pains, as penalties, with evil, as crime. It is of this purposiveness in the world that one asks whether, in this respect, everyone in the world gets his due. Consequently, yet a

IIIrd kind of counterpurposiveness must be thinkable in the world, namely the disproportion between crimes and penalties in the world.

---

* Although the proper concept of *wisdom* represents only a will's property of being in agreement with the highest good as the *final end* of all things, whereas [the concept of] *art* represents only competence in the use of the suitable means toward *optional ends*, yet, when art proves itself adequate to ideas the possibility of which surpasses every insight of human reason (e.g. when means and ends reciprocally produce one another, as in organic bodies), as a *divine art*, it can also, not incorrectly, be given the name of wisdom – or rather, not to mix up concepts, the name of an *artistic wisdom* of the author of the world, in distinction from his *moral wisdom*. Teleology (and, through it, physicotheology) gives abundant proof in experience of this artistic wisdom. But from it no inference is allowed to the moral wisdom of the author of the world, for the natural law and the moral law require principles of entirely different kinds, and the demonstration of the latter wisdom must be carried out totally *a priori*, and hence must in no way be founded on the experience of what goes on in the world. Now since the concept of God suited to religion must be a concept of him as a moral being (for we have no need of him for natural explanation, hence for speculative purposes); and since this concept can just as little be derived from the mere transcendental concept of an absolutely necessary being – a concept that totally escapes us – as be founded on experience; so it is clear enough that the proof of the existence of such a being can be none other than a moral proof.

[g] *das eigentliche Böse*
[h] *Übel*
[i] *Zweckmäßigkeit*

18

The attributes of the world-author's supreme wisdom against which these [three kinds of] counterpurposiveness stand out as objections are, therefore, likewise three:

> First, the *holiness* of the author of the world, as *law-giver* (creator), in opposition to the moral evil in the world.
> Second, his *goodness*, as *ruler* (preserver), in contrast[j] with the countless ills and pains of the rational beings of the world.
> Third, his *justice*, as *judge*, in comparison to the bad state which the disproportion between the impunity of the depraved and their crimes seems to indicate in the world.*

8:258

The case against those three charges must be presented, therefore, along the three above mentioned kinds [of counterpurposiveness], and must be tested against their validity.

I: Against the complaint over the holiness of the divine will for the moral evil which disfigures the world, God's work, the first vindication consists in this:

a) There is no such thing as an absolute counterpurposiveness which we take the trespassing of the pure laws of our reason to be, but there are violations only against human wisdom; divine wisdom judges these accord-

---

* These three attributes, none of which can in any way be reduced to the others – as, for instance, justice to goodness, and so the whole to a smaller number – together constitute the moral concept of God. Nor can their order be altered (as by making benevolence, for instance, the supreme condition of world creation to which the holiness of legislation is subordinated) without doing violence to religion, which has this very concept for foundation. Our own pure (hence practical) reason determines this order of rank, for if legislation accommodated itself to benevolence, its dignity would no longer be there, nor a firm concept of duties. Indeed the human being wishes to be happy first; but then he sees, and (though reluctantly) accepts, that the worthiness to be happy, i.e. the conformity of the employment of his freedom with the holy law, must in God's decision be the condition of his benevolence, and must, therefore, necessarily precede it. For the wish that has the subjective end (self-love) for foundation cannot determine the objective end (of wisdom) prescribed by the law that unconditionally gives the will its rule. Moreover, punishment in the exercise of justice is founded in the legislating wisdom not at all as mere means but as an end: trespass is associated with ills not that some other good may result from it, but because this connection is good in itself, i.e. morally and necessarily good. Justice indeed presupposes the benevo-

8:258 lence of the legislator (for if his will were not directed to the well-being of his subjects, neither could he bind them under duty to obey him); yet justice is not goodness but rather essentially different from it, even though included in the general concept of wisdom. Hence also the lament over the lack of justice shown in the wrongs which are the lot of human beings here on earth is directed not at the *well-being* which does not befall the good, but at the *ill* which does not befall the evil (although, if well-being occurs to the evil, then the contrast makes the offence all the greater). For under divine rule even the best of human beings cannot found his wish to fare well on divine justice but must found it on God's beneficence, for one who only does what he owes[k] can have no rightful claim on God's benevolence.

[j] *Kontraste*

[k] *seine Schuldigkeit*

ing to totally different rules, incomprehensible to us, where, what we with right find reprehensible with reference to our practical reason and its determination might yet perhaps be in relation to the divine ends and the highest wisdom precisely the most fitting means to our particular welfare and the greatest good of the world as well; the ways of the most high are not our ways[1] (*sunt supris sua iura*),[*l*] and we err whenever we judge what is law only relatively to human beings in this life to be so absolutely, and thus hold what appears counterpurposive to our view of things from so lowly a standpoint to be such also when considered from the highest. – This apology, in which the vindication is worse than the complaint, needs no refutation; surely it can be freely given over to the detestation of every human being who has the least feeling for morality.

b) The second alleged vindication would indeed allow for the actuality of moral evil in the world, but it would excuse the author of the world on the ground that it could not be prevented, because founded upon the limitations of the nature of human beings, as finite. – However, the evil would thereby be justified, and, since it could not be attributed to human beings as something for which they are to be blamed, we would have to cease calling it "a moral evil."

8:259

c) The third rejoinder, that even conceding that it is really a matter of what we call moral evil, a guilt resting on the human being, yet no guilt may be ascribed to God, for God has merely tolerated it for just causes as a deed of human beings: in no way has he condoned it, willed or promoted it – this rejoinder incurs one and the same consequence as the previous apology (b) (even if we take no offense at the concept of a mere *tolerating* on the part of a being who is the one and sole creator of the world): namely, since even for God it was impossible to prevent this evil without doing violence to higher and even moral ends elsewhere, the ground of this ill (for so we must now truly call it) must inevitably be sought in the essence of things, specifically in the necessary limitations of humanity as a finite nature; hence the latter can also not be held responsible for it.

II. With respect to the complaint brought against divine goodness for the ills, namely the pains, in this world, its vindication equally consists

a) in this: It is false to assume in human fates a preponderance of ill over the pleasant enjoyment of life, for however bad someone's lot, yet everyone would rather live than be dead, and those few who opt for the latter, so long as they themeslves postpone it, thereby still confess to that preference; and if they are insane enough for it,[*m*] even then they simply pass over into the state of insensibility where pain as well cannot be felt. – But surely the reply to this sophistry may be left to the sentence of every human being of sound mind who has lived and pondered over the value of

---

[*l*] Those on high have their own laws.
[*m*] *zum letztern* (i.e., the "be dead" option)

life long enough to pass judgment, when asked, on whether he had any inclination to play the game of life once more, I do not say in the same circumstances but in any other he pleases (provided they are not of a fairy world but of this earthly world of ours).

8:260

b) To the second vindication – namely, the preponderance of painful feelings over pleasant ones cannot be separated from the nature of an animal creature such as the human being (in the vein of what Count Veri claims in his book on the nature of pleasure) – ² the retort to this is that, if that is the way it is, then another question arises, namely why the creator of our existence called us into life when the latter, in our correct estimate, is not desirable to us. Ill humor would reply here as that Indian woman did to Genghis Khan, who could neither give her satisfaction for violence suffered nor afford security for the future: "If you will not protect us, why do you then conquer us?"

c) The third way of untying the knot is supposed to be this: God has put us here on earth for the sake of a future happiness, hence out of his goodness; yet an arduous and sorrowful state in the present life must without exception precede that hoped-for superabundant blessedness – a state in which we are to become worthy of that future glory precisely through our struggle with adversities. – But, that before the highest wisdom this time of trial (to which most succumb, and in which even the best is not happy about his life) must without exception be the condition of the joy eventually to be savored by us, and that it was not possible to let the creature be satisfied with every stage of his life – this can indeed be pretended but in no way can there be insight into it; in this way one can indeed cut the knot loose through an appeal to the highest wisdom which willed it, but one cannot untie the knot, which is what theodicy claims to be capable of accomplishing.

III. To the last charge, namely against the justice of the world's judge,* is replied:

8:261

a) The pretension that the depraved go unpunished in the world is ungrounded, for by its nature every crime already carries with it its due punishment, inasmuch as the inner reproach of conscience torments the depraved even more harshly than the Furies. – But in this judgment there obviously lies a misunderstanding. For here the virtuous man lends to the depraved the characteristic of his own constitution, namely, a conscientiousness in all its severity which, the more virtuous a human being is, all

---

* It is remarkable that of all the difficulties in reconciling the course of world events with the divinity of their creator, none imposes itself on the mind as starkly as that of the semblance in them of a lack of *justice*. If it comes about (although it seldom happens) that an unjust, especially violent, villain does not escape unpunished from the world, then the impartial spectator rejoices, now reconciled with heaven. No purposiveness of nature will so excite him in admiration of it and, as it were, make him detect God's hand in it. Why? Because nature is here moral, solely of the kind we seldom can hope to perceive in the world.

the more harshly punishes him because of the slightest indiscretion frowned upon by the moral law in him. But where this attitude of mind and the accompanying conscientiousness are totally absent, so too is the tormentor of crimes committed; and the depraved, if only he can escape the external floggings for his heinous deeds, laughs at the scrupulousness of the honest who inwardly plague themselves with self-inflicted rebukes; the small reproaches which from time to time he might make to himself are, however, either made not through conscience at all or, if he still has some of this conscience within him, are abundantly upset and made good by the pleasure of the senses for which alone he has a taste. – If that charge shall be further

b) refuted by this: It is indeed not to be denied that there is absolutely no relation according to justice between guilt and punishment in this world, and in the ways of this world one must often witness" with indignation a life led with crying injustice and yet happy to the end; this is not, however, something inherent in nature and deliberately promoted, hence not a moral dissonance, for it is a property of virtue that it should wrestle with adversities (among which is the pain that the virtuous must suffer through comparison of his own unhappiness with the happiness of the depraved), and sufferings only serve to enhance the value of virtue; thus this dissonance of undeserved ills resolves itself before reason into a glorious moral melody – the objection to this solution is that, although these ills, when they *precede* virtue or accompany it as its whetting stone, can indeed be represented as in moral harmony with it if at least the end of life crowns virtue and punishes the depraved; yet, if even such an end (as experience thereof gives many examples) fails against sense to material-   8:262
ize, then the suffering seems to have occurred to the virtuous, not *so that* his virtue should be pure, but *because* it was pure (and accordingly contrary to the rules of prudent self-love); and this is the very opposite of the justice of which the human being can form a concept for himself. For as regards the possibility that the end of this terrestrial life might not perhaps be the end of all life, such a possibility cannot count as *vindication* of providence; rather, it is merely a decree of morally believing reason which directs the doubter to patience but does not satisfy him.

c) If, finally, an attempt is made at the third resolution to this disharmonious relation between the moral worth of human beings and the lot that befalls them, by saying: In this world we must judge all well-being and ill merely as the consequence of the use of the human faculties according to the laws of nature, in proportion to the skill and the prudence of their application, and also in proportion to the circumstances they accidentally come by, but not according to their agreement with supersensible ends; in a future world a different order of things will obtain instead, and each will

" *wahrnehmen*

receive that which his deeds here below are worthy of according to moral judgment – [if this is said,] then this assumption too is arbitrary.*°* Rather, unless reason, as a faculty of moral legislation, is pronouncing a decree in accordance with this legislative interest, it must find it probable, according to the mere laws of theoretical cognition, that the way of the world determines our fates in the future just as it does here, according to the order of nature. For what else does reason have as a guide for its theoretical conjecture except natural law? And though it allowed itself, as asked for above (item b), an appeal to patience, and the hope of a future improvement, how can it expect – since even for it the way of things according to the order of nature is a wise one here – that in a future world this way would be unwise according to the same laws? Since according to the same reason there is absolutely no comprehensible relation between the inner grounds of determination of the will (namely of the moral way of thinking) according to the laws of freedom, and the (for the most part external) causes of our welfare independent of our will according to the laws of nature, so the presumption remains that the agreement of human fate with a divine justice, according to the concepts that we construe of the latter, is just as little to be expected there as here.

. .

8:263 Now the outcome of this juridical process before the forum of philosophy is this: Every previous theodicy has not performed what it promised, namely the vindication of the moral wisdom of the world-government against the doubts raised against it on the basis of what the experience of this world teaches – although, to be sure, as objections, so far as our reason's inherent insight regarding them goes, neither can these doubts prove the contrary. But again, whether in time yet more solid grounds of vindication will perhaps be found for the indicted reason – for absolving it not (as hitherto) merely *ab instantia*°*ᵖ* – this still remains undecided, if we do not succeed in establishing with certainty that our reason is absolutely incapable of insight into *the relationship in which any world as we may ever become acquainted with through experience stands with respect to the highest wisdom*; for then all further attempts by a putative human wisdom to gain insight into the ways of the divine wisdom are fully dismissed. Hence, in order to bring this trial to an end *once and for all,* it must yet be proven that at least a negative wisdom is within our reach – namely, insight into the necessary limitation of what we may presume with respect to that which is too high for us – and this may very well be done.

For in the arrangement of this world we have the concept of an *artistic wisdom* – a concept which, in order to attain to a physico-theology, is not

---

° *willkürlich*
ᵖ i.e., right there and then, without explanatory grounds

wanting in objective reality for our speculative faculty of reason. And we also have in the moral idea of our own practical reason a concept of a *moral wisdom* which could have been implanted in a world in general by a most perfect creator. – But of the *unity in the agreement* in a sensible world between that artistic and moral wisdom we have no concept; nor can we ever hope to attain one. For to be a creature and, as a natural being, merely the result of the will of the creator; yet to be capable of responsibility as a freely acting being (one which has a will independent of external influence and possibly opposed to the latter in a variety of ways); but again, to consider one's own deed at the same time also as the effect of a higher being – this is a combination of concepts which we must indeed 8:264 think together in the idea of a world and of a highest good, but which can be intuited only by one who penetrates to the cognition of the supersensible (intelligible) world and sees the manner in which this grounds the sensible world. The proof of the world-author's moral wisdom in the sensible world can be founded only on this insight – for the sensible world presents but the appearance of that other [intelligible] world – and that is an insight to which no mortal can attain.

. .

All theodicy should truly be an *interpretation* of nature insofar as God announces his will through it. Now every interpretation of the declared will of a legislator is either *doctrinal*[q] or *authentic*. The first is a rational inference of that will from the utterances of which the law-giver has made use, in conjunction with his otherwise recognized purposes; the second is made by the law-giver himself.

As a work of God, the world can also be considered by us as a divine publication of his will's *purposes*. However, in this respect the world is *often* a closed book for us, and it is so *every time* we look at it to extract from it God's *final aim* (which is always moral) even though it is an object of experience. Philosophical trials in this kind of interpretation are doctrinal; they constitute theodicy proper – which we can therefore call "doctrinal." – Yet we cannot deny the name of "theodicy" also to the mere dismissal of all objections against divine wisdom, if this dismissal is a *divine decree,* or (for in this case it amounts to the same thing) if it is a pronouncement of the same reason through which we form our concept of God – necessarily and prior to all experience – as a moral and wise being. For through our reason God then becomes himself the interpreter of his will as announced through creation; and we can call this interpretation an *authentic* theodicy. But that is not the interpretation of a *ratiocinating* (speculative) reason, but of an *efficacious*[r] practical reason which, just as in legislating it commands absolutely

[q] *doktrinal*
[r] *machthabend*

24

without further grounds, so it can be considered as the unmediated definition and voice of God through which he gives meaning to the letter of his creation. Now I find such an authentic interpretation expressed allegorically in an ancient holy book.

8:265   Job is portrayed as a man whose enjoyment of life included everything which anyone might possibly imagine it as making it complete. He was healthy, well-to-do, free, master over others whom he can make happy, surrounded by a happy family, among beloved friends – and on top of all of this (what is most important) at peace with himself in a good conscience. A harsh fate imposed in order to test him suddenly snatched from him all these blessings, except the last. Stunned by this unexpected reversal, as he gradually regains his senses, he breaks out in lamentation over his unlucky star; whereupon a dispute soon develops between him and his friends – supposedly gathered to console him – in which the two sides expound their particular theodicy to give a moral explanation for that deplorable fate, each side according to its particular way of thinking (above all, however, according to its station). Job's friends declare themselves for that system which explains all ills in the world from God's *justice*, as so many punishments for crimes committed; and, although they could name none *for* which the unhappy man is guilty, yet they believed they could judge *a priori* that he must have some weighing upon him, for his misfortune would otherwise be impossible according to divine justice. Job – who indignantly protests that his conscience has nothing to reproach him for in his whole life; and, so far as human unavoidable mistakes are concerned, God himself knows that he has made him a fragile creature – Job declares himself for the system of *unconditional divine decision.* "He has decided," Job says, "He does as he wills."*

There is little worthy of note in the subtle or hypersubtle reasonings⁵ of the two sides; but the spirit' in which they carry them out merits all the more attention. Job speaks as he thinks, and with the courage with which he, as well as every human being in his position, can well afford; his friends, on the contrary, speak as if they were being secretly listened to by the mighty one, over whose cause they are passing judgment, and as if gaining his favor through their judgment were closer to their heart than the truth. Their malice in pretending to assert things into which they yet must admit they have no insight, and in simulating a conviction which they in fact do not
8:266   have, contrasts with Job's frankness – so far removed from false flattery as to border almost on impudence – much to his advantage. "Will you defend God unjustly?" he asks;† "Will you give his person [special] consideration?

* Job 23:13.³
† Job 13:7–11, 16.⁴
⁵ *was beide Theile vernünfteln oder übervernunfteln*
' *der Character*

25

Will you plead for God? He shall punish you, if you secretly have consideration for persons! – There will be no hypocrite before him!"

The outcome of the story actually confirms this. For God deigned to lay before Job's eyes the wisdom of his creation, especially its inscrutability. He allowed him glimpses into the beautiful side of creation, where ends comprehensible to the human being bring the wisdom and the benevolent providence of the author of the world unambiguously to light; but also, by contrast, into the horrible side, by calling out to him the products of his might, among which also harmful and fearsome things, each of which appears indeed to be purposively arranged for its own sake and that of its species, yet, with respect to other things and to human beings themselves, as destructive, counterpurposive, and incompatible with a universal plan established with goodness and wisdom. And yet God thereby demonstrates an order and a maintenance of the whole which proclaim a wise creator, even though his ways, inscrutable to us, must at the same time remain hidden – indeed already in the physical order of things, and how much more in the connection of the latter with the moral order (which is all the more impenetrable to our reason). – The conclusion is this: Since Job admits having hastily spoken about things which are too high for him and which he does not understand – not *as if wantonly*, for he is conscious of his honesty, but only unwisely – God finds against his friends, for (as conscientiousness goes) they have not spoken as well of God as God's servant Job. If we now consider the theoretical position*" maintained by each side, that of Job's friends might convey more of an appearance of greater speculative reason and pious humility; before any court of dogmatic theologians, before a synod, an inquisition, a venerable congregation, or any higher consistory in our times (one alone excepted),[5] Job would have likely suffered a sad fate. Hence only sincerity of heart and not distinction of insight; honesty in openly admitting one's doubts; repugnance to pretending conviction where one feels none, especially before God (where this trick is pointless enough) – these are the attributes which, in the person of Job, have decided the preeminence of the honest man over the religious flatterer in the divine verdict.

8:267

The faith, however, which sprang in him for such a vexing resolution of his doubts – namely merely from being convicted of ignorance – could only arise in the soul of a man who, in the midst of his strongest doubts, could yet say (Job 27:5–6): "Till I die I will not remove mine integrity from me, etc."[6] For with this disposition he proved that he did not found his morality on faith, but his faith on morality: in such a case, however weak this faith might be, yet it alone is of a pure and true kind, i.e. the kind of faith that founds not a religion of supplication, but a religion of good life conduct.

*" *die Theorie*

26

CONCLUDING REMARK

Theodicy, as has been shown here, does not have as much to do with a task in the interest of science as, rather, with a matter of faith. From the authentic theodicy we saw that in these matters, less depends on subtle reasoning than on sincerity in taking notice of the impotence of our reason, and on honesty in not distorting our thoughts in what we say, however pious our intention. – This leads to yet the following brief reflection on a big subject, namely sincerity, which is the principal requirement in matters of faith, as contrasted with the propensity to falsehood and impurity which is the principal affliction of human nature.

One cannot always stand by the *truth* of what one says to oneself or to another (for one can be mistaken); however, one can and must stand by the *truthfulness* of one's declaration or confession, because one has immediate consciousness of this. For in the first instance we compare what we say with the object in a logical judgment (through the understanding), whereas in the second instance, where we declare what we hold as true, we compare what we say with the subject (before conscience). Were we to make our declaration with respect to the former without being conscious of the latter, then we lie, since we pretend something else than what we are conscious of. – The observation that there is such an impurity in the human heart is not new (for Job already made it); yet one is tempted to believe that attention to it is new to the teachers of morality and religion, one so seldom finds them making a sufficient use of it despite the difficulty associated with a purification of the dispositions in human beings even when they *want* to act according to duty. We can call this truthfulness "formal conscientiousness"; "material conscientiousness" consists in the caution of not venturing anything on the danger that it might be wrong, whereas "formal" conscientiousness consists in the consciousness of having applied this caution in a given case. – Moralists speak of an "erring conscience." But an erring conscience is an absurdity;[v] and, if there were such a thing, then we could never be certain we have acted rightly, since even the judge in the last instance can still be in error. I can indeed err in the judgment *in which I believe* to be right, for this belongs to the understanding which alone judges objectively (rightly or wrongly); but in the judgment *whether I in fact believe* to be right (or merely pretend it) I absolutely cannot be mistaken, for this judgment – or rather this proposition – merely says that I judge the object in such-and-such a way.

Now the formal conscientiousness which is the ground of truthfulness consists precisely in the care in becoming conscious of this belief (or unbelief) and not pretending to hold anything as true we are not conscious of holding as true. Hence, if someone says to himself (or – what is one and the

8:268

[v] *Unding*

27

IMMANUEL KANT

same in religious professions – before God) that *he believes*, without perhaps casting even a single glimpse into himself – whether he is in fact conscious of thus holding a truth or at least of holding it to some degree – * then such a person *lies*. And not only is his lie the most absurd (before a reader of hearts): it is also the most sinful, for it undermines the ground of every virtuous intention. It is not difficult to see how quickly these blind and external *professions* (which can very easily be reconciled with an internal profession just as false) can, if they yield *means of gain*, bring about a certain falsehood in a community's very way of thinking. – Since a purification of this public way of thinking must in all likelihood be deferred to a distant future – until some day, perhaps under the protection of freedom of thought, it will become a general principle of upbringing and education – we may in the meantime dedicate yet a few lines to the consideration of that vice apparently so deeply rooted in human nature.

8:269

There is something moving and edifying in the depiction of a character which is sincere, and distant from all falsehood and deliberate^x dissemblance. But, since honesty (mere simplicity and straightforward-

8:270

---

* The means for extorting truthfulness in external declarations, *the oath* (*tortura spiritualis*),^w is held by any human court as not only permissible but as indispensable – a sad proof of the little respect of human beings for the truth even in the temple of public justice, where the mere idea of it should by itself instill the greatest respect. Human beings, however, also feign conviction – which is at least not of the kind, or in the degree, as they pretend – even in their inner profession; and since this dishonesty can also have external harmful consequences (for it gradually forges actual persuasion), this means for extorting truthfulness – the oath (which is, to be sure, only an internal means of extortion, i.e. the trial whether holding something as true can withstand the test of an internal hearing of the profession *under oath*) – can likewise very well be used, if not to put a stop to the impudence of bold and in the end also externally violent assertions, at least to make it suspect. – Nothing more is expected by the human court from the conscience of one taking an oath than the admission that, *if there is* a future judge of the world (hence God and a future life), the taker of the oath wills to answer to him for the truth of his external profession; there is no necessity for the court to require him to profess *that there is such a judge of the world*, because, if the first declaration cannot prevent a lie, a second false profession would cause even fewer scruples. By any such inner sworn statement one would be asking himself: Do you now, by everything which is dear and holy to you, venture to guarantee the truth of that important proposition of faith or of some other equally so held? At such an unreasonable demand conscience would be startled, because of the danger to which one is exposed of pretending more than one can assert with certainty – where holding something as true involves an object which is not attainable by way of knowledge (theoretical insight), though its assumption, while still always free, is commendable above all things because it alone makes possible the union into one system of the highest principles of practical reason with those of theoretical cognition of nature (hence reason's agreement with itself). – Professions of faith whose source is historical must, however, all the more be submitted to this trial of truthfulness by fire if they are set down as rules to others: for here the impurity and the simulated conviction is propagated among many, and the blame for it is the onus of whoever is the guarantor as it were of other consciences (for human beings are gladly passive with their conscience).⁷

8:269

^w Spiritual torture
^x *positiven*

ness of mind) is the least that we can possibly require of a good character (especially if we waive candor of heart) and it is therefore difficult to see on what that admiration which we reserve for such a character is based; it must be that sincerity is the property farthest removed from human nature – a sad comment, since all the remaining properties, to the extent that they rest on principles, can have a true inner value only through that one. None but a contemplative misanthrope (who wishes evil to nobody, yet is inclined to believe every evil of all) can hesitate whether to find human beings to *deserve hatred* or rather *contempt*. The properties for which he would judge them qualified for the first finding are those through which they do deliberate harm. That property, however, which appears to him to expose them to the second estimate, could be none other than a propensity which is *in itself evil* even if it harms no one – a propensity for something which cannot be used as means for any purpose; something which, objectively, is good in no respect.[y] The first evil would indeed be none other than the evil of *hostility* (or, to put it mildly, of lack of love); the second can be none other than *mendacity* (falsity, even without any intention to harm). The *first* inclination has a purpose whose function[z] is yet permissible and good in certain farther connections,[a] e.g. hostility against incorrigible disturbers of the peace. The *second* propensity, however, is to use a means (the lie) which is good in no respect,[b] whatever its aim, since it is evil and reprehensible in itself. The *evil* with which competence for good ends in certain external relations can yet be associated is in the constitution of a human being of the first kind;[c] it is a sinning in means, which are not, however, reprehensible in every respect. The evil of the second kind is *baseness*,[d] whereby all character is denied to the human being. – I am here restricting myself principally to the impurity that lies deep in what is hidden, where the human being knows how to distort even inner declarations before his own conscience. The inclination to external deception should be all the less surprising; it must then be that, although we are all aware of the falsity of the coin with which we trade, that coin still manages to maintain itself in circulation.

I remember reading in M. de Luc's *Letters concerning Mountain Ranges, the History of the Earth and Humanity* the following result of the author's partly anthropological voyage.[8] This philanthropist had set out presupposing the original goodness of our species, and sought verification of his

[y] *zu nichts*

[z] *Gebrauch*

[a] *andern Beziehungen.* A few lines later, with respect to the same inclination, Kant speaks of *äußern Verhältnissen.* One wonders if this earlier *andern* is a printer's error and ought to be read, rather, as *äußern,* i.e., "external."

[b] *zu nichts*

[c] i.e., as deserving hate

[d] *Nichtswürdigkeit*

presupposition in places where urban luxury cannot have such influence as to corrupt minds – in mountain ranges, from the Swiss mountains all the way to the Harz[9] and, after his faith in an unselfish inclination to help became somewhat shaky through an experience on the Swiss side,*ᵉ* yet at the ends he draws this conclusion: *As regards benevolence the human being is good enough* (no wonder, since benevolence rests on an innate inclination of which God is the creator) *provided that no bad propensity to subtle deception dwells in him* (which is also not to be wondered at, because to refrain from deception rests on the character which the human being himself must build within himself). And this result of the investigation is one which, even without traveling to the mountains, everyone could have met with among his fellow citizens – indeed, yet closer to home, in his own heart.

ᵉ in den erstern

Religion within the boundaries of mere reason

Preface to the first edition

So far as morality is based on the conception of the human being as one who is free but who also, just because of that, binds himself through his reason to unconditional laws, it is in need neither of the idea of another being above him in order that he recognize his duty, nor, that he observe it, of an incentive other than the law itself. At least it is the human being's own fault if such a need is found in him; but in this case too the need could not be relieved through anything else: for whatever does not originate from himself and his own freedom provides no remedy for a lack in his morality. – Hence on its own behalf morality in no way needs religion (whether objectively, as regards willing, or subjectively, as regards capability) but is rather self-sufficient by virtue of pure practical reason. – For, since its laws bind through the mere form of universal lawfulness of the maxims to be adopted in accordance with this lawfulness as the highest condition (itself unconditional) of all ends, morality needs absolutely no material determining ground of the free power of choice,* that is no end, either in order to recognize what duty is or to impel its performance; on the contrary, when duty is the issue, morality can perfectly well abstract from ends altogether, and ought so to do. For example, to know whether I should (or even can) be truthful in my testimony before a court of justice, or faithful when someone else's goods entrusted to me are being re-

---

* Those for whom the merely formal determining ground as such (lawfulness) will not suffice as the determining ground in the concept of duty, nonetheless admit that this ground is not to be found in *self-love* directed to one's own *comfort*. But then there are only two determining grounds left: one that is rational, namely, one's own *perfection;* and another that is empirical, the *happiness* of others.[1] Now, if by the first they do not already understand moral perfection, which can only be one thing (namely a will unconditionally obedient to the law), in which case they would however be defining in a circle, then they must mean the human being's natural perfection inasmuch as it is capable of enhancement; and of this perfection there can be many aspects (such as skill in the arts and the sciences, taste, physical agility, etc.). But these are always only conditionally good, that is, good only on condition that their use does not conflict with the moral law (which alone commands unconditionally); hence natural perfection cannot be, when made into an end, the principle of the concepts of duty. The same also applies to an end when associated with the happiness of other human beings. For an action must first be weighed in itself according to the moral law before it can be associated with the happiness of others. The action's promotion of this happiness, therefore, is duty only conditionally, and cannot serve as the supreme principle of moral maxims.

claimed, there is no need to demand an end which I might perhaps propose to myself to realize by my declaration, for what sort of end this would be does not matter at all; rather, one who still finds it necessary to look around for some end when his testimony is rightfully demanded of him, is in this respect already contemptible.

But although on its own behalf morality does not need the representation of an end which would have to precede the determination of the will, it may well be that it has a necessary reference to such an end, not as the ground of its maxims but as a necessary consequence accepted in conformity to them. – For in the absence of all reference to an end no determination of the will can take place in human beings at all, since no such determination can occur without an effect, and its representation, though not as the determining ground of the power of choice nor as an end that comes first in intention, must nonetheless be admissible as the consequence of that power's determination to an end through the law (*finis in consequentiam veniens*);[a] without this end, a power of choice which does not [thus] add to a contemplated action the thought of either an objectively or subjectively determined object (which it has or should have), instructed indeed as to *how* to operate but not as to the *whither*, can itself obtain no satisfaction. So morality really has no need of an end for right conduct; on 6:5 the contrary, the law that contains the formal condition of the use of freedom in general suffices to it. Yet an end proceeds from morality just the same; for it cannot possibly be a matter of indifference to reason how to answer the question, *What is then the result of this right conduct of ours?* nor to what we are to direct our doings or nondoings, even granted this is not fully in our control, at least as something with which they are to harmonize. And this is indeed only the idea of an object that unites within itself the formal condition of all such ends as we ought to have (duty) with everything which is conditional upon ends we have and which conforms to duty (happiness proportioned to its observance), that is, the idea of a highest good in the world, for whose possibility we must assume a higher, moral, most holy, and omnipotent being who alone can unite the two elements of this good. This idea is not (practically considered) an empty one; for it meets our natural need, which would otherwise be a hindrance to moral resolve, to think for all our doings and nondoings taken as a whole some sort of ultimate end which reason can justify. What is most important here, however, is that this idea rises out of morality and is not its foundation; that it is an end which to make one's own already presupposes ethical principles. It cannot be a matter of indifference to morality, therefore, whether it does or does not fashion for itself the concept of an ultimate end of all things (although, to be sure, harmonizing with this end does not increase the number of morality's virtues but rather provides

[a] an end occurring by way of consequence.

these with a special point of reference for the unification of all ends); for only in this way can an objective practical reality be given to the combination, which we simply cannot do without, of the purposiveness [deriving] from freedom and the purposiveness of nature. Assume a human being who honors the moral law, and who allows himself to think (as he can hardly avoid doing) what sort of world he would *create*, were this in his power, under the guidance of practical reason – a world within which, moreover, he would place himself as a member. Now, not only would he choose a world precisely as the moral idea of the highest good requires, if the choice were entrusted to him alone, but he would also will the very existence of [such] a world, since the moral law wills that the highest good possible through us be actualized, even though, in following this idea, he 6:6 might see himself in danger of forfeiting much in the way of personal happiness, for it is possible that he might not be adequate to what reason makes the condition for it. He would thus feel himself compelled by reason to acknowledge this judgment with complete impartiality, as if rendered by somebody else yet at the same time his own, and in this way the human being evinces the need, effected in him by morality, of adding to the thought of his duties an ultimate end as well, as their consequence.

Morality thus inevitably leads to religion, and through religion it extends itself* to the idea of a mighty moral lawgiver outside the human

---

* The proposition, "There is a God, hence there is a highest good in the world," if it is to proceed (as proposition of faith) simply from morality, is a synthetic *a priori* proposition; for although accepted only in a practical context, it yet exceeds the concept of duty that morality contains (and which does not presuppose any matter of the power of choice, but only this power's formal laws), and hence cannot be analytically evolved out of morality. *But how is such a proposition* a priori *possible?* Agreement with the mere idea of a moral lawgiver for all human beings is indeed identical with the moral concept of duty in general, and to this extent the proposition commanding the agreement would be analytic. But the acceptance of the existence of this lawgiver means more than the mere possibility of such an object. I can only indicate here, but without developing it, the key to the resolution of this task, as far as I believe myself to have insight into it.[2]

An *end* is always the object of an *inclination*, that is, of an immediate desire to possess a thing by means of one's action, just as a *law* (which commands practically) is the object of *respect*. An objective end (i.e. an end which we ought to have) is one which is assigned to us as such by reason alone. The end that contains the inescapable, and at the same time sufficient, condition of all other ends is the *ultimate end*. One's own happiness is the subjective ultimate end of rational beings belonging to the world (they each *have* this end by virtue of their nature which is dependent upon sensible objects; it would therefore be otiose to say of that end that one *ought to* have it), and all practical propositions that have this ultimate end as their ground are synthetic yet at the same time empirical. But that every human being ought 6:7 to make the highest possible *good* in the world his own *ultimate end* is a synthetic practical proposition a priori, that is, an objective-practical proposition given through pure reason, since it is a proposition that exceeds the concept of the duties in this world, and adds a consequence (an effect) of these duties that is not contained in the moral laws and cannot, therefore, be evolved out of them analytically. For these laws command absolutely, whatever their consequences; indeed, they even require that we abstract from such consequences

being, in whose will the ultimate end (of the creation of the world) is what can and at the same ought to be the ultimate human end.

. .

If morality recognizes in the holiness of its law an object worthy of the highest respect, at the level of religion it represents an object of *worship* in the highest cause that brings this law to fruition, and thus morality appears in its majesty. Everything, however, even the most sublime object, is diminished under the hands of human beings whenever they apply its idea to their use. That which can be venerated truthfully only so far as respect for it is free, is forced to accommodate itself to forms which can be given authority only through coercive laws; and that which of itself exposes itself to the public criticism of all, must submit to a criticism which has coercive power, i.e., to a censorship.

However, since the command: Obey authority! is also a moral one and

entirely whenever a particular action is concerned, and thereby they make of duty an object of the highest respect, without proposing to us, or assigning, an end (and an ultimate end) such as would constitute some sort of inducement for it and an incentive to the fulfillment of our duty. All human beings could sufficiently partake of this incentive too if they just adhered (as they should) to the rule of pure reason in the law. What need have they to know of the outcome of their doings and nondoings that the world's course will bring about? It suffices for them that they do their duty, even if everything were to end with life in this world, and in this life too happiness and desert perhaps never converge. Yet it is one of the inescapable limitations of human beings and of their practical faculty of reason (perhaps of that faculty in all other worldly beings as well) to be concerned in every action with its result, seeking something in it that might serve them as an end and even prove the purity of their intention – which result would indeed come last in practice (*nexu effectivo*)[b] but first in representation and intention (*nexu finali*).[c] Now, in this end human beings seek something that they can *love*, even though it is being proposed to them through reason alone. Hence the law that only inspires *respect* in them, though it does not recognize this sought-after something as [its own] need, nonetheless extends itself on its behalf to include the moral ultimate end of reason among its determining grounds. That is, the proposition, "Make the highest possible good in this world your own ultimate end," is a synthetic proposition *a priori* which is introduced by the moral law itself, and yet through it practical reason reaches beyond the law. And this is possible because the moral law is taken with reference to the characteristic, natural to the human being, of having to consider in every action, besides the law, also an end (this characteristic of the human being makes him an object of experience). The proposition itself is possible (just like the theoretical yet synthetic propositions *a priori*) only because it contains the *a priori* principle of the cognition of the determining grounds of a power of free choice in experience in general, so far as experience, by exhibiting the effects of morality in its ends, gives an objective, although only practical, reality to the concept of morality as having causality in the world. – But now, if the strictest observance of the moral laws is to be thought of as the cause of the ushering in of the highest good (as end), then, since human capacity does not suffice to effect happiness in the world proportionate to the worthiness to be happy, an omnipotent moral being must be assumed as ruler of the world, under whose care this would come about, i.e., morality leads inevitably to religion.
[b] according to the concatenation of efficiency
[c] according to the concatenation of finality

36

its observance, like that of any duty, can be extended to religion, it is fitting that a treatise dedicated to the definition of the concept of religion should itself offer an example of this obedience – which, however, cannot be demonstrated merely by attending to the law in a single state regulation while [remaining] blind to all others, but concomitantly, only through coherent respect for all regulations. Now the theologian who judges on books can be appointed either as one who is to care simply for the welfare of souls, or as one who at the same time is to care for the welfare of the sciences: the first judges simply as divine, the second as scholar as well. It rests with the latter, as a member of a public institution to which (under the name of "university") all the sciences are entrusted for cultivation and protection against encroachments, whether to restrict the prerogatives of the first so that his censorship shall not disrupt the field of the sciences. And if the two are biblical theologians, then primacy in censorship pertains to the second as a member of the university in a faculty charged with the treatment of this theology; for, as regards the first concern (the welfare of souls), both have one and the same mandate, whereas, as regards the second (the welfare of the sciences), the theologian in the capacity of university scholar has in addition another special function to discharge. If we deviate from this rule things must finally come to the pass where they have already once been (for example, at the time of Galileo), namely that the biblical theologian, to humble the pride of the sciences and spare himself effort on them, might venture incursions even into astronomy or   6:9 other sciences such as the ancient history of the earth, and [thus] take charge of all the endeavors of the human understanding – just like those peoples who, finding in themselves neither ability nor resolution enough to defend themselves against threats of attack, transform all about them into a wilderness.

Over against biblical theology, however, there stands on the side of the sciences a philosophical theology which is a property held in trust by another faculty. This theology must have complete freedom to expand as far as its science reaches, provided that it stays within the boundaries of mere reason and makes indeed use of history, languages, the books of all peoples, even the Bible, in order to confirm and explain its propositions, but only for itself, without carrying these propositions over into biblical theology or wishing to modify its public doctrines, which is a privilege of divines. And although the right of censorship of the theologian (considered as a divine) cannot be disputed where it has been established that philosophical theology has truly trespassed across its boundaries and encroached on biblical theology, yet, as soon as this is in doubt again and the question therefore arises whether the trespass has occurred through a writing or some other public dissertation of the philosopher, the superior censorship can only fall to the biblical theologian as *member of his faculty;*

for as such he^d has also been charged with the care of the second interest of the community, namely the flourishing of the sciences, and has been appointed with just as much validity as [has] the first.^e

Indeed, in a case like this the primary censorship is the prerogative of this faculty [of theology] and not of the faculty of philosophy; for with respect to certain doctrines the former alone holds privilege, whereas the latter deals with its own openly and freely; only the former, therefore, can make complaints that its exclusive right has been impinged upon. However, in spite of the verging of the two bodies of doctrine on one another and the anxiety about a transgression of boundaries by philosophical theology, doubt about an encroachment can easily be averted if it is only borne in mind that any such mischief does not occur because the philosopher *borrows* something from biblical theology to use for his own purpose (for biblical theology itself will not want to deny that it contains much in common with the doctrines of mere reason and, in addition, much that belongs to the science of history or linguistic scholarship and is subject to the censorship of these [disciplines]); rather, even granted that the philosopher uses whatever he borrows from biblical theology in a meaning suited to mere reason but perhaps not pleasing to this theology, [the mischief occurs] only because the philosopher *brings* something *into* biblical theology itself and thereby seeks to fit it for other ends than it is fitted for. – Thus we cannot say, for instance, that the teacher of natural right encroaches on the Codex of Roman Law3 just because he borrows from it many a classical expression and formula for his philosophical doctrine of natural right, even when, as often happens, he employs them in not quite the same sense in which, according to the interpreters of the Codex, they are to be taken, so long as he does not wish that the jurists proper, or perhaps the courts of law, should also use them that way. For if that were not within his competence, we could conversely also accuse the biblical theologian, or the statutory jurist, of having countless times encroached upon the domain of philosophy, because both must often borrow from it, though only to their respective advantage, since they cannot do without reason nor, where science is at issue, without philosophy. And, were the biblical theologian to consider having absolutely nothing to do wherever possible with reason in things religious, we can easily foresee on which side the loss would be; for a religion that rashly declares war on reason will not long endure against it. – I will even venture to ask whether it would not be beneficial, upon completion of the academic instruction in

6:10

^d "as such he" = *dieser* (i.e. "this")

^e *der erstere*, literally, "the first." Kant's text is ambiguous. The Greene/Hudson translation glosses, "the theologian regarded as divine." Although this is a likely interpretation, the "first" could just as well refer to the "philosophical theologian." Cf. the sentence immediately following.

biblical theology, always to add by way of conclusion, as requisite to the complete preparation of the candidate, a special course on the pure *philosophical* doctrine of religion (which would avail itself of everything, the Bible included) somewhat along the lines of this book (or any other, if a better one of the same kind can be had). – For the sciences profit simply from being set apart, insofar as each science first constitutes a whole by itself; only after that shall the experiment be made of considering them in association. Now whether the theologian agrees with the philosopher or believes himself obliged to oppose him: let him just hear him out. For in this way alone can the theologian be forearmed against all the difficulties that the philosopher may cause him. To conceal these difficulties, however, or indeed to decry them as ungodly is a mean expedient that will not wash; to mix the two [disciplines] and for the biblical theologian to direct only the occasional fleeting glance at [philosophy], constitutes a lack of 6:11 thoroughness where in the end nobody knows exactly how they stand in the whole with respect to the doctrine of religion.

Of the following four essays in which, to make apparent the relation of religion to a human nature partly laden with good dispositions and partly with evil ones, I represent the relationship of the good and the evil principles as two equally self-subsisting transient causes affecting men, the first was already inserted in the *Berlin Monthly* of April 1792⁴ but could not be omitted here, because of the rigorous coherence of the materials in this work which, in the three essays now to be added, contains the complete development of the first. –

The reader will excuse the orthography (different from mine) of the first sheets in view of the different hands that have worked on the copy, and the shortness of the time left to me for revision.

Preface to the second edition

Except for misprints and certain few expressions that have been corrected, nothing has been altered in this edition. Newly added supplements have been placed at the foot of the text, marked with a dagger (†).

Regarding the title of this work (since doubts have been expressed also regarding the intention hidden behind it) I note: Since, after all, *revelation* can at least comprise also the pure *religion of reason*, whereas, conversely, the latter cannot do the same for what is historical in revelation, I shall be able to consider the first as a *wider* sphere of faith that includes the other, a *narrower* one, within itself (not as two circles external to one another but as concentric circles); the philosopher, as purely a teacher of reason (from mere principles *a priori*), must keep within the inner circle and, thereby, also abstract from all experience. From this standpoint I can also make this second experiment, namely, to start from some alleged revelation or other and, abstracting from the pure religion of reason (so far as it constitutes a system on its own), to hold fragments of this revelation, as a *historical system*, up to moral concepts, and see whether it does not lead back to the same pure *rational system* of religion [from which I have abstracted]. The latter, though not from the theoretical point of view (under which must also be reckoned the technicopractical point of view of pedagogical method, as a *technology*) may yet, from the morally practical point of view, be independent and sufficient to genuine religion, which, as a rational concept *a priori* (remaining after everything empirical has been removed), only obtains in this relation. If this is the case, then we shall be able to say that between reason and Scripture there is, not only compatibility but also unity, so that whoever follows the one (under the guidance of moral concepts) will not fail to come across the other as well. Were this not so, we would either have two religions in one person, which is absurd, or a *religion* and a *cult*, in which case, since the latter is not (like religion) an end in itself but has value only as a means, the two would have to be often shaken up together that they might, for a short time, combine; like oil and water, however, they would soon have to separate again and let the purely moral religion (the religion of reason) float to the top.

I noted in the first Preface that this unification, or the attempt at it, is a task to which the philosophical researcher of religion has perfect right, and not an encroachment on the exclusive right of the biblical theologian.

Since then I have found this claim advanced in the *Ethics*[5] (Part I, pp. 5–11) of the late Michaelis – a man well versed in both disciplines – and applied throughout his entire work, without the higher faculty finding anything in this prejudicial to its rights.

In this second edition I have not been not able to take cognizance, as I would have wished to do, of the judgments passed upon this text by worthy men, named and unnamed, since (as with all foreign literature) these arrive in our regions very late. [I say this] especially with reference to the *Annotationes quaedam theologicae etc.* of the renowned Hr. Dr. Storr of Tübingen,[6] who has examined the text with his accustomed sagacity and with a diligence and fairness deserving the greatest thanks; I plan a reply to him, but do not venture to promise it because of the difficulties that old age poses especially in the way of working with abstract ideas. – But there is a review in Number 29 of *Recent Critical News*, from Greifswald, which I can dispose of just as expeditiously as the reviewer did the text itself.[7] For in his opinion my writing is nothing but the answer to this question which I myself posed to myself: "How is the ecclesiastical system of dogmatics possible, in its concepts and doctrines, according to pure (theoretical and practical) reason?" – Hence this investigation is of no concern at all to those who have no more acquaintance and understanding of his (Kant's) 6:14 system than desire to be capable of them; for them the system might as well not exist. – To this I answer: Only common morality is needed to understand the essentials of this text, without venturing into the critique of practical reason, still less into that of theoretical reason. For instance, whenever virtue, as a facility in *actions* conforming to duty (according to their legality), is called *virtus phaenomenon* but, as a constant *disposition* toward such actions from *duty* (because of their morality), is called *virtus noumenon*, these expressions are used only because of the schools; the matter itself is contained, though in other words, in the most popular instruction for children or in sermons, and is easily understood. If only one could boast as much regarding the mysteries of divine nature, which are considered part of religious doctrine and are imported into the catechisms as though they were entirely popular but must eventually be transformed into moral concepts if they are to become intelligible to everyone.

Königsberg, 26 January 1794.

Table of contents

f Service = *Dienst;* counterfeit service = *Afterdienst. After* in German can mean "anus."

The philosophical doctrine of religion
Part one

Part One
Concerning the indwelling of the evil principle alongside the good
or
Of the radical evil in human nature

That "the world lieth in evil"[8] is a complaint as old as history, even as old as the older art of poetic fiction; indeed, just as old as that oldest among all fictions, the religion of the priests. All allow that the world began with something good: with the Golden Age, with life in Paradise, or an even happier life in communion with heavenly beings. But then they make this happiness disappear like a dream, and they spitefully hasten the decline into evil (moral evil, with which the physical always went hand in hand) in an accelerating fall,* so that now (this "now" is, however, as old as history) we live in the final age; the Last Day and the destruction of the world are knocking at the door, and in certain regions of India the Judge and Destroyer of the world, Rutra (otherwise known as Shiva or Shiwa), already is worshipped as the God now holding power, after Vishnu, the Sustainer of the World, grown weary of the office he had received from Brahma the Creator, resigned it centuries ago.[9]

More recent, though far less widespread, is the opposite heroic opinion,[10] which has gained standing only among philosophers and, in our days, especially among the pedagogues: that the world steadfastly (though hardly noticeably) forges ahead in the very opposite direction, namely from bad to better; that at least there is in the human being the predisposition to move in this direction. But surely, if the issue is *moral* good or evil (not just growth in civilization), they have not drawn this view from experience, for the history of all times attests far too powerfully against it; and we may

6:20

*
Aetas parentum peior avis tulit
Nos nequiores, mox daturos
Progeniem vitiosiorem.
Horace[g]

[8] *Odes*, III, 6: "The age of our parents (who were worse than our forefathers) brought us forth yet more dishonest, and we are now ready to issue an even more vicious progeny."

45

presume that it is, rather, just an optimistic presupposition on the part of
the moralists, from Seneca to Rousseau, intended to encourage the inde-
fatigable cultivation of that seed of goodness that perhaps lies in us, if one
could only count on any such natural foundation of goodness in the human
kind. Yet this is also to be said: Since we must assume that the human
being is sound of body by nature (i.e., in the way he is usually born), there
is cause not to assume that he is equally sound and good of soul by nature as well. Nature itself would then be promoting the cultivation in us of
this ethical predisposition toward goodness.[11] As Seneca says: *Sanabilibus
aegrotamus malis, nosque in rectum genitos natura, si sanari, velimus, adiuvat.*[h]

But since it well may be that we have erred in both these ways of
reading experience, the question arises whether a middle ground may not
at least be possible, namely that, as a species, the human being can neither
be good nor evil, or, at any rate, that he can be the one just as much as the
other, partly good, partly evil. – We call a human being evil, however, not
because he performs actions that are evil (contrary to law), but because
these are so constituted that they allow the inference of evil maxims in
him. Now through experience we can indeed notice unlawful actions, and
also notice (at least within ourselves) that they are consciously contrary to
law. But we cannot observe maxims, we cannot do so unproblematically
even within ourselves; hence the judgment that an agent is an evil human
being cannot reliably be based on experience. In order, then, to call a
human being evil, it must be possible to infer *a priori* from a number of
consciously evil actions, or even from a single one, an underlying evil
maxim, and, from this, the presence in the subject of a common ground,
itself a maxim, of all particular morally evil maxims.

6:21   But lest anyone be immediately scandalized by the expression *nature*,
which would stand in direct contradiction to the predicates *morally* good
or *morally* evil if taken to mean (as it usually does) the opposite of the
ground of actions [arising] from *freedom*, let it be noted that by "the nature
of a human being" we only understand here the subjective ground –
wherever it may lie – of the exercise of the human being's freedom in
general (under objective moral laws) antecedent to every deed that falls
within the scope of the senses. But this subjective ground must, in turn,
itself always be a deed [i] of freedom (for otherwise the use or abuse of the
human being's power of choice with respect to the moral law could not be
imputed to him, nor could the good or evil in him be called "moral").
Hence the ground of evil cannot lie in any object *determining* the power of
choice through inclination, not in any natural impulses, but only in a rule
that the power of choice itself produces for the exercise of its freedom,

[h] *De ira*, II:13.1: "We are sick with curable diseases, and if we wish to be cured, nature comes
to our aid, *for we are born to health*." The quote is also found on the title page of J.-J.
Rousseau's *Émile*.
[i] *Actus*

i.e., in a maxim. One cannot, however, go on asking what, in a human being, might be the subjective ground of the adoption of this maxim rather than its opposite. For if this ground were ultimately no longer itself a maxim, but merely a natural impulse, the entire exercise of freedom could be traced back to a determination through natural causes – and this would contradict freedom. Whenever we therefore say, "The human being is by nature good," or, "He is by nature evil," this only means that he holds within himself a first ground* (to us inscrutable) for the adoption of good or evil (unlawful) maxims, and that he holds this ground *qua* human, universally – in such a way, therefore, that by his maxims he expresses at the same time the character of his species.

We shall say, therefore, of one of these [two] characters (which distinguish the human being from other possible rational beings) that it is *innate* in him; and yet we shall always be satisfied that nature is not to blame for it (if the character is evil), nor does it deserve praise (if it is good), but that the human being is alone its author. But since the first ground of the adoption of our maxims, which must itself again lie in the free power of choice, cannot be any fact*j* possibly given in experience, the good or the evil in the human being is said to be innate (as the subjective first ground of the adoption of this or that maxim with respect to the moral law) only *in the sense* that it is posited as the ground antecedent to every use of freedom given in experience (from the earliest youth as far back as birth) and is thus represented as present in the human being at the moment of birth – not that birth itself is its cause. 6:22

Remark

At the basis of the conflict between the two hypotheses presented above there lies a disjunctive proposition: *The human being is* (by nature) *either morally good or morally evil.* It will readily occur to anyone to ask, however, whether this disjunction is accurate; and whether some might not claim that the human being is by nature neither of the two, others, that he is both at once, that is, good in some parts and evil in others. Experience even seems to confirm this middle position between the two extremes.

It is of great consequence to ethics in general, however, to preclude, so far as possible, anything morally intermediate, either in actions (*adia-*

---

* That the first subjective ground of the adoption of moral maxims is inscrutable can be seen provisionally from this: Since the adoption is free, its ground (e.g. why I have adopted an evil maxim and not a good one instead) must not be sought in any incentive of nature, but always again in a maxim; and, since any such maxim must have its ground as well, yet apart from a maxim no *determining ground* of the free power of choice ought to, or can, be adduced, we are endlessly referred back in the series of subjective determining grounds, without ever being able to come to the first ground.
j *Factum* (i.e. "something done")

phora)^k or in human characters; for with any such ambiguity all maxims run the risk of losing their determination and stability. Those who adhere to this strict way of thinking are commonly called *rigorists* (a name intended to carry reproach, but in fact a praise); so we can call *latitudinarians* those at the opposite extreme. These latter, again, are either latitudinarians of neutrality and may be called *indifferentists*, or latitudinarians of coalition and can then be called *syncretists*.[12]*

6:23   On the rigorist's criteria,† the answer to the question just posed is

---

* If the good = a, the opposite contradicting it is the not-good. Now, this not-good is the consequence either of the mere lack of a ground of the good, = o, or of a positive ground antagonistic to the good, = −a; in this latter case, the not-good can also be called positive evil. (With respect to pleasure and pain there is a similar middle term, whereby pleasure = a, pain = −a, and the state in which neither of the two obtains is indifference, = o.) Now, if the moral law in us were not an incentive of the power of choice, the morally good (the agreement of the power of choice with the law) would be = a, and the not-good, = o; the latter, however, would be just the consequence of the lack of a moral incentive, = a × o. In us, however, the law is incentive, = a. Hence the lack of the agreement of the power of choice with it (= o) is possible only as the consequence of a real and opposite determination of the power of choice, i.e. of a *resistance* on its part, = −a; or again, it is only possible through an evil power of choice. And so between an evil and a good disposition (the inner principle of maxims) according to which the morality of an action must be judged, there is no intermediate position.[13]

†A morally indifferent action (*adiaphoron morale*) would be one that merely follows upon the laws of nature, and hence stands in no relation at all to the moral law as law of freedom – for such an action is not a *factum*,[l] and with respect to it neither *command*, nor *prohibition*, nor yet *permission* (*authorization* according to law), intervenes or is necessary.

† Professor Schiller, in his masterful treatise on *gracefulness* and *dignity* in morality (*Thalia*, 1793, 3rd issue),[14] disapproves of this way of representing obligation, because it carries with it the frame of mind of a Carthusian. Since we are however at one upon the most important principles, I cannot admit disagreement on this one, if only we can make ourselves clear to one another. – I readily grant that I am unable to associate *gracefulness* with the *concept of duty*, by reason of its very dignity. For the concept of duty includes unconditional necessitation, to which gracefulness stands in direct contradiction. The majesty of the law (like the law on Sinai) instills awe (not dread, which repels; and also not fascination, which invites familiarity); and this awe rouses the respect of the subject toward his master, except that in this case, since the master lies in us, it rouses a *feeling of the sublimity* of our own vocation that enraptures us more than any beauty. – But *virtue*, i.e. the firmly grounded disposition to fulfill one's duty strictly, is also *beneficent* in its consequences, more so than anything that nature or art might afford in the world. Hence the glorious picture of humanity, as portrayed in the figure of virtue, does allow the attendance of the *graces*, who, however, maintain a respectful distance when duty alone is at issue. And if we consider the gracious consequences that virtue would spread throughout the world, should it gain entry everywhere, then the morally oriented reason (through the imagination) calls sensibility into play. Hercules becomes *Musagetes*^m only after subduing monsters, a labor at which those good sisters^n shrink back in fear and trembling. These same attendants of Venus Urania^o become wanton sisters in the train of

^k morally indifferent

^l "deed," in the sense of "something done."

^m leader of the muses

^n i.e. the muses

^o Heavenly Venus

based on the morally important observation that freedom of the power of choice has the characteristic, entirely peculiar to it, that it cannot be determined to action through any incentive *except so far as the human being has incorporated it into his maxim* (has made it into a universal rule for himself, according to which he wills to conduct himself); only in this way can an incentive, whatever it may be, coexist with the absolute spontaneity of the power of choice (of freedom). But the moral law is itself an incentive in the judgment of reason, and whoever makes it his maxim is *morally* good. Now, if the law fails nevertheless to determine somebody's free power of choice with respect to an action relating to it, an incentive opposed to it must have influence on the power of choice of the human being in question; and since, by hypothesis, this can only happen because this human being incorporates the incentive (and consequently also the deviation from the moral law) into his maxim (in which case he is an evil human being), it follows that his disposition as regards the moral law is never indifferent (never neither good nor bad).[15]

6:24

Nor can a human being be morally good in some parts, and at the same time evil in others. For if he is good in one part, he has incorporated the moral law into his maxim. And were he, therefore, to be evil in some other part, since the moral law of compliance with duty in general is a single one and universal, the maxim relating to it would be universal yet particular at the same time: which is contradictory.*

6:25

Venus Dione[p] as soon as they meddle in the business of determining duties and try to provide incentives for them. – Now, if we ask, "What is the *aesthetic* constitution, the *temperament* so to speak *of virtue:* is it courageous and hence *joyous*, or weighed down by fear and dejected?" an answer is hardly necessary. The latter slavish frame of mind can never be found without a hidden *hatred* of the law, whereas a heart joyous in the *compliance* with its duty (not just complacency in the *recognition* of it) is the sign of genuineness in virtuous disposition, even where *piety* is concerned, which does not consist in the self-torment of a remorseful sinner (a torment which is very ambiguous, and usually only an inward reproach for having offended against prudence), but in the firm resolve to improve in the future. This resolve, encouraged by good progress, must needs effect a joyous frame of mind, without which one is never certain of having *gained* also *a love* for the good, i.e. of having incorporated the good into one's maxim.

* The ancient moral philosophers, who have pretty well exhausted all that can be said concerning virtue, have also not left the two questions above untouched. They expressed the first thus: Whether virtue must be learned (the human being, therefore, would by nature be indifferent to virtue and vice?) The second was: Whether there is more than one virtue (and hence the human being can perhaps[q] be virtuous in some parts, and vicious in others)? To both they replied with rigoristic precision in the negative; and rightly so, for they were considering virtue *in itself*, in the *idea* of reason (how the human being ought to be). If, however, we want to pass moral judgment on this moral being, the human being *as he appears*, such as experience lets us cognize him, we can then answer both questions in the positive. For then he would be judged, not by the scales of pure reason (before a divine court of justice), but according to empirical standards (by a human judge). More about this in what follows.

6:25

[p] Venus as mother

[q] The text reads "nicht etwa." I am omitting the "nicht," which does not seem to make any difference.

Moreover, to have the one or the other disposition by nature as an innate characteristic does not mean here that the disposition has not been earned by the human being who harbors it, i.e. that he is not its author, but means rather that it has not been earned in time (that he has been the one way or the other *always, from his youth on*). The disposition, i.e. the first subjective ground of the adoption of the maxims, can only be a single one, and it applies to the entire use of freedom universally. This disposition too, however, must be adopted through the free power of choice, for otherwise it could not be imputed. But there cannot be any further cognition of the subjective ground or the cause of this adoption (although we cannot avoid asking about it), for otherwise we would have to adduce still another maxim into which the disposition would have to be incorporated, and this maxim must in turn have its ground.' Hence, since we cannot derive this disposition, or rather its highest ground, from a first act of the power of choice in time, we call it a characteristic of the power of choice that pertains to it by nature (even though the disposition is in fact grounded in freedom). However, that by the "human being" of whom we say that he is good or evil by nature we are entitled to understand not individuals (for otherwise one human being could be assumed to be good, and another evil, by nature) but the whole species, this can only be demonstrated later on, if it transpires from anthropological research that the grounds that justify us in attributing one of these two characters to a human being as innate are of such a nature that there is no cause for exempting anyone from it, and that the character therefore applies to the species.

6:26

I

CONCERNING THE ORIGINAL PREDISPOSITION
TO GOOD IN HUMAN NATURE

We may justifiably bring this predisposition, with reference to its end, under three headings, as elements of the determination of the human being:

1. The predisposition to the *animality* of the human being, as a *living being;*
2. To the *humanity* in him, as a living and at the same time *rational* being;
3. To his *personality*, as a rational and at the same time *responsible* being.*[16]

---

* We cannot consider this predisposition as already included in the concept of the preceding one, but must necessarily treat it as a special predisposition. For from the fact that a being

' I have amended the text by moving the closing parenthesis from the end of the sentence, where it is in the Academy text, to after "asking about it." The clause starting with "for otherwise" provides no explanation why we should not be asking about the cause, but it makes sense as an explanation of why no further cause can be known.

1. The predisposition to animality in the human being may be brought under the general title of physical or merely *mechanical* self-love, i.e. a love for which reason is not required.[17] It is threefold: *first*, for self-preservation; *second*, for the propagation of the species, through the sexual drive, and for the preservation of the offspring thereby begotten through breeding; *third*, for community with other human beings, i.e. the social drive. – On these three can be grafted all sorts of vices (which, however, do not of themselves issue from this predisposition as a root). They can be named vices of the *savagery* of nature, and, at their greatest deviation from the natural ends, are called the *bestial vices of gluttony, lust and wild lawlessness* (in relation to other human beings).   6:27

2. The predispositions to humanity can be brought under the general title of a self-love which is physical and yet *involves comparison* (for which reason is required); that is, only in comparison with others does one judge oneself happy or unhappy. Out of this self-love originates the inclination *to gain worth in the opinion of others*, originally, of course, merely *equal worth:* not allowing anyone superiority over oneself, bound up with the constant anxiety that others might be striving for ascendancy; but from this arises gradually an unjust desire to acquire superiority for oneself over others.[18] – Upon this, namely, upon *jealousy* and *rivalry,* can be grafted the greatest vices of secret or open hostility to all whom we consider alien to us. These vices, however, do not really issue from nature as their root but are rather inclinations, in the face of the anxious endeavor of others to attain a hateful superiority over us, to procure it for ourselves over them for the sake of security, as preventive measure; for nature itself wanted to use the idea of such a competitiveness (which in itself does not exclude reciprocal love) as only an incentive to culture. Hence the vices that are grafted upon this inclination can also be named vices of *culture,* and in their extreme degree of malignancy (where they are simply the idea of a maximum of evil that surpasses humanity), e.g. in *envy, ingratitude, joy in others' misfortunes,* etc., they are called *diabolical vices.*

---

has reason does not at all follow that, simply by virtue of representing its maxims as suited to universal legislation, this reason contains a faculty of determining the power of choice unconditionally, and hence to be "practical" on its own;[*] at least, not so far as we can see. The most rational being of this world might still need certain incentives, coming to him from the objects of inclination, to determine his power of choice. He might apply the most rational reflection to these objects – about what concerns their greatest sum as well as the means for attaining the goal determined through them – without thereby even suspecting the possibility of such a thing as the absolutely imperative moral law which announces to be itself an incentive, and, indeed, the highest incentive. Were this law not given to us from within, no amount of subtle reasoning on our part would produce it or win our power of choice over to it. Yet this law is the only law that makes us conscious of the independence of our power of choice from determination by all other incentives (of our freedom) and thereby also of the accountability of all our actions.
[*] *für sich*

51

3. The predisposition to personality is the susceptibility to respect for the moral law *as of itself a sufficient incentive to the power of choice*. This susceptibility to simple respect for the moral law within us would thus be the moral feeling, which by itself does not yet constitute an end of the natural predisposition but only insofar as it is an incentive of the power of choice. But now this is possible only because the free power of choice incorporates moral feeling into its maxim: so a power of choice so constituted is a good character, and this character, as in general every character of the free power of choice, is something that can only be acquired; yet, for its possibility there must be present in our nature a predisposition onto which nothing evil can be grafted. The idea of the moral law alone, together with the respect that is inseparable from it, cannot be properly called a *predisposition to personality;* it is personality itself (the idea of humanity considered wholly intellectually). The subjective ground, however, of our incorporating this ·incentive into our maxims seems to be an addition to personality, and hence seems to deserve the name of a predisposition on behalf of it.

6:28

If we consider the three predispositions just named according to the conditions of their possibility, we find that the *first* does not have reason at its root at all; that the *second* is rooted in a reason which is indeed practical, but only as subservient to other incentives; and that the *third* alone is rooted in reason practical of itself, i.e. in reason legislating unconditionally. All these predispositions in the human being are not only (negatively) *good* (they do not resist the moral law) but they are also predispositions *to the good* (they demand compliance with it). They are *original,* for they belong to the possibility of human nature. The human being can indeed use the first two inappropriately, but cannot eradicate either of the two. By the predispositions of a being we understand the constituent parts required for it as well as the forms of their combination that make for such a being. They are *original* if they belong with necessity to the possibility of this being, but *contingent* if the being in question is possible in itself also without them. It should be noted, finally, that there is no question here of other predispositions except those that relate immediately to the faculty of desire and the exercise of the power of choice.

II.
CONCERNING THE PROPENSITY TO EVIL IN HUMAN NATURE

6:29

By *propensity* (*propensio*) I understand the subjective ground of the possibility of an inclination (habitual desire, *concupiscentia*), insofar as this possibility is contingent for humanity in general.* It is distinguished from a

---

*† *Propensity* is actually only the *predisposition* to desire an enjoyment which, when the subject has experienced it, arouses *inclination* to it. Thus all savages have a propensity for intoxi-

predisposition in that a propensity can indeed be innate yet *may* be represented as not being such: it can rather be thought of (if it is good) as *acquired*, or (if evil) as *brought* by the human being *upon* himself. – Here, however, we are only talking of a propensity to genuine evil, i.e. moral evil, which, since it is only possible as the determination of a free power of choice and this power for its part can be judged good or evil only on the basis of its maxims, must reside in the subjective ground of the possibility of the deviation of the maxims from the moral law. And, if it is legitimate to assume that this propensity belongs to the human being universally (and hence to the character of the species), the propensity will be called a *natural* propensity of the human being to evil. – We can further add that the will's[u] capacity or incapacity arising from this natural propensity to adopt or not to adopt the moral law in its maxims can be called *the good or the evil heart*.

We can think of three different grades of this natural propensity to evil. *First*, it is the general weakness of the human heart in complying with the adopted maxims, or the *frailty* of human nature; *second*, the propensity to adulterate moral incentives with immoral ones (even when it is done with good intention, and under maxims of the good), i.e. *impurity*; *third*, the propensity to adopt evil maxims, i.e. the *depravity* of human nature, or of the human heart.

First, the frailty (*fragilitas*) of human nature is expressed even in the complaint of an Apostle: "What I would, that I do not!"[19] i.e. I incorporate the good (the law) into the maxim of my power of choice; but this good, which is an irresistible incentive objectively or ideally (*in thesi*), is subjectively (*in hypothesi*) the weaker (in comparison with inclination) whenever the maxim is to be followed.

Second, the *impurity* (*impuritas, improbitas*)[v] of the human heart consists   6:30 in this, that although the maxim is good with respect to its object (the intended compliance with the law) and perhaps even powerful enough in practice, it is not purely moral, i.e. it has not, as it should be [the case], adopted the law *alone* as its *sufficient* incentive but, on the contrary, often (and perhaps always) needs still other incentives besides it in order to

cants; for although many of them have no acquaintance at all with intoxication, and hence absolutely no desire for the things that produce it, let them try these things but once, and there is aroused in them an almost inextinguishable desire for them. – Between propensity and inclination (the latter presupposes acquaintance with the object of desire) there is yet *instinct*. It is a felt need to do or enjoy something of which we still do not have a concept (such as the drive in animals to build[t] or the drive to sex). Above inclination there is, finally, still another level of the faculty of desire, *passion* (not *emotional agitation*, for this belongs to the feeling of pleasure and aversion), or an inclination that excludes mastery over oneself.

[t] *kunsttrieb*

[u] *Willkür*

[v] *improbitas:* disgracefulness

53

determine the power of choice for what duty requires; in other words, actions conforming to duty are not done purely from duty.

Third, the depravity (*vitiositas,*[m] *pravitas*) or, if one prefers, the *corruption* (*corruptio*) of the human heart is the propensity of the power of choice to maxims that subordinate the incentives of the moral law to others (not moral ones). It can also be called the *perversity* (*perversitas*) of the human heart, for it reverses the ethical order as regards the incentives of a *free* power of choice; and although with this reversal there can still be legally good (*legale*) actions, yet the mind's attitude is thereby corrupted at its root (so far as the moral disposition is concerned), and hence the human being is designated as evil.

It will be noted that the propensity to evil is here established (as regards actions) in the human being, even the best; and so it also must be if it is to be proved that the propensity to evil among human beings is universal, or, which here amounts to the same thing, that it is woven into human nature.

So far as the agreement of actions with the law goes, however, there is no difference (or at least there ought to be none) between a human being of good morals (*bene moratus*)[x] and a morally good human being (*moraliter bonus*), except that the actions of the former do not always have, perhaps never have, the law as their sole and supreme incentive, whereas those of the latter *always* do. We can say of the first that he complies with the law according to the *letter* (i.e. as regards the action commanded by the law); but of the second, that he observes it according to the *spirit* (the spirit of the moral law consists in the law being of itself a sufficient incentive). *Whatever is not of this faith is sin*[20] (in attitude). For whenever incentives other than the law itself (e.g. ambition, self-love in general, yes, even a kindly instinct such as sympathy) are necessary to determine the power of choice to *lawful* actions, it is purely accidental that these actions agree with the law, for the incentives might equally well incite its violation. The maxim, by the goodness of which all the moral worth of the person must be assessed, is therefore still contrary to law, and the human being, despite all his good actions, is nevertheless evil.

6:31

The following elucidation is also necessary in order to define the concept of this propensity. Every propensity is either physical, i.e. it pertains to a human's power of choice as natural being; or moral, i.e. it pertains to a human's power of choice as moral being. – In the first sense, there is no propensity to moral evil, for the latter must originate from freedom; a physical propensity (one based on sensory inducements) to whatever use of freedom, be it for good or evil, is a contradiction. Hence a propensity to evil can only attach to the moral faculty of choice.[y] Nothing

---

[m] being given to vice
[x] well behaved
[y] *dem moralischen Vermögen der Willkür*

54

Chack

is, however, morally (i.e. imputably) evil but that which is our own deed. And yet by the concept of a propensity is understood a subjective determining ground of the power of choice *that precedes every deed*, and hence is itself not yet a *deed*. There would then be a contradiction in the concept of a simple propensity to evil, if this expression could not somehow be taken in two different meanings, both nonetheless reconcilable with the concept of freedom. Now, the term "deed" can in general apply just as well to the use of freedom through which the supreme maxim (either in favor of, or against, the law) is adopted in the power of choice, as to the use by which the actions themselves (materially considered, i.e. as regards the objects of the power of choice) are performed in accordance with that maxim. The propensity to evil is a deed in the first meaning (*peccatum originarium*),[z] and at the same time the formal ground of every deed contrary to law according to the second meaning, [i.e. of a deed] that resists the law materially and is then called vice (*peccatum derivativum*);[a] and the first indebtedness remains even though the second may be repeatedly avoided (because of incentives that are not part of the law). The former is an intelligible deed, cognizable through reason alone apart from any temporal condition; the latter is sensible, empirical, given in time (*factum phenomenon*).[b] Now the first one is said to be a bare propensity especially when compared with the second, and to be innate, because it cannot be eradicated (for the supreme maxim for that would have to be the maxim of the good, whereas in this propensity the maxim has been assumed to be evil). But the chief reason is   6:32 that we are just as incapable of assigning a further cause for why evil has corrupted the very highest maxim in us, though this is our own deed, as we are for a fundamental property that belongs to our nature. – In what has just been said can be found the reason why in this section, from the very start, we sought the three sources of moral evil solely in that which affects the ultimate ground for the acceptance or the observance of our maxims according to the laws of freedom, not in what affects sensibility (as receptivity).

III.

THE HUMAN BEING IS BY NATURE EVIL

VITIIS NEMO SINE NASCITUR, HORACE[c]

In view of what has been said above, the statement, "The human being is *evil*," cannot mean anything else than that he is conscious of the moral law and yet has incorporated into his maxim the (occasional) deviation from it.

[z] original sin
[a] derivative sin
[b] phenomenal deed
[c] *Satires* I:iii.68. Nobody is born without vice.

"He is evil *by nature*" simply means that being evil applies to him considered in his species; not that this quality may be inferred from the concept of his species ([i.e.] from the concept of a human being in general, for then the quality would be necessary), but rather that, according to the cognition we have of the human being through experience, he cannot be judged otherwise, in other words, we may presuppose evil as subjectively necessary in every human being, even the best. Now, since this propensity must itself be considered morally evil, hence not a natural predisposition but something that a human being can be held accountable for, and consequently must consist in maxims of the power of choice contrary to the law and yet, because of freedom, such maxims must be viewed as accidental, a circumstance that would not square with the universality of the evil at issue unless their supreme subjective ground were not in all cases somehow entwined with humanity itself and, as it were, rooted in it: so we can call this ground a natural propensity to evil, and, since it must nevertheless always come about through one's own fault, we can further even call it a *radical* innate *evil* in human nature (not any the less brought upon us by ourselves).

6:33　We can spare ourselves the formal proof that there must be such a corrupt propensity rooted in the human being, in view of the multitude of woeful examples that the experience of human *deeds* parades before us. If we wish to draw our examples from that state in which many a philosopher especially hoped to meet the natural goodliness of human nature, namely from the so-called *state of nature,* let one but compare with this hypothesis the scenes of unprovoked cruelty in the ritual murders of Tofoa, New Zealand, and the Navigator Islands,[21] and the never-ending cruelty (which Captain Hearne reports)[22] in the wide wastes of northwestern America from which, indeed, no human being derives the least benefit,* and we find vices of savagery more than sufficient to distance us from any such opinion. If we are however disposed to the opinion that we can have a better cognition of human nature known in its civilized state (where its predispositions can be more fully developed), we must then hear out a long melancholy litany of charges against humankind – of secret falsity even in the most intimate friendship, so that a restraint on trust in the

*† Thus the perpetual war between the Arathapescaw Indians and the Dog Rib Indians has no other aim than mere slaughter. In the savages' opinion, bravery in war is the highest virtue. In the civilized state too, bravery is an object of admiration and one reason for the special respect commanded by that estate in which bravery is the sole merit; and this is not without basis in reason. For that a human being should be capable of possessing and adopting as his goal something (honor) which he values more highly still than his life, and of sacrificing all self-interest to it, this surely bespeaks a certain sublimity in his predisposition. Yet we see in the complacency with which the victors boast of their grandiose deeds (the butchery, the merciless killing, and the like) that it is in their mere superiority, and in the havoc that they can wreak, with no other end, that they really place their good.

56

mutual confidence of even the best friends is reckoned a universal maxim of prudence in social dealings; of a propensity to hate him to whom we are indebted, to which a benefactor must always heed; of a hearty goodwill that nonetheless admits the remark that "in the misfortunes of our best friends there is something that does not altogether displease us"[23]; and of many other vices yet hidden under the appearance of virtue, let alone those of which no secret is made, for to us someone already counts as good when *his evil is common to a class*[24] – and we shall have enough of the vices of *culture* and civilization (the most offensive of all) to make us rather turn our eyes away from the doings of human beings, lest we be dragged ourselves into another vice, namely that of misanthropy. And if we are not satisfied yet, we need but consider a state wondrously compounded from both the others, namely that of a people in its external relations, where civilized peoples stand vis-à-vis one another in the relation of raw nature (the state of constant war) and have also firmly taken it into their heads not to get out of it, and we shall become aware of fundamental principles in the great societies we call *states** directly in contradiction to official policy yet never abandoned, principles which no philosopher has yet been able to bring into agreement with morality or else (what is terrible) suggest [how to replace with]*d* better ones, reconcilable with human nature: So *philosophical chiliasm*, which hopes for a state of perpetual peace based on a federation of nations united in a world-republic, is universally derided as sheer fantasy as much as *theological chiliasm*, which awaits for the completed moral improvement of the human race.

6:34

Now, the ground of this evil cannot (1) be placed, as is commonly done, in the sensuous nature*e* of the human being, and in the natural inclinations originating from it. For not only do these bear no direct relation to evil (they rather give the occasion for what the moral disposition can demon-

6:35

---

*† If we look at the history of these simply as a phenomenon of inner predispositions of humanity for the most part concealed from us, we then become aware of a certain machinelike progression of nature according to ends which are not theirs (the peoples') but nature's own. So long as a state has a neighboring one which it can hope to subdue, it strives to aggrandize itself by subjugating it. It thus strives for a universal monarchy – a state constitution in which all freedom would necessarily expire, and, together with it, virtue, taste and science (which follow upon freedom). Yet after this monster (in which the laws gradually lose their force) has swallowed up all its neighbors, it ultimately disintegrates all by itself. It divides through rebellion and factionalism into many smaller states which, instead of striving after a union of states (a republic of free federated peoples), in turn begin the same game all over again, so that war (that scourge of the human race) will not cease. Although not so incurably evil as the grave of universal despotism (or even as a federation of nations pitted against the relaxation of despotism in any state), war, as an ancient said,[25] nonetheless creates more evil men than it takes away.

d I am adding "[how to replace with]" in an effort to retain Kant's loose sentence structure yet abide by English syntax.

e *Sinnlichkeit*

strate in its power, for virtue): we also cannot presume ourselves responsible for their existence (we cannot because, as conatural to us, natural inclinations do not have us for their author), though we can well be responsible for the propensity to evil which, since it concerns the morality of the subject and hence is to be found in the latter as a freely acting being, must be capable of being imputed to the subject as itself guilty of it – this despite the deep roots the propensity has in the power of choice, on account of which we must say that it is found in the human being by nature. – The ground of this evil can also not be placed (2) in a *corruption* of the morally legislative reason, as if reason could extirpate within itself the dignity of the law itself, for this is absolutely impossible. To think of oneself as a freely acting being, yet as exempted from the one law commensurate to such a being (the moral law), would amount to the thought of a cause operating without any law at all (for the determination according to natural law is abolished on account of freedom): and this is a contradiction. – *Sensuous nature*[f] therefore contains too little to provide a ground of moral evil in the human being, for, to the extent that it eliminates the incentives originating in freedom, it makes of the human a purely *animal* being; a reason exonerated from the moral law, an *evil reason* as it were (an absolutely evil will), would on the contrary contain too much, because resistance to the law would itself be thereby elevated to incentive (for without any incentive the power of choice cannot be determined), and so the subject would be made a *diabolical* being. – Neither of these two is however applicable to the human being.

But even though the existence of this propensity to evil in human nature can be established through experiential demonstrations of the actual resistance in time of the human power of choice against the law, these demonstrations still do not teach us the real nature of that propensity or the ground of this resistance; that nature rather, since it has to do with a relation of the free power of choice (the concept of which is not empirical) to the moral law (of which the concept is equally purely intellectual), must be cognized *a priori* from the concept of evil, so far as the latter is possible according to the laws of freedom (of obligation and imputability). What follows is the development of this concept.

6:36 The human being (even the worst) does not repudiate the moral law, whatever his maxims, in rebellious attitude (by revoking obedience to it). The law rather imposes itself on him irresistibly, because of his moral predisposition; and if no other incentive were at work against it, he would also incorporate it into his supreme maxim as sufficient determination of his power of choice, i.e. he would be morally good. He is, however, also dependent on the incentives of his sensuous nature[g] because of his equally

[f] *Sinnlichkeit*
[g] *Sinnlichkeit*

58

innocent natural predisposition, and he incorporates them too into his maxim (according to the subjective principle of self-love). If he took them into his maxim *as of themselves sufficient* for the determination of his power of choice, without minding the moral law (which he nonetheless has within himself), he would then become morally evil. But now, since he naturally incorporates both into the same maxim, whereas he would find each, taken alone, of itself sufficient to determine the will, so, if the difference between maxims depended simply on the difference between incentives (the material of the maxims), namely, on whether the law or the sense impulse provides the incentive, he would be morally good and evil at the same time – and this is a contradiction (as we saw in the Introduction). Hence the difference, whether the human being is good or evil, must not lie in the difference between the incentives that he incorporates into his maxim (not in the material of the maxim) but in their *subordination* (in the form of the maxim): *which of the two he makes the condition of the other.* It follows that the human being (even the best) is evil only because he reverses the moral order of his incentives in incorporating them into his maxims. He indeed incorporates the moral law into those maxims, together with the law of self-love; since, however, he realizes that the two cannot stand on an equal footing, but one must be subordinated to the other as its supreme condition, he makes the incentives of self-love and their inclinations the condition of compliance with the moral law – whereas it is this latter that, as *the supreme condition* of the satisfaction of the former, should have been incorporated into the universal maxim of the power of choice as the sole incentive.

In this reversal of incentives through a human being's maxim contrary to the moral order, actions can still turn out to be as much in conformity to the law as if they had originated from true principles – as when reason uses the unity of the maxims in general, which is characteristic of the moral law, merely to introduce into the incentives of inclination, under the name of *happiness*, a unity of maxims which they cannot otherwise have. (For example, when adopted as principle, truthfulness spares us the anxiety of maintaining consistency in our lies and not being entangled in their serpentine coils.) The empirical character is then good but the intelligible character still evil.

Now if a propensity to this [inversion] does lie in human nature, then there is in the human being a natural propensity to evil; and this propensity itself is morally evil, since it must ultimately be sought in a free power of choice, and hence is imputable. This evil is *radical*, since it corrupts the ground of all maxims; as natural propensity, it is also not to be *extirpated* through human forces, for this could only happen through good maxims – something that cannot take place if the subjective supreme ground of all maxims is presupposed to be corrupted. Yet it must equally be possible to *overcome* this evil, for it is found in the human being as acting freely.

6:37

59

The depravity of human nature is therefore not to be named *malice*,[h] if we take this word in the strict sense, namely as a disposition (a subjective *principle* of maxims) to incorporate evil *qua evil* for incentive into one's maxim (since this is *diabolical*), but should rather be named *perversity* of the heart, and this heart is then called *evil* because of what results. An evil heart can coexist with a will which in the abstract[i] is good. Its origin is the frailty of human nature, in not being strong enough to comply with its adopted principles, coupled with its dishonesty in not screening incentives (even those of well-intentioned actions) in accordance with the moral guide, and hence at the end, if it comes to this, in seeing only to the conformity of these incentives to the law, not to whether they have been derived from the latter itself, i.e. from it as the sole incentive. Now, even though a lawless action and a propensity to such contrariety, i.e. *vice*, do not always originate from it, the attitude of mind that construes the absence of vice as already being conformity of the *disposition* to the law of duty (i.e. as *virtue*) is nonetheless itself to be named a radical perversity in the human heart (for in this case no attention at all is given to the incentives in the maxim but only to compliance with the letter of the law).

6:38   This *innate* guilt (*reatus*), which is so called because it is detectable as early as the first manifestation of the exercise of freedom in the human being, but which must nonetheless have originated from freedom and is therefore imputable, can be judged in its first two stages (those of frailty and impurity) to be unintentional guilt (*culpa*); in the third, however, as deliberate guilt (*dolus*), and is characterized by a certain *perfidy* on the part of the human heart (*dolus malus*) in deceiving itself as regards its own good or evil disposition and, provided that its actions do not result in evil (which they could well do because of their maxims), in not troubling itself on account of its disposition but rather considering itself justified before the law. This is how so many human beings (conscientious in their own estimation) derive their peace of mind when, in the course of actions in which the law was not consulted or at least did not count the most, they just luckily slipped by the evil consequences; and [how they derive] even the fancy that they deserve not to feel guilty of such transgressions as they see others burdened with, without however inquiring whether the credit goes perhaps to good luck, or whether, on the attitude of mind they could well discover within themselves if they just wanted, they would not have practiced similar vices themselves, had they not been kept away from them by impotence, temperament, upbringing, and tempting circumstances of time and place (things which, one and all, cannot be imputed to us). This dishonesty, by which we throw dust in our own eyes and which hinders the establishment in us of a genuine moral disposition, then extends itself also

[h] depravity = *Bösartigheit;* malice = *Bösheit*
[i] *im Allgemeinen*

60

externally, to falsity or deception of others. And if this dishonesty is not to be called malice, it nonetheless deserves at least the name of unworthiness. It rests on the radical evil of human nature which (inasmuch as it puts out of tune the moral ability to judge what to think of a human being, and renders any imputability entirely uncertain, whether internal or external) constitutes the foul stain of our species – and so long as we do not remove it, it hinders the germ of the good from developing as it otherwise would.

A member of the English Parliament exclaimed in the heat of debate: "Every man has his price, for which he sells himself."[26] If this is true (and everyone can decide by himself), if nowhere is a virtue which no level of temptation can overthrow, if whether the good or evil spirit wins us over only depends on which bids the most and affords the promptest pay-off, then, what the Apostle says might indeed hold true of human beings universally, "There is no distinction here, they are all under sin – there is none righteous (in the spirit of the law), no, not one."[27]*

6:39

IV.
CONCERNING THE ORIGIN OF EVIL
IN HUMAN NATURE

Origin (the first origin) is the descent of an effect from its first cause, i.e. from that cause which is not in turn the effect of another cause of the same kind. It can be considered as either *origin according to reason*, or *origin according to time*. In the first meaning, only the effect's *being*[l] is considered; in the second, its *occurrence*, and hence, as an event, it is referred to its *cause in time*. If an effect is referred to a cause which is however bound to it according to the laws of freedom, as is the case with moral evil, then the determination of the power of choice to the production of this effect is

---

* The appropriate proof of this sentence of condemnation by reason sitting in moral judgment is contained not in this section, but in the previous one. This section contains only the corroboration of the judgment through experience – though experience can never expose the root of evil in the supreme maxim of a free power of choice in relation to the law, for, as *intelligible*[j] deed, the maxim precedes all experience. – From this, i.e. from the unity of the supreme maxims under the unity of the law to which it relates, we can also see why the principle of the exclusion of a mean between good and evil must be the basis of the intellectual judgment of humankind, whereas, for the empirical judgment, the principle can be laid down on the basis of *sensible*[k] *deed[s]* (actual doing or not doing) that there is a mean between these extremes – on the one side, a negative mean of indifference prior to all education; on the other, a positive mean, a mixture of being partly good and partly evil. This second judgment, however, concerns only human morality as appearance, and in a final judgment must be subordinated to the first.

[j] *intelligibile*
[k] *sensibler*
[l] *Dasein*

61

thought as bound to its determining ground not in time but merely in the representation of reason; it cannot be derived from some *preceding* state or

6:40 other, as must always occur, on the other hand, whenever the evil action is referred to its natural cause as *event* in the world. To look for the temporal origin of free actions as free (as though they were natural effects) is therefore a contradiction; and hence also a contradiction to look for the temporal origin of the moral constitution of the human being, so far as this constitution is considered as contingent, for constitution here means the ground of the *exercise of* freedom which (just like the determining ground of the free power of choice in general) must be sought in the representations of reason alone.

Whatever the nature, however, of the origin of moral evil in the human being, of all the ways of representing its spread and propagation through the members of our species and in all generations, the most inappropriate is surely to imagine it as having come to us by way of *inheritance* from our first parents; for then we could say of moral evil exactly what the poet says of the good: *genus et proavos, et quae non fecimus ipsi, vix ex nostra puto.*[m]* – We should note further that, when we enquire into the origin of evil, at the beginning we still do not take into account the propensity to it (as *peccatum in potentia*)[n] but only consider the actual evil of given actions according to

6:41 the evil's inner possibility, and according to all that must conspire within the power of choice for such actions to be performed.

Every evil action must be so considered, whenever we seek its rational origin, as if the human being had fallen into it directly from the state of innocence. For whatever his previous behavior may have been, whatever the natural causes influencing him, whether they are inside or outside

* The three so-called "higher faculties" (in the universities) would explain this transmission each in its own way, namely, either as *inherited disease,* or *inherited guilt,* or *inherited sin.* (1) The Faculty of Medicine would represent the inherited evil somewhat as it represents the tapeworm, concerning which certain natural scientists are actually of the opinion that, since it is not otherwise found either in an element outside us nor (of this same kind) in any other animal, it must already have been present in our first parents. (2) The *Faculty of Law* would regard it as the legal consequence of our accession to an *inheritance* bequeathed to us by these first parents but weighted down because of a serious crime (for to be born is just to inherit the use of the goods of the earth, inasmuch as these are indispensable to our survival). We must therefore make payment (atone) and, at the end, shall still be evicted (by death) from this possession. This is how the justice of law works! (3) The *Theological Faculty* would regard this evil as the personal participation by our first parents in the *fall* of a condemned rebel: either we were at the time ourselves accomplices (though not now conscious of it); or even now, born under the rebel's dominion (as Prince of this World), we prefer his goods to the supreme command of the heavenly master and lack sufficient faith to break loose from him, hence we shall eventually have to share in his doom.
[m] Ovid, *Metamorphoses*, XIII:140–141: "Race and ancestors, and those things which we did not make ourselves, I scarcely consider as our own."
[n] potential sin

them, his action is yet free and not determined through any of these causes; hence the action can and must always be judged as an *original* exercise of his power of choice. He should have refrained from it, whatever his temporal circumstances and entanglements; for through no cause in the world can he cease to be a free agent. It is indeed rightly said that to the human being are also imputed the *consequences* originating from his previous free but lawless actions. All that is thereby meant, however, is this: It is not necessary to get sidetracked into the prevarication of establishing whether such actions may have been free or not, since there is choice already sufficient ground for the imputation in the admittedly free action which was their cause. However evil a human being has been right up to the moment of an impending free action (evil even habitually, as second nature), his duty to better himself was not just in the past: it still is his duty *now;* he must therefore be capable of it and, should he not do it, he is at the moment of action just as accountable, and stands just as condemned, as if, though endowed with a natural predisposition to the good (which is inseparable from freedom), he had just stepped out of the state of innocence into evil. – Hence we cannot inquire into the origin in time of this deed but must inquire only into its origin in reason, in order thereby to determine and, where possible, to explain the propensity [to it], if there is one, i.e. the subjective universal ground of the adoption of a transgression into our maxim.

Now, the mode of representation which the Scriptures use to depict the origin of evil, as having a *beginning* in human nature, well agrees with the foregoing; for the Scriptures portray this beginning in a narrative, where what must be thought as objectively first by nature[o] (without regard to the condition of time) appears as a first in time. Evil begins, according to the Scriptures, not from a fundamental propensity to it, for otherwise its beginning would not result from freedom, but from *sin* (by which is 6:42 understood the transgression of the moral law as *divine command*); the state of human beings prior to any propensity to evil is however called the state of innocence. The moral law moved forward in the form of *prohibition* (Genesis II:16–17),[28] as befits a being who, like the human, is not pure but is tempted by inclinations. But, instead of following this law absolutely as sufficient incentive (which alone is unconditionally good, and with which there cannot be further hesitation), the human being looked about for yet other incentives (III:6)[29] which can be good only conditionally (i.e. so far as they do not infringe the law). And he made it his maxim – if one thinks of action as originating from freedom with consciousness – to follow the law of duty, not from duty but, if need be, also with an eye to other aims. He thereby began to question the strin-

[o] *der Natur der Sache nach*

gency of the command that excludes the influence of every other incentive, and thereupon to rationalize* downgrading his obedience to the command to the status of the merely conditional obedience as a means (under the principle of self-love), until, finally, the preponderance of the sensory inducements over the incentive of the law was incorporated into the maxim of action, and thus sin came to be (III:6). *Mutato nomine de te fabula narratur.*[p] It is clear from the above that this is what we do daily, and that hence "in Adam we have all sinned"[31] and still sin – except that a prior innate propensity to transgression is presupposed in us but not in the first human being, in whom rather innocence is presupposed with respect to time; hence his transgression is called a *fall into sin*, whereas ours is represented as resulting from a prior innate depravity of our nature. This propensity, however, means nothing more than this: if we wish to engage in an explanation of evil with respect to its *beginning in time*, we must trace the causes of every deliberate transgression in a previous time of our life, all the way back to the time when the use of reason had not yet developed, hence the source of evil back to a propensity (as natural foundation) to evil which is therefore called innate; in the case of the first human being, who is represented with full control of the use of his reason from the beginning, this is neither necessary nor expedient, for otherwise the foundation [of sin] (the evil propensity) would have to be co-created; hence we construe his sin as generated directly from innocence. – We must not however seek an origin in time of a moral character for which we are to be held accountable, however unavoidable this might be if we want to *explain* the contingent existence of this character (hence the Scriptures, in accordance with this weakness of ours, have perhaps so portrayed its origin in time).

The rational origin, however, of this disharmony in our power of choice with respect to the way it incorporates lower incentives in its maxims and makes them supreme, i.e. this propensity to evil, remains inexplicable to us, for, since it must itself be imputed to us, this supreme ground of all maxims must in turn require the adoption of an evil maxim. Evil can have originated only from moral evil (not just from the limitations of our nature); yet the original predisposition (which none other than the human being himself could have corrupted, if this corruption is to be imputed to him) is a predisposition to the good; there is no conceivable ground for us, therefore, from which moral evil could first have come in us. – The

6:43

---

* Any profession of reverence for the moral law which in its maxim does not however grant to the law – as self-sufficient incentive – preponderance over all other determining grounds of the power of choice is hypocritical, and the propensity to it is inward deceit, i.e. a propensity to lie to oneself in the interpretation of the moral law, to its prejudice (III:5); wherefore the Bible too (the Christian part of it) calls the author of evil (who is even within us) the Liar from the beginning,[30] and thus characterizes the human being as regards what seems to be the main ground of evil in him.

[p] Horace, *Satires*, I:1: "Change but the name, of you the tale is told."

Scriptures express this incomprehensibility in a historical narrative,* which adds a closer determination of the depravity of our species, by projecting evil at the beginning of the world, not, however, within the human being, but in a *spirit* of an originally more sublime destiny.[32] The absolutely *first* beginning of all evil is thereby represented as incomprehensible to us (for whence the evil in that spirit?); the human being, however, is represented as having lapsed into it only *through temptation,*[33] hence not as corrupted *fundamentally* (in his very first predisposition to the good) but, on the contrary, as still capable of improvement, by contrast to a tempting *spirit,* i.e. one whom the temptation of the flesh cannot be accounted as a mitigation of guilt. And so for the human being, who despite a corrupted heart yet always possesses a good will, there still remains hope of a return to the good from which he has strayed.

6:44

General remark
Concerning the restoration to its power of the original predisposition to the good

The human being must make or have made *himself* into whatever he is or should become in a moral sense, good or evil. These two [characters] must be an effect of his free power of choice, for otherwise they could not be imputed to him and, consequently, he could be neither *morally* good nor evil. If it is said, The human being is created good, this can only mean nothing more than: He has been created for the *good* and the original *predisposition* in him is good; the human being is not thereby good as such, but he brings it about that he becomes either good or evil, according as he either incorporates or does not incorporate into his maxims the incentives contained in that predisposition (and this must be left entirely to his free choice). Granted that some supernatural cooperation is also needed to his becoming good or better, whether this cooperation only consist in the diminution of obstacles or be also a positive assistance, the human being must nonetheless make himself antecedently worthy of receiving it; and

* What is being said here must not be regarded as though intended for Scriptural exegesis, which lies outside the boundaries of the competence of mere reason. We can explain how we put a historical account to our moral use without thereby deciding whether this is also the meaning of the writer or only our interpretation, if this meaning is true in itself, apart from all historical proof, and also the only meaning according to which we can derive something edifying from a text which would otherwise be only a barren addition to our historical cognition. We should not quarrel over an issue unnecessarily, and over its historical standing, when, however we understand it, the issue does not contribute anything to our becoming a better human being – if what can make a contribution in this respect is just as well known without historical demonstration and must even be known without it. Historical cognition that has no intrinsic relation, valid for everyone, to this [moral improvement], belongs among the *adiaphora,* which each may treat as one finds edifying.

6:44

he must *accept* this help (which is no small matter), i.e. he must incorporate this positive increase of force into his maxim: in this way alone is it possible that the good be imputed to him, and that he be acknowledged a good human being.

6:45 How it is possible that a naturally evil human being should make himself into a good human being surpasses every concept of ours. For how can an evil tree bear good fruit? But, since by our previous admission a tree which was (in its predisposition) originally good did bring forth bad fruits,* and since the fall from good into evil (if we seriously consider that evil originates from freedom) is no more comprehensible than the ascent from evil back to the good, then the possibility of this last cannot be disputed. For, in spite of that fall, the command that we *ought* to become better human beings still resounds unabated in our souls; consequently, we must also be capable of it, even if what we can do is of itself insufficient and, by virtue of it, we only make ourselves receptive to a higher assistance inscrutable to us. – Surely we must presuppose in all this that there is still a germ of goodness left in its entire purity, a germ that cannot be extirpated or corrupted. And it certainly cannot be self-love,† which, when

---

* The tree, good in predisposition, is not yet good in deed; for, if it were so, it surely could not bring forth bad fruit. Only when a human being has incorporated into his maxim the incentive implanted in him for the moral law, is he called a good human being (the tree, a good tree absolutely).

† Words susceptible of two entirely different meanings often long delay the achievement of conviction on even the clearest grounds. Like *love* in general, *self-love* too can be divided into love of *good will* and love of *good pleasure* (*benevolentiae et complacentiae*), and both (as is self-evident) must be rational. To incorporate the first into one's maxim is natural (for who would not want that things always go well for him?). This love is however rational to the extent that with respect to the end only what is consistent with the greatest and most abiding well-being is chosen, and that also the most apt means for each of these components of happiness are chosen. Reason only occupies here the place of a servant of natural inclination; the maxim that one adopts has absolutely no relation to morality. Let this maxim, however, become an unconditional principle of the power of choice, and it is the source of an incalculably great resistance to morals. – A rational love of *good pleasure in oneself* can be understood in either [of two senses: in one,] that we take pleasure in those maxims, already mentioned, which have for end the satisfaction of natural inclination (so far as this end can be attained by complying with them); and then it is one and the same with the love of good will toward oneself: one takes pleasure in oneself, just as a businessman who has done well in his business speculations rejoices over his good discernment because of the maxims he adopted

6:46 in them. [In the second sense,] the maxim of self-love, of *unconditional good pleasure* in oneself (independent of gain or loss resulting from action), is however the inner principle of a contentment only possible for us on condition that our maxims are subordinated to the moral law. No human being, to whom morality is not indifferent can take pleasure in himself, or can even avoid a bitter sense of dislike about himself, if he is conscious of such maxims in him as do not conform to the moral law. We could call this love a *rational love* of oneself that prevents any adulteration of the incentives of the power of choice by other causes of contentment consequent upon one's actions (under the name of happiness to be procured through them). But, since this denotes unconditional respect for the law, why needlessly

adopted as the principle of all our maxims, is precisely the source of all evil.

The restoration of the original predisposition to good in us is not 6:46 therefore the acquisition of a *lost* incentive for the good, since we were never able to lose the incentive that consists in the respect for the moral law, and were we ever to lose it, we would also never be able to regain it. The restoration is therefore only the recovery of the *purity* of the law, as the supreme ground of all our maxims, according to which the law itself is to be incorporated into the power of choice, not merely bound to other incentives, nor indeed subordinated to them (to inclinations) as conditions, but rather in its full purity, as the self-*sufficient* incentive of that power. The original good is *holiness of maxims* in the compliance to one's duty, hence merely out of duty, whereby a human being, who incorporates this purity into his maxims, though on this account still not holy as such 6:47 (for between maxim and deed there still is a wide gap), is nonetheless upon the road of endless progress toward holiness.[34] When the firm resolve to comply with one's duty has become a habit, it is called *virtue* also in a legal sense, in its *empirical character* (*virtus phaenomenon*). Virtue here has the abiding maxim of *lawful* actions, no matter whence one draws the incentives that the power of choice needs for such actions. Virtue, in this sense, is accordingly acquired *little by little*, and to some it means a long habituation (in the observance of the law), in virtue of which a human being, through gradual reformation of conduct and consolidation of his maxims, passes from a propensity to vice to its opposite. But not the slightest *change of heart* is necessary for this; only a change of *mores.*[q] A human being here considers himself virtuous whenever he feels himself stable in his maxims of observance to duty – though not by virtue of the supreme ground of all maxims, namely duty, but [as when], for instance, an immoderate human being converts to moderation for the sake of health; a liar to truth for the sake of reputation; an unjust human being to civic righteousness for the sake of peace or profit, etc., all in conformity with the prized principle of happiness. However, that a human being

render more difficult the clear understanding of the principle with the expression *rational self-love*, when this self-love is however *moral* only under the latter condition, and we thus go around in a circle (for we can love ourselves morally only to the extent that we are conscious of our maxim to make respect for the law the highest incentive of our power of choice)? For us – dependent as we are on objects of the senses – happiness is by *nature* the first that we desire and desire unconditionally. Yet by our nature (if this is how we want to name something innate in us) as a substance endowed with reason and freedom, this very happiness is not the first by far, nor is it indeed the object of our maxims unconditionally: this is rather the *worthiness of being happy*, i.e., the agreement of all our maxims with the moral law. Now, that this worthiness is objectively the condition under which alone the wish for happiness can conform with the law-giving reason, in this consists every ethical advance; and in the disposition to wish only under such condition, the ethical frame of mind.
[q] *Sitten*

should become not merely *legally* good, but *morally* good (pleasing to God) i.e. virtuous according to the intelligible character [of virtue] (*virtus noumenon*) and thus in need of no other incentive to recognize a duty except the representation of duty itself – that, so long as the foundation of the maxims of the human being remains impure, cannot be effected through gradual *reform* but must rather be effected through a *revolution* in the disposition of the human being (a transition to the maxim of holiness of disposition). And so a "new man"[35] can come about only through a kind of rebirth, as it were a new creation (John, 3:5;[36] compare with Genesis, 1:2[37]) and a change of heart.

But if a human being is corrupt in the very ground of his maxims, how can he possibly bring about this revolution by his own forces and become a good human being on his own? Yet duty commands that he be good, and duty commands nothing but what we can do. The only way to reconcile this is by saying that a revolution is necessary in the mode of thought[r] but a gradual reformation in the mode of sense[s] (which places obstacles in the way of the former), and [that both] must therefore be possible also to the human being. That is: If by a single and unalterable decision a human being reverses the supreme ground of his maxims by which he was an evil human being (and thereby puts on a "new man"),[38] he is to this extent, by principle and attitude of mind, a subject receptive to the good; but he is a good human being only in incessant laboring and becoming; i.e. he can hope – in view of the purity of the principle which he has adopted as the supreme maxim of his power of choice, and in view of the stability of this principle – to find himself upon the good (though narrow) path of constant *progress* from bad to better. For him who penetrates to the intelligible ground of the heart (the ground of all the maxims of the power of choice), for him to whom this endless progress is a unity, i.e. for God, this is the same as actually being a good human being (pleasing to him); and to this extent the change can be considered a revolution. For the judgment of human beings, however, who can assess themselves and the strength of their maxims only by the upper hand they gain over the senses in time, the change is to be regarded only as an ever-continuing striving for the better, hence as a gradual reformation of the propensity to evil, of the perverted attitude of mind.

From this it follows that a human being's moral education must begin, not with an improvement of mores, but with the transformation of his attitude of mind and the establishment of a character, although it is customary to proceed otherwise and to fight vices individually, while leaving their universal root undisturbed. But now, even the most limited human being is capable of all the greater a respect for a dutiful action the

6:48

[r] *Denkungsart*
[s] *Sinnesart*

68

more he removes from it, in thought, other incentives which might have influence upon its maxim through self-love. And even children are capable of discovering even the slightest taint of admixture of spurious incentives: for in their eyes the action then immediately loses all moral worth. This predisposition to the good is cultivated in no better way than by just adducing the *example* of good people (as regards their conformity to law), and by allowing our apprentices in morality to judge the impurity of certain maxims on the basis of the incentives actually behind their actions. And so the predisposition gradually becomes an attitude of mind, so that *duty* merely for itself begins to acquire in the apprentice's heart a noticeable importance. To teach only *admiration* for virtuous actions, however great a sacrifice these may have cost, falls short of the right spirit that ought to support the apprentice's feeling' for the moral good. For, however virtuous someone is, all the good that he can ever perform still is   6:49
merely duty; to do one's duty, however, is no more than to do what lies in the common moral order and is not, therefore, deserving of wonder. This admiration is, on the contrary, a dulling of our feeling for duty, as if to give obedience to it were something extraordinary and meritorious.

Yet there is one thing in our soul which, if we duly fix our eye on it, we cannot cease viewing with the highest wonder, and for which admiration is legitimate and uplifting as well. And that is the original moral predisposition in us, as such. – What is this in us (one can ask oneself) in virtue of which we, beings ever dependent on nature through so many needs, are at the same time elevated so far above it in the idea of an original predisposition (in us) that we would hold the whole of nature as nothing, and ourselves as unworthy of existence, were we to pursue the enjoyment of nature – though this alone can make our life desirable – in defiance of a law through which our reason commands us compellingly, without however either promising or threatening anything thereby? Every human being who has been instructed in the holiness that lies in the idea of duty, even one of the most ordinary ability, must feel the force of this question deeply within himself, though he has not presumed to investigate the concept of freedom which first and foremost derives from this law.* The   6:50
very incomprehensibility of this predisposition, proclaiming as it does a

---

* We can quickly be convinced that the concept of the freedom of the power of choice does not precede in us the consciousness of the moral law but is only inferred from the determinability of our power of choice through this law as unconditional command. We have only to ask whether we are certainly and immediately conscious of a faculty enabling us to overcome, by firm resolve, every incentive to transgression, however great (*Phalaris licet imperet, ut sis falsus, et admoto dictet periuria tauro*)." Everybody must admit that *he does not*
' Gemüt
" Juvenal, *Satires* VIII:81–82: "[. . . T]hough Phalaris himself should command you to be false and, having brought up his bull, should dictate perjuries." Phalaris was a tyrant of Agrigent. According to legend, he tortured his enemies by putting them inside a hollow bull cast in iron ore, which was then heated red hot.

divine origin, must have an effect on the mind, even to the point of exaltation, and must strengthen it for the sacrifices which respect for duty may perhaps impose upon it. Often to arouse this feeling of the sublimity of our moral vocation is especially praiseworthy as a means of awakening moral dispositions, since it directly counters the innate propensity to pervert the incentives in the maxims of our power of choice. Thus it works, in the unconditional respect for the law which is the highest condition of all the maxims to be adopted, for the restoration of the original ethical order among the incentives and, thereby, for the restoration to its purity of the predisposition in the human heart to the good.

But does not the thesis of the innate corruption of the human being with respect to all that is good stand in direct opposition to this restoration through one's own effort? Of course it does, so far as the comprehensibility of, i.e. our *insight* into, its possibility is concerned, or, for that matter, the possibility of anything that must be represented as an event in time (change) and, to this extent, as necessary according to nature, though its opposite must equally be represented, under moral laws, as possible through freedom; it is not however opposed to the possibility of this restoration itself. For if the moral law commands that we *ought* to be better human beings now, it inescapably follows that we must be *capable* of being better human beings. The thesis of innate evil is of no use in moral *dogmatics*, for the precepts of the latter would include the very same duties, and retain the same force, whether there is in us an innate propensity to transgression or not. In moral *discipline*, however, the thesis means more, yet not more than this: We cannot start out in the ethical training of our conatural moral predisposition to the good with an innocence which is natural to us but must rather begin from the presupposition of a depravity of our power of choice in adopting maxims contrary to the original ethical predisposition; and, since the propensity to this [depravity] is inextirpable, with unremitting counteraction against it. Since this only leads to a pro-

6:51

know whether, were such a situation to arise, he would not waver in his resolve. Yet duty equally commands him unconditionally: he *ought* to remain true to his resolve; and from this he rightly *concludes* that he must also *be able* to do it, and that his power of choice is therefore free. Those who pretend that this inscrutable property is entirely within our grasp concoct an illusion through the word *determinism* (the thesis that the power of choice is determined through inner sufficient grounds) as though the difficulty consisted in reconciling these grounds with freedom – [an issue] that does not enter into anyone's mind. Rather, what we want to discern, but never shall, is this: how can *pre-determinism* co-exist with freedom, when according to predeterminism freely chosen[v] actions, as occurrences, have their determining grounds *in antecedent time* (which, together with what is contained therein, no longer lies in our control), whereas according to freedom the action, as well as its contrary, must be in the control of the subject at the moment of its happening.

6:50

† There is no difficulty in reconciling the concept of *freedom* with the idea of God as a
[v] *willkürlich*

gression from bad to better extending to infinity, it follows that the transformation of the disposition of an evil human being into the disposition of a good human being is to be posited in the change of the supreme inner ground of the adoption of all the human being's maxims in accordance with the ethical law, so far as this new ground (the new heart) is itself now unchangeable. Assurance of this cannot of course be attained by the human being naturally, neither via immediate consciousness nor via the evidence of the life he has hitherto led, for the depths of his own heart (the subjective first ground of his maxims) are to him inscrutable. Yet he must be able to *hope* that, by the exertion of *his own* power, he will attain to the road that leads in that direction, as indicated to him by a fundamentally improved disposition. For he ought to become a good human being yet cannot be judged *morally* good except on the basis of what can be imputed to him as done by him.

Against this expectation of self-improvement, reason, which by nature finds moral labor vexing, now conjures up, under the pretext of natural impotence, all sorts of impure religious ideas (among which belongs falsely imputing to God the principle of happiness as the supreme condition of his commands). All religions, however, can be divided into *religion of rogation* (of mere cult) and *moral religion*, i.e. the religion of *good life-conduct*. According to the first, the human being either flatters himself that God can make him eternally happy (through the remissions of his debts) without any necessity on his part *to become a better human being;* or else, if this does not seem possible to him, that *God* himself *can make him a better human being* without his having to contribute more than to *ask* for it, and, since before an omniscient being asking is no more than *wishing*, this would amount in fact to doing nothing, for, if improvement were a matter of mere wishing, every human being would be good. According to moral religion, however (and, of all the public religions so far known, the Christian alone is of this type), it is a fundamental principle that, to become a better human being, everyone must do as much as it is in his powers to do; and only then, if a human being has not buried his innate talent (Luke 19:12–16),[39] if he has made use of the original predisposition to the good in order to become a better human being, can he hope that what does not lie in his power will be made good by cooperation from above. Nor is it absolutely necessary that the human being know in what this cooperation

6:52

necessary being, for freedom does not consist in the contingency of an action (in its not being determined through any ground at all), i.e. not in indeterminism ([the thesis] that God must be equally capable of doing good or evil, if his action is to be called free) but in absolute spontaneity. The latter is at risk only with predeterminism, where the determining ground of an action lies *in antecedent time*, so that the action is no longer in *my* power but in the hands of nature, which determines me irresistibly; since in God no temporal sequence is thinkable, this difficulty has no place.

consists; indeed, it is perhaps unavoidable that, were the way it occurs revealed at a given time, different people would, at some other time, form different conceptions of it, and that in all sincerity. For here too the principle holds, "It is not essential, and hence not necessary, that every human being know what God does, or has done, for his salvation"; but it is essential to know *what a human being has to do himself* in order to become worthy of this assistance.

†This General Remark is the first of four which are appended, one to each Part of this writing, and which could bear the labels 1) Of Effects of Grace; 2) Miracles; 3) Mysteries; and 4) Means of Grace. – These are, as it were, *parerga* to religion within the boundaries of pure reason; they do not belong within it yet border on it. Reason, conscious of its impotence to satisfy its moral needs, extends itself to extravagant ideas which might make up for this lack, though it is not suited to this enlarged domain. Reason does not contest the possibility or actuality of the objects of these ideas; it just cannot incorporate them into its maxims of thought and action. And if in the inscrutable field of the supernatural there is something more than it can bring to its understanding, which may however be necessary to make up for its moral impotence, reason even counts on this something being made available to its good will even if uncognized, with a faith which (with respect to the possibility of this something) we might call *reflective*, since the *dogmatic* faith which announces itself to be a *knowledge* appears to reason dishonest or impudent: for to remove difficulties that obstruct what stands firm on its own (practically), when these difficulties touch upon transcendent questions, is only a secondary occupation (*parergon*). As regards the disadvantages that result from these ideas (which are also *morally* transcendent), when we wish to introduce them into religion, their effects, in the order of the four classes mentioned above, are as follows: (1) supposed inner experience (effects of grace), *enthusiasm*; (2) alleged outer experiences (miracles), *superstition;* (3) presumed enlightenment of the understanding with respect to the supernatural (mysteries), *illumination,* the delusion of the initiates; (4) adventurous attempts at influencing the supernatural (means of grace), *thaumaturgy,* sheer aberrations of a reason that has strayed beyond its limits, indeed for a supposed moral aim (one pleasing to God). – Regarding this General Remark to the first Part of our treatise in particular, the summoning of the *effects of grace* belongs to the last class and cannot be incorporated into the maxims of reason, if the latter keeps to its boundaries; nor, in general, can anything supernatural, because all use of reason ceases precisely with it. – For it is impossible to make these effects *theoretically* cognizable (that they are effects of grace and not of immanent nature), because our use of the concept of cause and effect cannot be extended beyond the objects of experience, and hence beyond nature; moreover, the presupposition of a *practical* employment of this idea is wholly self-contradictory. For the

6:53

employment would presuppose a rule concerning what good we ourselves must *do* (with a particular aim [in mind]) in order to achieve something; to expect an effect of grace means, however, the very contrary, namely that the good (the morally good) is not of our doing, but that of another being – that we, therefore, can only *come by* it by *doing nothing,* and this contradicts itself. Hence we can admit an effect of grace as something incomprehensible but cannot incorporate it into our maxims for either theoretical or practical use.

The philosophical doctrine of religion
Part two

Part two

Concerning the battle of the good against the evil principle for dominion over the human being

To become a morally good human being it is not enough simply to let the germ of the good which lies in our species develop unhindered; there is in us an active and opposing cause of evil which is also to be combatted. It was especially the Stoics who among the ancient moralists called attention to this through their watchword *virtue*, which designates courage and valor (in Greek as well as in Latin)⁴⁰ and hence presupposes the presence of an enemy. In this respect the name *virtue* is a glorious one, and the fact that people have often boastfully misused and derided it (as of late the word "Enlightenment") can do it no harm. – For to require courage is already halfway to instilling it; whereas the lazy and timid cast of mind (in morality and religion), which has not the least trust in itself and waits for external help, unharnesses all the forces of a human being and renders him unworthy even of this help.

However, those valiant men [the Stoics] mistook their enemy, who is not to be sought in the natural inclinations, which merely lack discipline and openly display themselves unconcealed to everyone's consciousness,⁴¹ but is rather as it were an invisible enemy, one who hides behind reason and hence all the more dangerous. They send forth *wisdom* against *folly*, which lets itself be deceived by inclinations merely because of carelessness, instead of summoning it against the *malice* (of the human heart) which secretly undermines the disposition with soul-corrupting principles.*

* These philosophers derived their universal moral principle from the dignity of human nature, from its freedom (as an independence from the power of the inclinations), and they could not have laid down a better or nobler principle for foundation.⁴² They then drew the moral laws directly from reason, the sole legislator, commanding absolutely through its laws. And so was everything quite correctly apportioned – objectively, as regards the rule, and also subjectively, with respect to the incentive – provided that one attributes to the human being an uncorrupted will, unhesitatingly incorporating these laws into its maxims. The mistake of those philosophers, however, lay in just this last presupposition. For no matter how far back we direct our attention to our moral state, we find that this state is no longer *res integra*,ᵖ and
ᵖ i.e. a complete thing

77

6:58   *Considered in themselves* natural inclinations are *good,* i.e. not reprehensible, and to want to extirpate them would not only be futile but harmful and blameworthy as well; we must rather only curb them, so that they will not wear each other out but will instead be harmonized into a whole called happiness. Now the reason that accomplishes this is called *prudence.* Only what is unlawful is evil in itself, absolutely reprehensible, and must be eradicated. And the reason which teaches this, all the more so when it also puts it in actual practice, alone deserves the name of *wisdom,* in comparison to which vice may indeed also be called *folly,* but only when reason feels enough strength within itself to *despise* it (and every stimulation to it), not just to *hate* it as something to be feared, and arm itself against it.

6:59   Thus when the Stoic thought of the human moral battle simply as a human being's struggle with his inclinations, so far as these (innocent in themselves) must be overcome as obstacles in the compliance to his duty, he could locate the cause of the transgression only in the *omission* to combat them, since he did not assume any special positive principle (evil in itself);[44] since this omission is, however, itself contrary to duty (a transgression) and not just a natural error, and its cause cannot in turn be sought (without arguing in a circle) in the inclinations but, on the contrary, only in that which determines the power of choice as free power of choice (in the first and inmost ground of the maxims which are in agreement with the inclinations), we can well understand how philosophers – to whom the basis of an explanation remains forever shrouded in darkness[†] and, though absolutely

that we must rather start by dislodging from its possession the evil which has already taken up position there (as it could not have done, however, if it had not been incorporated by us into our maxims). That is, the first really good thing that a human being can do is to extricate himself from an evil which is to be sought not in his inclinations but in his perverted maxims, and hence in freedom itself. Those inclinations only make more difficult the *execution* of the good maxims opposing them; whereas genuine evil consists in our *will* not to resist the inclinations when they invite transgression, and this disposition is the really true enemy. The inclinations are opponents of the basic principles only in general (be these principles good or bad), and to this extent that high-minded principle of morality [of the Stoics] is beneficial as a preliminary exercise (the discipline of the inclinations in general) that renders the subject tractable at the hand of basic principles. But, to the extent that specific principles of *moral-goodness* ought to be present yet, as maxims, are not, we must presuppose in the subject somebody else opposing them, in the struggle with which virtue must hold its own; without it all virtues, though indeed not splendid *vices,* as one Church Father has it,[43] would certainly be *splendid frailties,* for through them rebellion is indeed often stilled, though never the rebel himself conquered and extirpated.

[†] It is a very common presupposition of moral philosophy that the presence in the human being of moral evil can very easily be explained, namely by the power of the incentives of sensibility, on the one hand, and the impotence of the incentive of reason (respect for the law) on the other, i.e. by *weakness.* But then the moral good in him (in his moral predisposition) would have to be even more easily explainable, for to comprehend the one without comprehending the other is quite unthinkable. Now reason's ability to become master over all the inclinations striving against it through the mere idea of a law is absolutely inexplicable; hence it is also incomprehensible how the senses could have the ability to become master

necessary, is nonetheless unwelcome – could mistake the real opponent of goodness with whom they believed they had to stand in combat.*

We should not therefore be disconcerted if an apostle represents this *invisible* enemy – this corrupter of basic principles recognizable only through his effects upon us – as being outside us, indeed as an evil *spirit:* "We have to wrestle not against flesh and blood (the natural inclinations) but against principalities and powers, against evil spirits.⁴⁵ This expression does not appear to be intended to extend our cognition beyond the world of the senses but only to make intuitive, *for practical use,* the concept of something to us unfathomable. It is at any rate all the same to us, so far as this practical use is concerned, whether we locate the tempter simply in   6:60 ourselves, or also outside us; for guilt touches us not any the less in the latter case than in the former, inasmuch as we would not be tempted by him were we not in secret agreement with him.* – We will divide this whole examination into two sections.

Section one.
Concerning the rightful claimʸ of the good principle to dominion over the human being

A. THE PERSONIFIED IDEA OF THE GOOD PRINCIPLE

That which alone can make a world the object of divine decree and the end of creation is *Humanity* (rational being in general as pertaining to the world)ᶻ *in its full moral perfection,*⁴⁶ from which happiness follows in the will of the Highest Being directly as from its supreme condition. – This hu-

---

over a reason which commands with such authority on its side. For if all the world proceeded in accordance with the precept of the law, we would say that everything occurred according to the order of nature, and nobody would think even of inquiring after the cause.

* It is a peculiarity of Christian morality to represent the moral good as differing from the moral evil, not as heaven from earth, but as heaven from hell. This is indeed a figurative representation and, as such, a stirring one, yet not any the less philosophically correct in meaning. – For it serves to prevent us from thinking of good and evil, the realm of light and the realm of darkness, as bordering on each other and losing themselves into one another by gradual steps (of greater and lesser brightness); but rather to represent them as separated by an immeasurable gap. The total dissimilarity of the basic principles by which one can be subject to either one or the other of these two realms, and also the danger associated with the illusion of a close relationship between the characteristics that qualify somebody for one or the other, justify this form of representation which, though containing an element of horror, is nonetheless sublime.

ˣ Kant's sentence does not parse. I have had to drop a comma and a *welcher* to make sense of it.

ʸ *Rechtsanspruch; Recht* also translates as "law."

ᶻ *Weltwesen* = . . . being . . . as pertaining to the world

79

man being, alone pleasing to God, "is in him from all eternity";[47] the idea of him proceeds from God's being; he is not, therefore, a created thing but God's only-begotten Son, "the *Word*" (the *Fiat!*) through which all other things are, and without whom nothing that is made would exist[48] (since for him, that is, for a rational being in the world, as can be thought according to its moral determination, everything was made). – "He is the reflection of his glory."[49] – "In him God loved the world,"[50] and only in

6:61 him and through the adoption of his dispositions can we hope "to become children of God";[51] etc.

Guilt

Now it is our universal human duty to *elevate* ourselves to this ideal of moral perfection, i.e. to the prototype of moral disposition in its entire purity, and for this the very idea, which is presented to us by reason for emulation, can give us force. But, precisely because we are not its authors but the idea has rather established itself in the human being without our comprehending how human nature could have even been receptive of it, it is better to say that that *prototype* has *come down* to us from heaven, that it has taken up humanity (for it is not just as possible to conceive how the *human being, evil* by nature, would renounce evil on his own and *raise* himself up to the ideal of holiness, as it is that the latter take up humanity – which is not evil in itself – by *descending* to it). This union with us may therefore be regarded as a state of *abasement* of the Son of God[52] if we represent to ourselves this God-like human being, our prototype, in such a way that, though himself holy and hence not bound to submit to sufferings, he nonetheless takes these upon himself in the fullest measure for the sake of promoting the world's greatest good. The human being, on the contrary, who is never free of guilt even when he has taken on the very same disposition, can regard himself as responsible for the sufferings that come his way, whatever the road, and hence unworthy of the union of his disposition with such an idea, even though this idea serves him as prototype.

Sense of morals can only be achieved by overcoming temptation

We cannot think the ideal of a humanity pleasing to God (hence of such moral perfection as is possible to a being pertaining to this world and dependent on needs and inclinations) except in the idea of a human being willing not only to execute in person all human duties, and at the same time to spread goodness about him as far wide as possible through teaching and example, but also, though tempted by the greatest temptation, to take upon himself all sufferings, up to the most ignominious death, for the good of the world and even for his enemies. – For human beings cannot form for themselves any concept of the degree and the strength of a force like that of a moral disposition except by representing it surrounded by obstacles and yet – in the midst of the greatest possible temptations – victorious.

x 6:62 In the *practical faith in this Son of God* (so far as he is represented as having taken up human nature) the human being can thus hope to become pleasing to God (and thereby blessed); that is, only a human being conscious of such a moral disposition in himself as enables him to *believe* and self-assuredly trust that he, under similar temptations and afflictions (so far as these are made the touchstone of that idea), would steadfastly cling to the prototype of humanity and follow this prototype's example in loyal emulation, only such a human being, and he alone, is entitled to consider himself not an unworthy object of divine pleasure.

B. THE OBJECTIVE REALITY OF THIS IDEA

From the practical point of view this idea has complete reality within itself. For it resides in our morally-legislative reason. We *ought* to conform to it, and therefore we must also *be able* to. If we had to demonstrate in advance that it is possible to be a human being conforming to this prototype, as is absolutely necessary in the case of concepts of nature (lest we run the risk of being stalled by empty concepts), we would have to entertain reservations about allowing even to the moral law the authority of unconditional and yet sufficient determining ground of our power of choice. For how it is possible that the mere idea of conformity to law in general be an even more powerful incentive of that power than any conceivable as deriving from [individual] advantages, can neither be understood by reason nor verified by examples from experience. For, as regards the first, the law commands unconditionally; and, as regards the second, even if there never had been one human being capable of unconditional obedience to the law, the objective necessity that there be such a human being would yet be undiminished and self-evident. There is no need, therefore, of any example from experience to make the idea of a human being morally pleasing to God a model to us; the idea is present as model already in our reason. – If anyone, in order to accept for imitation a human being as such an example of conformity to that idea, asks for more than what he sees, i.e. more than a course of life entirely blameless and as meritorious as indeed one may ever wish; and if, in addition, he also asks for miracles as credentials, to be brought about either through that human being or on   6:63
his behalf – he who asks for this thereby confesses to his own moral *unbelief,* to a lack of faith in virtue which no faith based on miracles (and thus only historical) can remedy, for only faith in the practical validity of the idea that lies in our reason has moral worth. (And moreover, such faith alone can validate miracles, if need be, as effects coming from the good principle; it cannot borrow its validation from them.)

Just for this reason an experience must be possible in which the example of such a human being is given (to the extent that one can at all expect and ask for evidence of inner moral disposition from an external experience). For, according to the law, each and every human being should furnish in his own self an example of this idea. And the required prototype always resides only in reason, since outer experience yields no example adequate to the idea; as outer, it does not disclose the inwardness of the disposition but only allows inference to it, though not with strict certainty. (Indeed, even a human being's inner experience of himself does not allow him so to fathom the depths of his heart as to be able to attain, through self-observation, an entirely reliable cognition of the basis of the maxims which he professes, and of their purity and stability).

Now if a human being of such a truly divine disposition had descended, as it were, from heaven to earth at a specific time, and had he exhibited in his self, through teaching, conduct, and suffering, the _example_ of a human being well-pleasing to God, to the extent that such an example can at all be expected from outer experience (for, in fact, the _prototype_ of any such human being is nowhere to be sought except in our reason); had he brought about, through all this, an incalculably great moral good in the world, through a revolution in the human race: even then we would have no cause to assume in him anything else except a naturally begotten human being (because he too feels to be under the obligation to exhibit such an example in himself). Not that we would thereby absolutely deny that he might indeed also be a supernaturally begotten human being. But, from a practical point of view[a] any such presupposition is of no benefit to us, since the prototype which we see embedded in this apparition must be sought in us as well (though natural human beings), and its presence in the human soul is itself incomprehensible enough that we should also assume, besides its supernatural origin, its hypostatization in a particular human being. On the contrary, the elevation of such a Holy One above every frailty of human nature would rather, from all that we can see, stand in the way of the practical adoption of the idea of such a being for our imitation. For let the nature of this human being well-pleasing to God be thought as human, inasmuch as he is afflicted by just the same needs and hence also the same sufferings, by just the same natural inclinations and hence also the same temptations to transgression, as we are. Let it also be thought as superhuman, however, inasmuch as his unchanging purity of will, not gained through effort but innate, would render any transgression on his part absolutely impossible. The consequent distance from the natural human being would then again become so infinitely great that the divine human being could no longer be held forth to the natural human being as _example._ The natural human being would say: If I were given a perfectly holy will, every temptation to evil would of itself founder in me; if I were given the most complete inner assurance that, after a short life on earth, I should at once become partaker (by virtue of this holiness) in all the eternal glory of the Kingdom of Heaven, I would then take all sorrows upon myself, however grave they might be, even to the most ignominious death, not only willingly but also joyfully, since I would have the glorious and imminent outcome before my eyes. To be sure, the thought that this

6:64

[a] _in praktischer Absicht_

82

divine human being had actual possession of his eminence and blessedness from eternity (and did not need to earn them first through such sorrows), and that he willingly divested himself of them for the sake of plainly unworthy individuals, even for the sake of his enemies, to deliver them from eternal damnation – this thought must attune our mind to admiration, love and thankfulness toward him. Likewise the idea of a conduct in accordance with so perfect a rule of morality could no doubt also be valid for us, as a precept to be followed. Yet he himself could *not* be presented to us *as an example to be emulated,* hence also not as proof that so pure and exalted a moral goodness can be practised and attained *by us.**

Yet such a divinely disposed teacher, though in fact totally human,   6:65
would nonetheless be able to speak truly of himself as if the ideal of   6:66
goodness were displayed incarnate in him (in his teaching and conduct).

---

* It is plainly a limitation of human reason, one which is ever inseparable from it, that we cannot think of any significant moral worth in the actions of a person without at the same time   6:65
portraying this person or his expression in human guise, even though we do not thereby mean to say that this is how things are in themselves ($\chi\alpha\tau'\,\dot{\alpha}\lambda\acute{\eta}\vartheta\varepsilon\iota\alpha\nu$)^b for we always need a certain analogy with natural being in order to make supersensible characteristics comprehensible to us. Thus a philosophical poet assigns to the human being, inasmuch as he has to do battle against a propensity to evil within himself, just because he might overpower it, a higher rung on the moral ladder of beings than to the very inhabitants of heaven who, by virtue of the holiness of their nature, are raised above all possibility of being led astray ("The world with its defects/ is better than a realm of will-less angels."[53]) – The Scriptures too, to make the extent of God's love for the human race comprehensible to us, adapt themselves to this manner of representation, by attributing to God the highest sacrifice a living being can ever perform in order to make even the unworthy happy ("God so loved the world, etc."[54]), although through reason we cannot form any concept of how a self-sufficient being could sacrifice something that belongs to his blessedness, thus robbing himself of a perfection. We have here (as means of elucidation) a *schematism of analogy,* with which we cannot dispense. To transform it, however, into a *schematism of object-determination* (as means for expanding our cognition) constitutes *anthropomorphism,* and from the moral point of view (in religion) this has most injurious consequences. – Here I also want to remark incidentally that, in the ascent from the sensible to the supersensible, we can indeed *schematize* (render a concept comprehensible through analogy with something of the senses) but in no way infer by analogy that what pertains to the sensible must also be attributed to the supersensible (thus *expanding* the concept of the latter): we cannot, for the utterly simple reason that it would run *counter* to all analogy to conclude that, since we must necessarily use a schema for a concept to render it comprehensible to us (to support it with an example), this schema must necessarily belong to the object too as its predicate. Thus I cannot say: Just as I cannot make the cause of a plant *comprehensible* to me (or the cause of any organic creature, or in general of the purposive world) in any other way than on the analogy of an artificer in relation to his work (a clock), namely by attributing understanding to the cause, so too must the cause itself (of the plant, of the world in general) *have* understanding; i.e. attributing understanding to it is not just a condition of my capacity to comprehend but of the possibility itself to be a cause. But between the relationship of a schema to its concept and the relationship of this very schema of the concept to the thing itself there is no analogy, but a formidable leap ($\mu\varepsilon\tau\acute{\alpha}\beta\alpha\sigma\iota\varsigma$ $\varepsilon\grave{\iota}\varsigma$ $\check{\alpha}\lambda\lambda o$ $\gamma\acute{\varepsilon}\nu o\varsigma$)^c which leads straight into anthropomorphism. Of this I have given proof elsewhere.

^{b} according to truth
^{c} passage into another genus

[handwritten margin note: of the possibility itself to be the cause requires not an analogy but formidable leap "leap of faith"]

For he would be speaking only of the disposition which he makes the rule of his actions but which, since he cannot make it visible as an example to others in and of itself, he places before their eyes externally through his teachings and actions: "Which of you convinceth me of sin?"[55] And it is only proper that, in the absence of proof to the contrary, a teacher's irreproachable example of what he teaches – when this is, moreover, a matter of duty for everyone – be attributed to no other disposition in him except the purest one. Now, when expressed in thought as the ideal of humankind, such a disposition, in conjunction with all the sufferings undertaken for the sake of the world's highest good, is perfectly valid for all human beings, at all times, and in all worlds, before the highest righteousness, whenever a human being makes his own like unto it, as he ought. To be sure, it will ever remain a righteousness which is not our own, inasmuch as ours would have to come into existence in a life conduct completely and unfailingly in accord with that disposition. Yet an appropriation of it for the sake of our own must be possible, provided that ours is associated with the disposition of the prototype, even though rendering this appropriation comprehensible to us is still fraught with great difficulties. These difficulties we now want to consider.

C. DIFFICULTIES THAT STAND IN THE WAY OF THE REALITY OF THIS IDEA, AND THEIR SOLUTION

The first difficulty which makes doubtful the possibility of realizing in us the idea of a humanity well-pleasing to God, considering the *holiness* of the Lawgiver and the lack of righteousness on our part, is the following. The law says: "Be ye holy (in the conduct of your lives) as your Father in Heaven is holy,"[56] for this is the ideal of the Son of God which is being placed before us as model. The distance between the goodness which we ought to effect in ourselves and the evil from which we start is, however, infinite, and, so far as the deed is concerned – i.e. the conformity of the conduct of one's life to the holiness of the law – it is not exhaustible in any time. Nevertheless, the human being's moral constitution ought to agree with this holiness. The latter must therefore be assumed in his disposition, in the universal and pure maxim of the agreement of conduct with the law, as the germ from which all good is to be developed – [in a disposition] which proceeds from a holy principle adopted by the human being in his supreme maxim. And this is a change of heart which must itself be possible because it is a duty. – Now the difficulty lies here: How can this disposition count for the deed itself, when this deed is *every time* (not generally, but at each instant) defective? The solution rests on the following: According to our mode of estimation, [to us] who are unavoidably restricted to temporal conditions in our conceptions of the relation-

6:67

ship of cause to effect, the deed, as a continuous advance *in infinitum* from a defective good to something better, always remains defective, so that we are bound to consider the good as it appears in us, i.e. according to the *deed*, as *at each instant* inadequate to a holy law. But because of the *disposition* from which it derives and which transcends the senses, we can think of the infinite progression of the good toward conformity to the law as being judged by him who scrutinizes the heart (through his pure intellectual intuition) to be a perfected whole even with respect to the deed (the life conduct).* And so notwithstanding his permanent deficiency, a human being can still expect to be *generally* well-pleasing to God, at whatever point in time his existence be cut short.

The *second* difficulty that arises whenever we consider the human being, as he strives toward the good, with respect to the relation of his moral good to the divine *goodness*, has to do with *moral happiness*, by which we do not here mean the assurance of the everlasting possession of contentment in one's *physical state* (freedom from evils and enjoyment of ever mounting pleasures), i.e. *physical happiness*, but the assurance of the reality and *constancy* of a disposition that always advances in goodness (and never falters from it). For, *if one were absolutely assured of the unchangeableness of such a disposition*, the constant "seeking after the Kingdom of God" would be equivalent to knowing oneself already in possession of this kingdom, 6:68 inasmuch as a human being thus disposed would from himself derive the confidence that "all things else (i.e. what relates to physical happiness) will be added to him."[57]

Now one could indeed refer a human being anxious on this score, and his wish, to: "His (God's) Spirit gives witness to our spirit,"[58] etc.; that is, whoever possesses as pure a disposition as is required will feel of himself that he can never fall so low as to regain a liking for evil. There is, however, something awkward about such feelings of a presumed supernatural origin: one is never more easily deceived than in what promotes a good opinion of oneself. Moreover, it seems never advisable to be encouraged to such a state of confidence but much more beneficial (for morality) to "work out one's salvation with *fear* and *trembling*"[59] (a hard saying which, if misunderstood, can drive one to the darkest enthusiasm). Yet

---

* It must not be overlooked that we do not thereby mean to say that the disposition should serve to *compensate* for any lack of conformity to duty, hence for the actual evil, in this infinite series (the presupposition is rather that the human moral constitution pleasing to God is actually to be found in the series), but rather that the disposition, which takes the place of the totality of the series of approximations carried on *in infinitum*, makes up only for the deficiency which is in principle inseparable from the existence of a temporal being, [namely] never to be able to become quite fully what he has in mind.[d] For as regards the compensation for the transgressions incurred in this progression, we shall consider it in connection with the solution to the *third* difficulty.

[d] *im Begriffe*

without *any* confidence in the disposition once acquired, perseverance in it would hardly be possible. We can, however, find this confidence, without delivering ourselves to the sweetness or the anxiety of enthusiasm, by comparing our life conduct so far pursued with the resolution we once embraced. – For [take] a human being who, from the time of his adoption of the principles of the good and throughout a sufficiently long life henceforth, has perceived the efficacy of these principles on what he does, i.e. on the conduct of his life as it steadily improves, and from that has cause to infer, but only by way of conjecture, a fundamental improvement in his disposition: [he] can yet also reasonably hope that in this life he will no longer forsake his present course but will rather press in it with ever greater courage, since his advances, provided that their principle is good, will always increase his *strength* for future ones; nay, if after this life another awaits him, that he will persevere in it (in all appearances under different circumstances, yet according to the very same principle) and come ever closer to his goal of perfection, though it is unattainable; for, on the basis of what he has perceived in himself so far, he can legitimately assume that his disposition is fundamentally improved. By contrast, one who has always found himself unable to stand fast by his often repeated resolutions to be good but has always relapsed into evil, or who has been forced to acknowledge that in the course of his life he has gone from bad to worse, slipping ever further down as though on a slope: [such a one] 6:69 can reasonably entertain no hope of improving, even if he still had to live longer in this world, or a future life stood ahead of him, for, from all indications, he would have to regard the corruption as rooted in his disposition. Now, the first is a glimpse into a *boundless* future which is, however, desirable and happy; the second, by contrast, into a *misery* which is just as *boundless*, i.e. for human beings, from what they can judge, the two [glimpse] into either a blessed or a cursed*ᵉ* *eternity*. And these are representations powerful enough to serve to one part [of humanity] as reassurance and confirmation in the good, and, to the other, for rousing conscience to judgment, to make yet a break with evil so far as is possible, hence as incentives, without any necessity to presuppose *dogmatically*, as an item of doctrine, that an eternity of good or evil is the human lot also objectively:* with supposed cognitions and assertions of this sort reason

---

* Among those questions which, even if they could be answered, would not in the least enlighten the questioner (and which we may therefore call *childish questions*) is this: Will the punishment of hell be finite or everlasting? Teach the first alternative, and there is cause to fear that many would say (like all those who believe in purgatory, or like the sailor in Moore's *Travels*⁶⁰): "Well, I hope that I will be able to last it out." Assert the second instead, and count it as tenet of faith, and the unintended result may be the hope of complete impunity after a most dastardly life. For a clergyman, though sought for advice and consolation only in the brief moments of a belated remorse at the end of such a dastardly life, must yet find it cruel
ᵉ unselig

86

simply transgresses the limitations of its insight. The good and pure 6:70
disposition of which we are conscious (and which we can call a good spirit 6:71
that presides over us) thus carries confidence in its own perseverance and
stability, though indirectly, and is our Comforter (Paraclete) whenever our

and inhuman to proclaim eternal damnation to the [dying] one; and since the clergyman
admits no middle ground between eternal damnation and complete absolution (on the
contrary, either there is eternal punishment or no punishment at all), he will have to hold out
to him the hope of not being punished at all, i.e. he must promise to transform him in a hurry
into a human being well-pleasing to God; but, since there is no time left then for the
conversion to a life of good conduct, professions of remorse, formulas of faith, even vows of
a new life just in case the end of the present one is somewhat delayed, will have to take the
place of the means. – Such is the unavoidable consequence when the *eternity* of [one's]
future destiny, conformable to the conduct of [one's] present life, is set forth as *dogma*, and a
human being is not rather instructed to form a concept of his future moral state on the basis
of his state up to the present, and to come *on his own* to a conclusion regarding it as the
[totality of the] naturally foreseeable consequences of his present one. For then the *immeasur-
ableness* of the series of such consequences under the dominion of evil will work on him the
same moral effect (of inciting him before the end of his life to undo whatever has happened
as much as he can, through reparation or compensation proportionate to his actions) as can
be expected from proclaiming the eternity of the evil, without however entailing the disadvantages of the dogma of this eternity (which, moreover, is warranted by neither rational insight
nor scriptural exegesis), namely that the wicked human being counts in advance, even *during* 6:70
his life, on an easily obtainable pardon, or that, at life's close, he believes he only has to
reckon with the claims of heavenly justice upon him, and these he can satisfy with words
alone, and human rights are meanwhile left begging, and nobody will get back what belongs
to him (this is an outcome so common to this kind of expiation that an example to the
contrary is almost unheard of). – Furthermore, should anyone fear that his reason, through
conscience, will judge him too leniently, he errs, I believe, seriously. For reason is incorrupt-
ible just because it is free, and must pass judgment over him (the human being) precisely as
reason; and if we simply tell him, under such circumstances, that it is at least possible that
soon he must stand before a judge, we need but leave him to his own reflection, which will in
all probability judge him with the greatest severity. – To this I want to add a couple of further
comments. The common saying, "All's well that ends well," can indeed be applied to moral
cases, but only if by the "good ending" we understand that a human being becomes a
genuinely good human being. Yet where is he to recognize himself to be such, since he can
draw this conclusion only from the constancy of his consequent good conduct, and, at the
end of life, there is no time left for this? With respect to *happiness* the saying can more easily
be conceded, but here too only by assuming the standpoint of someone who looks at his life,
not from the starting point, but at its close, and reviews it from there. Griefs once endured,
when we feel safe from them, leave no painful reminiscences behind but rather a feeling of
gladness that makes the enjoyment of the supervening good fortune all the sweeter. For
pleasure and pain (since they belong to the senses) are both included in the temporal series,
and disappear with it; they do not constitute a totality with the present enjoyment of life but
are rather displaced by it as it succeeds them. If we however apply the same saying to the
judgment of the moral worth of the life we have led up to the present, we may be wide of the
truth in our judgment, even if, in conclusion, we have given to our life a totally good new
turn. For the moral subjective principle of the *disposition* by which our life is to be judged is
(as transcending the senses) not of the kind that its existence can be thought as divisible into
temporal segments but rather only as an absolute unity. And since we can draw inferences
regarding the disposition only on the basis of actions (which are its appearances), for the

87

lapses make us anxious about its perseverance. Certainty with respect to the latter is neither possible to the human being, nor, so far we can see, morally beneficial. For (be it well noted) we cannot base this confidence upon an immediate consciousness of the immutability of our disposition, since we cannot see through to the latter but must at best infer it from the consequence that it has on the conduct of our life. And since our inference is drawn from perceptions that are only appearances of a good or bad disposition, our inference never reveals with any certainty especially the *strength* of the disposition, least of all when, in the face of impending death, we think that we have improved ours. For then, in the absence of further conduct upon which to base our judgment of our moral worth, even those empirical proofs of the genuineness of an improved disposition are entirely lacking, and the unavoidable consequence of a rational estimate of our moral state is a feeling of hopelessness (which, however, human nature itself, because of the obscurity of all views that transcend the limits of this life, takes care that it does not turn into wild despair).

6:72 The *third* and apparently the greatest difficulty – which would have^f every human being, even after he has entered upon the path of goodness, still a reprobate in the sentencing of his entire life conduct before a divine *righteousness* – is as follows. – Whatever his state in the acquisition of a good disposition, and, indeed, however steadfastly a human being may have persevered in such a disposition in a life conduct conformable to it, *he nevertheless started from evil*, and this is a debt which is impossible for him to wipe out. He cannot regard the fact that, after his change of heart,

---

purpose of a [moral] estimate our life is to be viewed only as a *temporal unity*, i.e. a *whole*. But then the reproaches [arising] from the first part of our life (before the improvement) join in with just as loud a voice as the approval in the *concluding* part, and might indeed dampen the triumphant tone of the "All's well that ends well." – Finally, closely related to this doctrine 6:71 regarding the duration of punishment in another world, though not identical with it, is yet another, namely, that "All sins must be forgiven here," that at the end of life our account must be completely closed, and nobody may hope somehow to make up there for what was neglected here. This doctrine can no more proclaim itself to be dogma than the previous one, but is rather only a principle by which practical reason regulates itself in its use of the concept of the supersensible, while at the same time granting that it knows nothing of the objective composition of the latter. Practical reason is in fact saying only this much: We can conclude that we are human beings pleasing to God, or not, only on the basis of the conduct of the life we have led so far; and since this conduct ends with our life, so too does the reckoning, the balance of which alone must yield whether we may regard ourselves as justified or not. – In general, if, instead of [extending it to] the *constitutive* principles of the cognition of supersensible objects into which we cannot in fact have any insight, we restricted our judgment to the *regulative* principles, which content themselves with only their practical use, human wisdom would be better off in a great many respects, and there would be no breeding of would-be knowledge of something of which we fundamentally know nothing – groundless though indeed for a while glittering sophistry that it is, at the end unmasked as a detriment to morality.

^f *vorstellt*

88

he has not incurred new debts as equivalent to his having paid off the old ones. Nor can he produce, in the future conduct of a good life, a surplus over and above what he is under obligation to perform each time; for his duty at each instant is to do all the good in his power. – Moreover, so far as we can judge by our reason's standards of right, this original debt, or at any rate the debt that precedes whatever good a human being may ever do (this, and no more, is what we understood by *radical* evil; cf. the first Section), cannot be erased by somebody else. For it is not a *transmissible* liability which can be made over to somebody else, in the manner of a financial debt (where it is all the same to the creditor whether the debtor himself pays up, or somebody else for him), but the *most personal* of all liabilities, namely a debt of sins which only the culprit, not the innocent, can bear, however magnanimous the innocent might be in wanting to take the debt upon himself for the other. – Now, moral evil (transgression of the moral law, called sin when the law is taken *as divine command*) brings with it an *infinity* of violations of the law, and hence an *infinity* of guilt (though it is otherwise before a human court, which takes only the individual crime into account, hence only the act and anything related to it, not the universal disposition), not so much because of the *infinity* of the highest lawgiver whose authority is thereby offended (for we understand nothing of such intangible relations of the human being to the highest being) but because the evil is in the *disposition* and the maxims in general (in the manner of *universal principles* as contrasted with individual transgressions): consequently, every human being has to expect *infinite* punishment and exclusion from the Kingdom of God.

The resolution to this difficulty rests on the following consideration. The judicial verdict of one who knows the heart of the accused must be thought as based on the universal disposition of the latter, not on the [6:73] appearances of his disposition, [i.e.] on actions that either diverge from the law or agree with it. In this respect, however, we now presuppose in the human being a good disposition which has the upper hand over the evil principle formerly dominant in him. So the question is whether the moral consequence of his earlier disposition, [i.e.] punishment, (or in other words: the effect on the subject of God's displeasure) can be extended to reach even his present state, in his improved disposition in which he already is an object of divine pleasure. Now, since the question here is not whether, also *before* the human being's conversion, the punishment imposed upon him accorded with divine justice (as there is no doubt about this), the punishment *is not* to be thought (in this inquiry) as fully exacted before the human being's improvement. Also *after his conversion*, however, since he now leads a new life and has become a "new man,"[61] the punishment cannot be considered appropriate to his new quality (of thus being a human being well-pleasing to God). Yet satisfaction must be rendered to Supreme Justice, in whose sight no one deserving of punishment can go unpunished. But, since neither *before* nor *after* conversion is the punishment in accordance with divine wisdom but is nevertheless necessary, the punishment must be thought as adequately executed in the situation of conversion itself. We must therefore see whether, by means of the very concept of moral conversion, we can think that situation as entailing such ills as the new human being, whose disposition is good, can regard as having been incurred by himself (in a different context) and, [therefore],

6:74 as *punishment** whereby satisfaction is rendered to divine justice. – Now conversion is an exit from evil and an entry into goodness, "the putting off of the old man and the putting on of the new,"[64] since the subject dies unto sin (and thereby also the subject of all inclinations that lead to sin) in order to live unto justice. As an intellectual determination, however, this conversion is not two moral acts separated by a temporal interval but is rather a single act, since the abandonment of evil is possible only through the good disposition that effects the entrance into goodness, and *vice-versa*. The good principle is present, therefore, just as much in the abandonment of the evil as in the adoption of the good disposition, and the pain that by rights accompanies the first derives entirely from the second. The emergence from the corrupted disposition into the good is in itself already sacrifice (as "the death of the old man,"[65] "the crucifying of the flesh"[66]) and entrance into a long train of life's ills which the new human being undertakes in the disposition of the Son of God, that is, simply for the sake of the good, yet are still fitting *punishment* for someone else, namely the old human being (who, morally, is another human being). – *Physically* ([i.e.] considered in his empirical character as a sensible being) he still is the same human being liable to punishment, and he must be judged as such before a moral tribunal of justice and hence by himself as well. Yet, in his new disposition (as an intelligible being), in the sight of a divine judge for whom the disposition takes the place of the deed, he is *morally* another being. And this disposition which he has incorporated in

---

* We cannot assume that the hypothesis that all evils in the world are generally to be regarded as punishments for transgressions committed was devised for the sake of a theodicy or as a contrivance for the purposes of priestly religion (cult), for it is too common to have been artificially excogitated; we must rather presume that the hypothesis is closely allied to human reason, which is inclined to link the course of nature with the laws of morality, and hence quite naturally comes up with the idea that we should seek to become better human beings first, before we can request to be freed from the ills of life, or to be compensated for them with a superior good. – Hence the first man is represented (in Holy Scriptures) as condemned to work if he wishes to eat, his wife to bear children in pain, and both to die, *all on account of their transgression*, although there is no telling how animal creatures, fitted with their bodily limbs, could have expected any other destiny even if these transgressions had not been perpetrated.[62] For the Hindus human beings are but spirits (called "Dewas") locked up in animal bodies as punishment for previous crimes, and even a philosopher (Malebranche) preferred to attribute no soul, and hence no feelings, to nonrational animals rather than to admit that horses had to withstand so much torment "without having ever eaten of forbidden hay."[63]

all its purity, like unto the purity of the Son of God – or (if we personify this idea) this very **Son of God** – bears as *vicarious substitute* the debt of sin for him, and also for all who believe (practically) in him: as *savior*, he satisfies the highest justice through suffering and death, and, as *advocate*, he makes it possible for them to hope that they will appear justified before their judge. Only we must remember that (in this way of imagining) the suffering which the new human being must endure* while dying to the *old* human being throughout his life is depicted in the representative of the human kind as a death suffered once and for all. – Here, then, is that surplus over the merit from works for which we felt the need earlier, one which is imputed to us *by grace*. For what in our earthly life (and perhaps even in all future times and in all worlds) is always only in mere *becoming* (namely, our being a human being well-pleasing to God) is imputed to us as if we already possessed it here in full. And to this we indeed have no rightful claim† (according to the empirical cognition we have of ourselves), so far as we know[g] ourselves (estimate our disposition not directly

6:75

---

* Even the purest moral disposition elicits in the human being, regarded as a worldly creature, nothing more than the continuous becoming of a subject well pleasing to God in actions (such as can be met with in the world of the senses). In quality (since it must be thought as supersensibly *grounded*) this disposition can indeed be, and ought to be, holy and conformable to the archetype's disposition. In degree, however, (in terms of its manifestations in actions) it always remains deficient and infinitely removed from that of the archetype. Nevertheless, as an intellectual unity of the whole, the disposition takes *the place of* perfected *action*, since it contains the ground of its own steady progress in remedying its deficiency. But now it can be asked: Can he "in whom there is no condemnation,"[67] or [in whom there] must be [none], believe himself justified and, at the same time, count *as punishment* the sufferings that befall him on the way to an ever greater goodness, thus professing to deserve punishment and, by the same token, also to have a disposition displeasing to God? Yes indeed, but always in his quality as the "man" he is continually putting off. Whatever is due to him as punishment in that quality, i.e. as "the old man" (and this includes all the sufferings and ills of life in general) he gladly takes upon himself in his quality as "the new man," solely for the sake of the good; consequently, to that extent and as such a "new man," those sufferings are not ascribed to him as "punishments" but the term here rather means only this: In his quality as "the new man" he willingly takes upon himself, as so many opportunities to test and exercise his disposition for the good, all the ills and sufferings that befall him; these "the old man" would have to impute to himself as punishment, and he too actually imputes them to himself as such inasmuch as he still is in the process of dying to "the old man." This punishment is itself the cause and at the same time the effect of his disposition for the good, hence also of the contentment and *moral happiness* inherent in the consciousness of his progress in the good (and this progress is one and the same act as the abandonment of evil). In the old disposition, by contrast, these very ills would have counted exclusively as punishment, and would also have had to be *felt* as such, since, even when considered as mere ills, they would still be opposed to what, in the form of *physical happiness*, a human being in such a disposition takes as his exclusive goal.

†† Rather, *receptivity* is all that we, on our part, can attribute to ourselves, whereas a superior's decision to grant a good for which the subordinate has no more than (moral) receptivity is called *grace*.

[g] *erkennen*

6:75

6:76 but only according to our deeds), so that the accuser within us would still be more likely to render a verdict of guilty. It is always therefore only a decree of grace when we are relieved of all responsibility for the sake of this good in which we believe, though fully in accord with eternal justice (because based on a satisfaction that for us consists only in the idea of an improved disposition of which, however, God alone has cognition).

It can further be asked whether this deduction of the idea of a *justification* of a human being who is indeed guilty but has passed into a disposition well-pleasing to God has any practical use at all, and what such use could be. It is hard to see what *positive* use can be made of it for religion and for the conduct of life, for the fundamental condition of the inquiry is that the individual in question already actually is in the required good disposition for the sake of which (its development and encouragement) every practical employment of moral concepts is truly directed as end; as regards comfort, such a good disposition already brings it with it (as comfort and hope, not as certainty) to anyone conscious of it in himself. Thus the investigation is only an answer to a speculative question, but one that cannot therefore be passed over in silence, since reason could then be accused of being absolutely incapable of reconciling the human being's hope of absolution from his guilt with divine justice, and this accusation might be disadvantageous to reason in many respects, most of all morally. However, the *negative* use that can be derived from the investigation for religion and morality, on behalf of each and every human being, is very far-reaching. For from the deduction as adduced we see that it is possible to think of absolution for a human being burdened with guilt, before heavenly justice, only on the assumption of a total change of heart; that, therefore, no expiations, be they of the penitential or the ceremonial sort, no invocations or exaltations (even those of the vicarious ideal of God's Son) can make up for the lack of this change of heart or, if the change is there, in the least increase its validity before the heavenly tribunal; for that ideal must be adopted in our disposition before it can stand in place of the deed.[–]A different issue is raised by the question, What can a human being expect *at the end of his life*, or what can he fear, in virtue of his conduct during it? For this a human being must first of all have cognition of his own character, at least to some extent. Thus, though he may believe that

6:77 there has been an improvement in his disposition, he must be equally able to take the old (corrupted) one into consideration, the one from which he started, and examine what and how much of this disposition he has cast off, as well as the *quality* (whether pure or still impure) and the *grade* of the supposed new disposition for overcoming the old one and preventing relapse into it; he will thus have to look at his disposition throughout his whole life. But, since he can derive no certain and definite concept of his real disposition through immediate consciousness but only from the conduct he has actually led in life, he shall not be able to think of any other condition of being delivered to the verdict of a future judge (that is, his awakening consciousness, together with the empirical self-cognition produced by it) than that *his whole life* be one day placed before the judge's eyes, and not just a segment of it, perhaps the last and to him still the most advantageous; to it he would of his own accord add the prospect in a life further extended (without fixing limits for himself on this score), in case it lasted longer. Here he cannot allow the previously recognized disposition to take the place of the deed but, on the contrary, he must extract his disposition from the deed before him. What verdict, does the reader think, will this mere thought lead a human being to pronounce upon his future life on the base of his conduct so far, when this thought brings back to his recollection (though he is not of the worst sort) much which he has otherwise easily forgotten, even if no more were said to him than that he has cause to believe that one day he will stand before a judge? Address this question in a human being to the judge within him, and the human being will pronounce a stern judgment upon himself, for he cannot bribe his reason; but represent for him another judge, of whom news will be had through sources of information elsewhere, and he will have much with which to counter the judge's severity under the pretext of human frailty; he will think he can get around him, whether by forestalling his punishment through remorseful self-inflicted torments that do not, however, originate in any genuine disposition toward improvement or by mollifying him with prayers and entreaties, even with incantations and self-proclaimed professions of faith. And give him now encouragement (as with the proverb, "All is well that ends well") and from early on he will make his plans accordingly, with a view not to forfeit too much of life's pleasures unnecessarily and, by life's end, to settle his accounts with speed and to his advantage.*   6:78

---

*† The aim of those who have a clergyman summoned to them at the end of life is normally to find in him a *comforter*, not on account of their *physical* sufferings brought on by the last illness or even by the natural fear in the face of death (for on this score death itself, which puts an end to life, can be the comforter) but because of the *moral* sufferings, the reproaches of their conscience. At such time, however, conscience ought rather to be *stirred up* and *sharpened*, in order that whatever good yet to be done, or whatever consequences of past evil still left to be undone (repaired for), will not be neglected, in accordance with the warning, "Agree with thine adversary" (with him who has a legal right against you) "quickly, while thou art in the way with him" (i.e. so long as you still live), "lest he deliver thee to the judge" (after death), etc.[68] But to administer opium to conscience instead, as it were, is to be guilty of a crime against the human being himself and against those who survive him, and is totally contrary to the purpose for which such support given to conscience at life's end can be held necessary.

Section two
Concerning the evil principle's rightful claim to dominion over the human being, and the struggle of the two principles with one another

The Holy Scriptures (the Christian portion thereof) convey this intellectual moral relation in the form of a story in which two principles, opposed to each other like heaven to hell and represented as two persons outside the human being, not only test their respective power in him but also seek (the one party as his prosecutor, the other as advocate) to establish their claims *through law*,[^h] as it were before a supreme judge.

The human being was originally appointed the proprietor of all the goods of the earth (Genesis 1:28),[69] though he was to have only their usufruct (*dominium utile*)[^i] under his Creator and Lord as the supreme proprietor (*dominus directus*).[^j] At the same time an evil being is introduced (we have no cognition of how he became so evil as to betray his master, for originally he was good) who, through his fall, has lost whatever estate he might have had in heaven and now wants to acquire another on earth. But, since earthly and corporeal objects give him no pleasure (he is a being of a higher species – a spirit), he seeks to establish dominion *over minds* by causing our first parents to rebel against their overlord and become dependent on him. And so he succeeds in setting himself up as the supreme proprietor of all the goods on earth, i.e. as the prince of this world. Now, one might well wonder why God did not avail himself of his power against this traitor,* and did not prefer to destroy the kingdom which he intended to found at its very inception. But, in his domination and government over rational beings the Supreme Being deals with them in accordance with the principle of their freedom, and whatever good or evil befalls them, it ought to be theirs to ascribe to themselves. A Kingdom of Evil was thus set up here on earth in defiance of the good principle, and all of Adam's (natural) descendants were subjugated to it – and this with their own free consent, since the false show of this world's goods diverted their gaze from the abyss of perdition in store for them. Because of its rightful claim to dominion over the human being, the good principle did indeed retain a hold through the establishment of a form of government solely directed to

6:79

---

* Father Charlevoix reports that when he told his Iroquois catechumen the story of all the evil that the evil spirit wrought on a creation originally good, and how this spirit is still constantly seeking to thwart the best divine arrangements, the catechumen asked him with indignation: But why does not God strike the Devil dead? to which question he candidly admits that he was unable, on the spot, to find an answer.[70]

[^h]: Law = *Recht*

[^i]: The right to the enjoyment of the advantages of a property belonging to another, so far as may be had without damage or prejudice to the property.

[^j]: the immediate lord

the public and exclusive veneration of its name (in the *Jewish* theocracy). But, since in this government the subjects remained attuned in their minds to no other incentive except the goods of this world and only wished, therefore, to be ruled through rewards and punishments in this life – nor were they in this respect capable of other laws except such as were in part imposed by burdensome ceremonies and observances, in part indeed ethical but only inasmuch as they gave rise to external compulsion, hence were only civil, and the inferiority of the moral disposition was in no way at issue – so this institutional order did no substantial injury to the realm of darkness but only served to keep ever in remembrance the imprescriptible right of the first proprietor. – Now there suddenly appeared among these very people, at a time when they were feeling the full measure of all the evils of a hierarchical constitution, and were feeling it as well, perhaps, because of the Greek sages' moral doctrines on freedom 6:80 which, unsettling as they were for the slavish mind, had gradually gained influence over them and had induced most of them to reflection – they were thus ripe for a revolution – a person whose wisdom, even purer than that of the previous philosophers, was as though descended from heaven; and he announced himself indeed as a true human being, so far as his doctrines and example were concerned, yet also as an envoy of heavenly origin who was not implicated, at the time of original innocence, in the bargain with the evil principle into which the rest of the human race had entered through their representative (their first progenitor);* "in him,

---

*† To conceive the possibility of a person free from innate propensity to evil by having him born of a virgin mother is an idea of reason consistent with, as it were, a moral instinct difficult to explain and yet undeniable. For, since natural generation cannot take place without sensual pleasure on both sides and yet seems to relate us to the mating of animals generally far too closely (for human dignity), we look upon it as something to *be ashamed* of – an attitude[k] which certainly was the real cause of the belief in the sanctity of the monastic state – and imagine it, therefore, as something immoral, something not reconcilable with the perfection of a human being, yet grafted in his nature and hence also passed on to his followers as an evil predisposition. – Now, the idea of the birth, independent of any sexual intercourse (virginal), of a child untainted by moral blemish is well suited to this obscure representation (merely sensible on one side, yet moral and hence intellectual on the other), though not without its theoretical difficulties (with respect to which, however, it is not at all necessary to determine anything from a practical point of view). For, according to the hypothesis of epigenesis, the mother, who descended from her parents through *natural* birth, would still be tainted with this moral blemish and would pass it on to her child, at least half of it, even in a supernatural birth. To escape this consequence, therefore, we would have to assume the theory that the seeds [of the descendants] *pre-exist* in the progenitors, not, however, the theory that these seeds develop on the *female* side (for then the consequence is not escaped) but on the *male* side alone (not on the part of the *ova* but of the *spermatozoa*). So, since the male side has no part in a supernatural pregnancy, this mode of representation could be defended as theoretically consistent with the idea [of virginal birth]. – But what is the use of all this theorizing *pro* or *contra*, when it suffices for practical purposes to hold the idea itself before us as model, as symbol of humankind raising itself above temptation to evil (and withstanding it victoriously)?
[k] *Vorstellung*

95

therefore, the prince of this world had no part."[71] The sovereignty of this
prince was thereby put in jeopardy. For were this human being well-
pleasing to God to resist his temptations also to enter into that bargain [with
him], and were other human beings to believe in him and adopt his same
disposition, then the prince of the world would lose just that many subjects,
and his kingdom would run the risk of being totally destroyed. The prince
offered, therefore, to make him the vassal lord of his whole kingdom, if he
just would pay homage to him as the owner of it.[72] But, since this attempt did
not succeed, not only did he take away from this stranger in his territory
anything that could make his earthly life agreeable (to the point of direst
poverty): he also provoked against him every persecution by which evil
human beings could embitter him – sufferings that only one well disposed
can truly feel with depth, [such as] the slandering of his teaching's pure
intention (in order to deprive him of a following) – and he finally pursued
him to the most ignominious death, without achieving anything in the least
against him by this onslaught by unworthy people upon his steadfastness
and honesty in teaching, and example for the sake of the good. And now to
the outcome of this combat. Its result can be viewed in *legal*[l] terms, or in
physical terms. If one views the physical result (which belongs to the senses),
then the good principle is the worsted party; after enduring many sufferings, he had to give up his life in combat,* for he had provoked a revolt in a
foreign dominion (which, as such, had coercive power). However, since the
realm in which *principles* (be they good or evil) have power is not one of
nature but of freedom, i.e. it is a realm in which one can control things only
to the extent that one rules over minds, and where nobody is therefore slave

*† Not that (as in Dr. Bahrdt's fanciful fiction)[73] he *sought* death in order to promote a worthy
purpose through a shining and sensational example; that would be suicide. For one may
indeed dare something at the risk of losing one's life, or even endure death at the hand of
another, when one cannot avoid it, without betraying an irremissible duty. But one cannot
dispose of oneself and one's life as a means, whatever the end, and thus be the *author* of
one's death. – Nor (as the Wolfenbüttel fragmentarist suspects)[74] did he *stake* his life for just
a political though illegal purpose, and not a moral one, perhaps that of overthrowing the rule
of the priests in order to establish himself in their place with supreme temporal power. For in
opposition to this stands the admonition, "Do this in remembrance of me,"[75] which he gave
to his disciples at the last supper, when he had already given up the hope of attaining any
such power. This admonition, if intended as the remembrance of a worldly design that had
come to nought, would have been an offensive exhortation, such as to provoke ill-will against
its originator, and hence self-defeating. However, the remembrance could just as well refer
to the failure of a very good and purely moral design of the Master, namely, to bring about in
his own lifetime a *public* revolution (in religion), by overthrowing a morally repressive ceremonial faith and the authority of its priests (the preparations for the gathering together at Easter
of his disciples, scattered all over the land, might well have had this as end). And we may
indeed even now regret that the design did not succeed, even though it was not in vain, for
after the Master's death it gave way to a religious transformation that quietly spread everywhere, though in the midst of many sufferings.
[l] *rechtlicher*

96

(bondsman) but who wills to be one, and only so long as he wills it: so the master's very death (the last extreme of a human being's suffering) was the manifestation of the good principle, that is, of humanity in its moral perfection, as example for everyone to follow. The representation of this death ought to have had, and could have had, the greatest influence on human hearts at that time – indeed, so it can at any time – for it most strikingly displays the contrast between the freedom of the children of heaven and the bondage of a mere son of earth. However, the good principle did not descend among humans from heaven at one particular time but from the very beginning of the human race, in some invisible way (as anyone must grant who attentively considers the holiness of the principle, and the incomprehensibility as well of the union of this holiness with human sensible nature in the moral disposition) and has precedence of domicile in humankind by right. And, since the principle appeared in an actual human being as example for all others, this human being "came unto his own, and his own received him not, but as many as received him, to them gave he power to be called the sons of God, even to them that believe on his name";[76] that is, by exemplifying this principle (in the moral idea) that human being opened the doors of freedom to all who, like him, choose to die to everything that holds them fettered to earthly life to the detriment of morality; and among these he gathers unto himself "a people for his possession, zealous of good works,"[77] under his dominion, while he abandons to their fate all those who prefer moral servitude.

So the moral outcome of this conflict, on the part of the hero of the story (up to his death), is not really the *conquering* of the evil principle – for its kingdom still endures and, in any case, a new epoch must yet come in which it is to be destroyed – but only the breaking up of its controlling power in holding against their will those who have so long been subject to it, now that another moral dominion (since the human being must be subject to some dominion or other) has been revealed to them as freedom, and in it they can find protection for their morality if they want to forsake the old one. Moreover, the evil principle is still called the prince of this world, and those in this world who adhere to the good principle should always be prepared for physical sufferings, sacrifices, and mortifications of self-love, all of which are portrayed in this world by the evil principle as persecutions, since in his kingdom he has rewards only for those who have made earthly goods their ultimate aim.

It is easy to see, once we divest of its mystical cover this vivid mode of representing things, apparently also the only one at the time *suited to the common people*, why it (its spirit and rational meaning) has been valid and binding practically, for the whole world and at all times: because it lies near enough to every human being for each to recognize his duty in it. Its meaning is that there is absolutely no salvation for human beings except in the innermost adoption of genuine moral principles in their disposition,

6:83

97

[and] that to interfere with this adoption is surely not the so often blamed sensibility but a certain self-incurred perversity or, as we might otherwise also call this wickedness, fraud (*faussité*, the satanic guile through which evil came into the world): [this is] a corruption that lies in all human beings and cannot be overcome except through the idea of the moral good in its absolute purity, combined with the consciousness that this idea belongs to our original predisposition and we only need to be assiduous in keeping it free of any impure mixture, and to accept it deeply in our disposition, to become convinced by the gradual influence that it has on the mind that the dreaded powers of evil have nothing to muster against it ("the gates of hell shall not prevail")[78] and, lest we happen to compensate for a deficiency in this trust *by way of superstition*, through expiations that presuppose no change of heart, or *by way of enthusiasm*, through alleged (merely passive) inner illuminations, and thus ever be kept distant from the good based on self-activity, that we should not ascribe to this good any other distinguishing trait except that of a well-ordered conduct of life. – Finally, any attempt like the present to find a meaning in Scriptures in harmony with the *most holy* teachings of reason must be held not only as permissible but as duty;* and we may be reminded at this point of what the *wise teacher* said to his disciples regarding someone who went his own way, by which, however, he would have had eventually to come to the same goal: "Forbid him not; for he who is not against us is for us."[79]

6:84

General remark

If a moral religion (to be cast not in dogmas and observances but in the heart's disposition to observe all human duties as divine commands) must be established, eventually all the *miracles* which history connects with its inception must themselves render faith in miracles in general dispensable. For we betray a culpable degree of moral unbelief if we do not grant sufficient authority to duty's precepts, as originally inscribed in the heart by reason, unless they are in addition authenticated through miracles: "Except ye see signs and wonders, ye will not believe."[80] Yet, when a religion of mere cult and observances has run its course and one based on the spirit and the truth (on moral disposition) is to be introduced in its place, it is entirely conformable to the ordinary human way of thinking, though not required by the [new] religion, if the historical introduction of the latter be accompanied and as it were adorned by miracles, to announce the end of the previous one which without miracles would not have had any authority at all: indeed, even in such a way that, to win over the adherents of the earlier religion to the recent revolution, the older religion is interpreted as the ancient prefiguration, now come to fulfill-

*† And it may be admitted that it is not the only one.

ment, of the ultimate end of providence in the new. And it would not pay under these circumstances to contest those narratives or interpretations, now that the true religion, which in its time needed introduction through such aids, is finally here and from now on is able to hold its own on rational grounds. For we would then have to accept that the mere faith in things incomprehensible and their repetition (of which anyone is capable without being for that reason a better human being, or ever becoming one thereby) is a way, indeed the only way, of pleasing God – a claim that we   6:85
must dispute with all our might. It might well be that the person of the teacher of the one and only religion, valid for all worlds, is a mystery; that his appearance on earth, as well as his translation from it, his eventful life and his passion, are all but miracles – indeed, that the history that ought to testify to the account of these miracles is itself a miracle (a supernatural revelation). So we may leave the merit of these miracles, one and all, undisturbed; nay even venerate the external cover that has served to bring into public currency a doctrine whose authentication rests on a document indelibly retained in every soul and in need of no miracle: provided, however, that, as regards the use of these historical reports, we do not make it a tenet of religion that knowing, believing, and professing them are themselves something by which we can make ourselves well-pleasing to God.

As for miracles in general, there are rational human beings who, though not disposed to renounce belief in them, never allow this belief to intervene in practical matters; and this is as much as to say that, *in theory*, they do indeed believe that there are miracles, but avow none *in their practical affairs*. For this reason wise governments have always granted that miracles did occur *in ancient times*, and have even received this opinion among the doctrines of official religion, but have not tolerated *new* miracles.* For ancient miracles have already been little by little so defined and   6:86

---

* In this respect even those teachers of religion who link their articles of faith to the authority of the government (i.e. the orthodox) follow the same maxim as the latter does. Hence Herr Pfenniger,[81] in defending the claim of his friend Herr Lavater[82] that a faith in miracles is still possible, rightly accuses of inconsistency the orthodox (for he explicitly excepted those of a *naturalistic* bend of mind on this point), because, although they assert miracles that occurred in the Christian community some seventeen centuries ago, they are unwilling to sanction more now, without being able to prove from the Scriptures either that, or if, miracles ought at some point to cease altogether (for the subtle argument that miracles are no longer necessary presumes a greater insight than any human being ought to be thought capable of), and this is a proof which they still owe to him. It was therefore only a maxim of reason not to grant or allow miracles now, not an objective insight that there are none. But is not this maxim, which in this instance is directed to the threat of civil mischief, also valid for the fear of a similar mischief in the philosophical community and the rational community at large? – Those who do not grant *great* (sensational) miracles but freely allow *little* ones, under the title of *special [divine] governance* (since these last are merely for guidance and require only a little   6:86
application of force on the part of the supernatural cause), do not bear in mind that what

restricted by the authorities that they can cause no disturbance among the community, whereas there must be concern about new miracle workers, on account of the effects that they can have upon the public peace and the established order. If we however ask: What is to be understood by the word *miracles?* they can then be defined (since what really matters to us is only to know what they are *for us*, i.e. for our practical employment of reason) as events in the world, the causes and *effects* of which are absolutely unknown to us and so must remain. And we can think of either *theistic* or *demonic* miracles – the latter being divided into *angelic* miracles (miracles of good spirits) and *satanic* miracles (miracles of evil spirits), though of the demonic miracles only the satanic really come into question, for the *good* angels (I know not why) give us little or nothing at all to say about them.

Regarding *theistic* miracles, we can of course form a concept of the laws governing the actions of their cause (as an omnipotent etc. and hence moral being), but only a *general* concept, so far as we can think of him as the creator and ruler of the world, according to the order of nature as well as the moral order, for we can obtain immediate and independent cognition of the laws of these orders, and reason can then employ them for its own use. Should we, however, accept that from time to time, and in special cases, God allows nature to deviate from such laws, then we do not have the least conception, nor can we ever hope to attain one, of the law according to which God promotes any such occurrence (apart from the *general moral* law that whatever God does will all be good, in virtue of which, however, nothing precise is established with respect to the particular event). Here reason is as paralyzed, for it is held back in its affairs according to recognized laws while not being instructed in a new one; and neither can it ever hope to be thus instructed in the world. Among miracles, however, the demonic are the ones most irreconcilable with the employment of our reason. For, as regards the *theistic* miracles, reason can at least have a negative criterion at its disposal, namely, if something is represented as commanded by God in a direct manifestation of him yet is directly in conflict with morality, it cannot be a divine miracle despite every appearance of being one (e.g. if a father were ordered to kill his son who, so far as he knows, is totally innocent);[83] whereas in the case of a supposed demonic miracle even this criterion fails to apply, and should we, in these cases, seize upon the contrary positive criterion to put at reason's disposal – namely, if through the miracle there comes an invita-

6:87

matters here is not the effect or its magnitude but the form of the course of worldly events, i.e. the *way in which the effect occurs,* whether naturally or supernaturally, and that for God no distinction of easy or difficult is to be thought of. And as regards the *mystery* of supernatural influences, any such deliberate concealment of the importance of an occurrence of this kind is even less proper.

tion to a good action which in itself we already recognize as duty, this invitation has not come from an evil spirit – even then we could be mistaken, for the evil spirit often acts the part, as they say, of an angel of light.

In practical affairs, therefore, we cannot possibly count on miracles, or in any way take them into consideration in the employment of our reason (which is necessary in all circumstances of life). A judge (however much he might believe in miracles in the church) hears a delinquent's allegations of diabolical temptations to which he was subjected as though nothing were said, despite the fact that, if the judge regarded a case of this sort possible, it would be well worth some consideration that a simple-minded ordinary human being has fallen into the snares of a cunning villain. But the judge cannot summon the villain; he cannot have the two confront one another; in a word, he can make absolutely nothing rational out of the case. The rational clergyman will therefore be well on guard against cramming the heads of those committed to his spiritual care with stories from *The Hellish Protheus*,[84] and making their imagination run wild. Concerning, however, the good sort of miracles, these are used by people in practical affairs as mere turns of phrase. Thus the doctor says: Nothing will help the sick man, short of a miracle, i.e. he will surely die. – Now, to practical affairs also belongs the natural scientist's search for the causes of events in their own natural laws; in the natural laws of these events, I say, which he can therefore verify through experience, even though he must renounce cognition of that which brings about effects according to these laws, in itself, or of what these laws might be for us relative to some other possible sense. A human being's moral improvement is likewise a practical affair incumbent upon him, and heavenly influences may indeed always cooperate in this improvement, or be deemed necessary to explain its possibility. Yet he has no understanding of himself in the matter: neither how to distinguish with certainty such influences from the natural ones, nor how to bring them and so, as it were, heaven itself down to himself. And, since he knows not what to do with them, in no case does he *sanction** miracles but rather, should he pay heed to the precept of reason, he conducts himself as if every change of heart and all improvement depended solely on the application of his own workmanship. But that, through the gift of a *firm* theoretical faith in miracles, the human being himself could perform them and thus storm heaven, is a senseless notion that strays too far outside the limits of reason to dwell on.[†]

6:88

---

*† Which is the same as saying: He does not incorporate faith in miracles in his maxims (either of theoretical or practical reason), without however contesting their possibility or actuality.

† It is a common ruse of those who dupe the gullible with the arts of *magic*, or who at least want to render such people in general prone to believe, that they appeal to the scientists' own admission of *ignorance*. After all, they say, we have no cognition of the *cause* of gravity, of magnetic force and the like. – Yet we have cognition of the laws of these forces in sufficient

detail within determinate limitations on the conditions under which alone certain effects occur; and that is enough for the rational employment of the forces as well as the explanation of their appearances, *secundum quid*,^{*p*} [i.e.] for the *regressive* employment of their laws in the ordering of experiences under them, though not *simpliciter*,^{*q*} [i.e.] to gain insight into the causes themselves of the forces operating according to the laws. – From this an inner phenomenon of the human understanding becomes comprehensible: why so called "miracles of nature", i.e. sufficiently attested though absurd appearances or characteristics of things that show up unexpectedly contrary to the hitherto recognized^{*r*} laws of nature, are eagerly received and *stimulate* the mind so long as they are still held to be natural, whereas the announcement of a real miracle *dejects* the mind. The reason is that the first open up the prospect of a new acquisition of nourishment for reason; that is, they give *hope* of discovering new laws of nature, whereas the other arouses apprehension that we might lose confidence also in those already accepted in cognition.^{*s*} When reason is deprived of the laws of nature, it no longer is of any use in the resulting magical world, not even for moral employment in complying in it with our duty; for we no longer know whether, unbeknown to us, changes have occurred in our very moral incentives due to miracles, and nobody can decide whether to attribute these changes to ourselves or to some other obscure cause. – Those, whose judgement in these matters inclines them to the opinion that without miracles they can manage nothing, believe that they moderate reason's offence at miracles by assuming that they only happen *seldom*. If they thereby mean that this is already implicit in the concept of a miracle (for if any such event happened regularly, it could no longer be defined as miracle), we can, if necessary, let them get away with this sophistry (of transforming an objective question about what a thing is into a subjective one of what we mean by the word with which we signify it) and still ask: *How often?* Once in a hundred years perhaps? Or, indeed, in ancient times but no more now? We can determine nothing here on the basis of the cognition of the object (for on our own admission, the object escapes us) but only on the basis of the necessary maxims of our reason's employment: either miracles are to be admitted as *daily* [events] (though hidden under the appearance of natural occurrences), or *never*, and in this last case they are not to be used as foundation either of our rational explanations or of the maxims of our actions; and since the first [alternative] is in no way compatible with reason, nothing remains but to accept the latter maxim – for this principle always remains only a maxim of judgement, not a theoretical assertion. Nobody can have so exaggerated a conceit of his insight as to make bold to assert definitely that, for instance, the most admirable conservation of the species in the plant and animal kingdom, where every spring a new generation once more displays its original undiminished, with all the inner perfection of mechanism, and even (as in the vegetable kingdom) with all the always so delicate beauty of colour, without the forces of inorganic nature, otherwise so destructive in the bad weather of autumn and winter, being able at this point to harm the seed – that this, I say, is a mere consequence of natural laws, and pretend to *understand* whether the creator's direct influence is not rather needed for it each time. – But these are experiences; *for us*, therefore, they are nothing other than effects of nature, and *ought* never to be judged otherwise. For this is what modesty requires of reason's claims, and to transcend these boundaries is presumptuousness and immodesty, even though in asserting miracles people often purport to demonstrate a humble and self-renouncing way of thinking.

6:89

^{*p*} in a certain respect
^{*q*} i.e. absolutely
^{*r*} *bekannt*
^{*s*} *als bekannt*

The philosophical doctrine of religion
Part three

Part three

The victory of the good principle over the evil principle, and the founding of a kingdom of God on earth

The battle that every morally well-disposed human being must withstand in this life, under the leadership of the good principle, against the attacks of the evil principle, can procure him, however hard he tries, no greater advantage than freedom from the *dominion* of evil. That he be *free*, that he "relinquish the bondage under the law of sins, to live for righteousness,"[85] this is the highest prize that he can win. He still remains not any the less exposed to the assaults of the evil principle; and, to assert his freedom, which is constantly under attack, he must henceforth remain forever armed for battle.

The human being is nevertheless in this perilous state through his own fault; hence he is *bound* at least to apply as much force as he can muster in order to extricate himself from it. But how? That is the question. – If he searches for the causes and the circumstances that draw him into this danger and keep him there, he can easily convince himself that they do not come his way from his own raw nature, so far as he exists in isolation, but rather from the human beings to whom he stands in relation or association. It is not the instigation of nature that arouses what should properly be called the *passions*, which wreak such great devastation in his originally good predisposition. His needs are but limited, and his state of mind in providing for them moderate and tranquil. He is poor (or considers himself so) only to the extent that he is anxious that other human beings will consider him poor and will despise him for it. Envy, addiction to power, avarice, and the malignant inclinations associated with these, assail his nature, which on its own is undemanding, *as soon as he is among human beings.* Nor is it necessary to assume that these are sunk into evil and are examples that lead him astray: it suffices that they are there, that they surround him, and that they are human beings, and they will mutually corrupt each other's moral disposition and make one another evil. If no means could be found to establish a union which has for its end the prevention of this evil and the promotion of the good in the human

6:94

105

being – an enduring and ever expanding society, solely designed for the preservation of morality by counteracting evil with united forces – however much the individual human being might do to escape from the dominion of this evil, he would still be held in incessant danger of relapsing into it. – Inasmuch as we can see, therefore, the dominion of the good principle is not otherwise attainable, so far as human beings can work toward it, than through the setting up and the diffusion of a society in accordance with, and for the sake of, the laws of virtue – a society which reason makes it a task and a duty of the entire human race to establish in its full scope. – For only in this way can we hope for a victory of the good principle over the evil one. In addition to prescribing laws to each individual human being, morally legislative reason also unfurls a banner of virtue as rallying point for all those who love the good, that they may congregate under it and thus at the very start gain the upper hand over evil and its untiring attacks.

An association of human beings merely under the laws of virtue, ruled by this idea, can be called an *ethical* and, so far as these laws are public, an *ethico-civil* (in contrast to a *juridico-civil*) society, or an *ethical community*. It can exist in the midst of a political community and even be made up of all the members of the latter (indeed, without the foundation of a political community, it could never be brought into existence by human beings). It has however a special unifying principle of its own (virtue) and hence a form and constitution essentially distinct from those of the other. There is nevertheless a certain analogy between the two, when considered in general as two communities, and with respect to this analogy the ethical community can also be called an *ethical state*, i.e. a *kingdom* of virtue (of the good principle). The idea of such a state has an entirely well-grounded, objective reality in human reason (in the duty to join such a state), even though we cannot subjectively ever hope of the good will of human beings that these will work harmoniously toward this end.

6:95

Division one
Philosophical representation of the victory of the good principle in the founding of a Kingdom of God on earth

I. CONCERNING THE ETHICAL STATE OF NATURE

A *juridico-civil* (political) *state* is the relation of human beings to each other inasmuch as they stand jointly under *public juridical laws* (which are all coercive laws). An *ethico-civil* state is one in which they are united under laws without being coerced, i.e. under *laws of virtue* alone.

Now, just as the rightful (but not therefore always righteous) *state of nature*, i.e. the *juridical state of nature*, is opposed to the first, so is the *ethical state of nature* distinguished from the second. In these two [states of nature] each individual prescribes the law to himself, and there is no external law to which he, along with the others, acknowledges himself to be subject. In both each individual is his own judge, and there is no effective *public* authority with power to determine legitimately, according to laws, what is in given cases the duty of each individual, and to bring about the universal execution of those laws.

In an already existing political community all the political citizens are, as such, still in the *ethical state of nature*, and have the right to remain in it; for it would be a contradiction (*in adjecto*)[q] for the political community to compel its citizens to enter into an ethical community, since the latter entails freedom from coercion in its very concept. Every political community may indeed wish to have available a dominion over minds as well, according to the laws of virtue; for where its means of coercion do not reach, since a human judge cannot penetrate into the depths of other human beings, there the dispositions to virtue would bring about the required result. But woe to the legislator who would want to bring about through coercion a polity directed to ethical ends! For he would thereby not only achieve the very opposite of ethical ends, but also undermine his political ends and render them insecure. – The citizen of the political community therefore remains, so far as the latter's lawgiving authority is concerned, totally free: he may wish to enter with his fellow citizens into an ethical union over and above the political one, or rather remain in a natural state of this sort. Only insofar as an ethical community must rest on *public* laws and have a constitution based on them, must those who freely commit themselves to enter into this state, not [indeed] allow the political power to command them how to order (or not order) such a constitution internally, but allow limitations, namely the condition that nothing be included in this constitution which contradicts the duty of its members as *citizens of the state* – even though, if the ethical bond is of the genuine sort, this condition need not cause anxiety.

Further, since the duties of virtue concern the entire human race, the concept of an ethical community always refers to the ideal of a totality of human beings, and in this it distinguishes itself from the concept of a political community. Hence a multitude of human beings united in that purpose cannot yet be called the ethical community as such but only a particular society that strives after the consensus of all human beings (indeed, of all finite rational beings) in order to establish an absolute ethical whole of which each partial society is only a representation or schema; for each of these societies can in turn be represented, in relation

6:96

---

[q] i.e., a contradiction generated by the juxtaposition of two mutually exclusive terms.

to others of this kind, as situated in the natural state, with all the imperfec-
tions of the latter (as is also the case with separate political states not
bound together through a public international law).

II.

THE HUMAN BEING OUGHT TO LEAVE THE
ETHICAL STATE OF NATURE IN ORDER TO
BECOME A MEMBER OF AN ETHICAL
COMMUNITY

6:97

Just as the juridical state of nature is a state of war of every human being
against every other, so too is the ethical state of nature one in which the
good principle, which resides in each human being, is incessantly attacked
by the evil which is found in him and in every other as well. Human beings
(as we remarked above) mutually corrupt one another's moral predisposition and, even with the good will of each individual, because of the lack of
a principle which unites them, they deviate through their dissensions from
the common goal of goodness, as though they were *instruments of evil,* and
expose one another to the danger of falling once again under its dominion.
Further, just as the state of a lawless external (brutish) freedom and
independence from coercive laws is a state of injustice and of war, each
against each, which a human being ought to leave behind in order to enter
into a politico-civil state,* so is the ethical state of nature a *public* feuding
between the principles of virtue and a state of inner immorality which the
natural human being ought to endeavor to leave behind as soon as
possible.

Now, here we have a duty *sui generis,*ᵛ not of human beings toward
human beings but of the human race toward itself. For every species of

---

* Hobbes's statement,[86] *status hominum naturalis est bellum omnium in omnes,*ʳ has no other
fault apart from this: it should say, *est status belli . . . etc.*ˢ For, even though one may not
concede that actual *hostilities* are the rule between human beings who do not stand under
external and public laws, their condition (*status iuridicus*),ᵗ i.e. the relationship in and through
which they are capable of rights (of their acquisition and maintenance) is nonetheless one in
which each of them wants to be himself the judge of what is his right vis-à-vis others, without
however either having any security from others with respect to this right or offering them
any: and this is a condition of war, wherein every man must be constantly armed against
everybody else. Hobbes's second statement,[87] *exeumdum esse e statu naturali,*ᵘ follows from
the first: for this condition is a continual violation of the rights of all others through the
presumption of being the judge in one's own affairs and of not allowing any security to other
human beings in theirs save one's own power of choice.
ʳ the natural state of men is a war of all against all
ˢ is a state of war . . . etc.
ᵗ juridical state
ᵘ one must exit from the natural state
ᵛ of a unique kind

rational beings is objectively – in the idea of reason – destined to a common end, namely the promotion of the highest good as a good common to all. But, since this highest moral good will not be brought about solely through the striving of one individual person for his own moral perfection but requires rather a union of such persons into a whole toward that very end, [i.e.] toward a system of well-disposed human beings in which, and through the unity of which alone, the highest moral good can come to pass, yet the idea of such a whole, as a universal republic based on the laws of virtue, differs entirely from all moral laws (which concern what we know to reside within our power), for it is the idea of working toward a whole of which we cannot know whether as a whole it is also in our power: so the duty in question differs from all others in kind and in principle. – We can already anticipate that this duty will need the presupposition of another idea, namely, of a higher moral being through whose universal organization the forces of single individuals, insufficient on their own, are united for a common effect. First of all, however, we must follow up the leading thread of that moral need and see where it will lead us. 6:98

III.
THE CONCEPT OF AN ETHICAL COMMUNITY IS THE CONCEPT OF A PEOPLE OF GOD UNDER ETHICAL LAWS

If an ethical community is to come into being, all individuals must be subjected to a public legislation, and all the laws binding them must be capable of being regarded as commands of a common lawgiver. Now if the community to be founded is to be a *juridical* one, the mass of people joining in a union must itself be the lawgiver (of constitutional laws), because legislation proceeds from the principle of *limiting the freedom of each to the conditions under which it can coexist with the freedom of everyone else, in conformity with a universal law,* * and the universal will thus establishes an external legal constraint. If, however, the community is to be an *ethical* one, the people, as a people, cannot itself be regarded as legislator. For in such a community all the laws are exclusively designed to promote the *morality* of actions (which is something *internal*, and hence cannot be subject to public human laws) whereas these public laws (and in this they constitute a juridical community) are on the contrary directed to the *legality* of actions, which is visible to the eye, and not to (inner) morality which alone is at issue here. There must therefore be someone other than the people whom we can declare the public lawgiver of an ethical community. But neither can ethical laws be thought of as proceeding *originally* 6:99

---

* This is the principle of all external right.

merely from the will of this superior (as statutes that would not be binding without his prior sanction), for then they would not be ethical laws, and the duty commensurate to them would not be a free virtue but an externally enforceable legal duty. Therefore only such a one can be thought of as the supreme lawgiver of an ethical community, with respect to whom all *true duties*, hence also the ethical,* must be represented as *at the same time* his commands; consequently, he must also be one who knows the heart,[89] in order to penetrate to the most intimate parts of the dispositions of each and everyone and, as must be in every community, give to each according to the worth of his actions. But this is the concept of God as a moral ruler of the world. Hence an ethical community is conceivable only as a people under divine commands, i.e. as a *people of God*,[90] and indeed *in accordance with the laws of virtue*.

We might of course also think of a people of God *in accordance with statutory laws*, that is to say, such laws as do not involve the morality of actions but only their legality. This would be a juridical community, of which God would indeed be the lawgiver (hence its *constitution* would be a 6:100 theocracy) – though priests, as human beings who receive their orders directly from him, would run an aristocratic *government*. Such a constitution, however, whose existence and form rest entirely on historical grounds, does not constitute the problem of a morally legislative reason which alone we are to bring to a resolution here. It will come up for examination in the historical section, as an institution under politico-civil laws, of which the lawgiver, though God, is yet external, whereas we only have to do here with an institution, of which the lawgiving is purely internal, a republic under laws of virtue, i.e. with a people of God "zealous of good works."[91]

To such a *people* of God we can oppose the idea of a *band* under the evil principle – a union of those who side with that principle for the propagation of evil. It is in the interest of evil to prevent the realization of the other union, even though here too the principle that battles the dispositions of virtue resides in our very self and is only figuratively represented as an external power.

---

* As soon as something is recognized as duty, even if it should be a duty imposed through the purely arbitrary will" of a human lawgiver, obeying it is equally a divine command. Of course we cannot call statutory civil laws divine commands; but if they are legitimate, their *observance* is equally a divine command. The proposition, "We ought to obey God rather than men,"[88] means only that when human beings command something that is evil in itself (directly opposed to the ethical law), we may not, and ought not, obey them. But, conversely, if an alleged divine statutory law is opposed to a positive civil law not in itself immoral, there is then cause to consider the alleged divine law as spurious, for it contradicts a clear duty, whereas that it is itself a divine command can never be certified sufficiently on empirical evidence to warrant violating on its account an otherwise established duty.
" *Willkür*

IV.

THE IDEA OF A PEOPLE OF GOD CANNOT BE REALIZED (BY HUMAN ORGANIZATION) EXCEPT IN THE FORM OF A CHURCH

The sublime, never fully attainable idea of an ethical community is greatly scaled down under human hands, namely to an institution which, at best capable of representing with purity only the form of such a community, with respect to the means for establishing a whole of this kind is greatly restricted under the conditions of sensuous* human nature. But how could one expect to construct something completely straight from such crooked wood?[92]

To found a moral people of God is, therefore, a work whose execution cannot be hoped for from human beings but only from God himself. Yet human beings are not permitted on this account to remain idle in the undertaking and let Providence have free rein, as if each could go after his private moral affairs and entrust to a higher wisdom the whole concern of the human race (as regards its moral destiny). Each must, on the contrary, so conduct himself as if everything depended on him. Only on this condition may he hope that a higher wisdom will provide the fulfillment of his well-intentioned effort.   6:101

The wish of all well-disposed human beings is, therefore, "that the kingdom of God come, that His will be done on earth";[93] but what preparations must they make in order that this wish come to pass among them?

An ethical community under divine moral legislation is a *church* which, inasmuch as it is not the object of a possible experience, is called the *church invisible* (the mere idea of the union of all upright human beings under direct yet moral divine world-governance, as serves for the archetype of any such governance to be founded by human beings). The *church visible* is the actual union of human beings into a whole that accords with this ideal. So far as every society under public laws entails a subordination of its members (in the relation of those who obey the society's laws with respect to those who oversee their observance), the mass of people united into that whole (of the church) is a *congregation* under superiors who (under the name of teachers or shepherds of souls) only administer the affairs of the church's invisible supreme head, and, in this respect, are called *servants* of the church, just as, in a political community, the visible head occasionally calls himself the supreme servant of the state, even though he does not acknowledge any other human being above himself (and, as a rule, not even the people as a whole). The true (visible) church is one that displays the (moral) kingdom of God on earth inasmuch as the latter can be realized through human beings. The requisites for a true church, and also its marks, are the following:[94]

sinnlichen

1. *Universality*, whence its numerical unity, for which it must be internally predisposed; to wit: though indeed divided and at variance with itself in accidental opinions, yet, as regards its essential purpose, it is founded on principles that necessarily lead it to universal union in a single church (hence, no sectarian schisms).

2. Its *make-up* (quality), i.e. *purity*: union under no other incentives than moral ones (cleansed of the nonsense of superstition and the madness of enthusiasm).

6:102

3. *Relation* under the principle of *freedom:* the internal relation of its members among themselves as well as the external relation of the church to the political power, both in a *free state* (hence neither a *hierarchy*, nor an *illuminatism* – which is a kind of *democracy* through individual inspirations, which can vary greatly from one another, according to each mind).

4. Its *modality*, the *unchangeableness* of its *constitution* – exception however made for the accidental regulations that only concern the *administration* of the church and must change according to times and circumstances, for which, however, the church must already possess secure principles within itself *a priori* (in the idea of its end, and hence in the form of primordial laws publicly laid down for instruction once and for all, as it were through a book of laws, not through arbitrary creeds which, since they lack authority, are fortuitous, exposed to contradiction, and changeable).

As church, therefore, i.e. considered as the mere *representative* of a state [ruled] by God, an ethical community really has nothing in its principles that resembles a political constitution. Its constitution is neither *monarchical* (under a pope or patriarch), nor *aristocratic* (under bishops and prelates), nor *democratic* (as of sectarian *illuminati*). It could best of all be likened to the constitution of a household (a family) under a common though invisible moral father, whose holy son, who knows the father's will and yet stands in blood relation with all the members of the family, takes his father's place by making the other members better acquainted with his will; these therefore honor the father in him and thus enter into a free, universal and enduring union of hearts.

V.

THE CONSTITUTION OF EACH AND EVERY
CHURCH ALWAYS PROCEEDS FROM SOME
HISTORICAL (REVEALED) FAITH, WHICH WE
CAN CALL ECCLESIASTICAL FAITH; AND THIS IS
BEST FOUNDED ON A HOLY SCRIPTURE

The only faith that can found a universal church is *pure religious faith*, for it
6:103   is a plain rational faith which can be convincingly communicated to every-

one, whereas a historical faith, merely based on facts, can extend its influence no further than the tidings relevant to a judgment on its credibility can reach. Yet, due to a peculiar weakness of human nature, pure faith can never be relied on as much as it deserves, that is, [enough] to found a Church on it alone.

Conscious of their impotence in the cognition of supersensible things, and though they allow every honor to be paid to faith in these things (as the faith which must carry conviction for them universally), human beings are yet not easily persuaded that steadfast zeal in the conduct of a morally good life is all that God requires of them to be his well-pleasing subjects in his Kingdom. They cannot indeed conceive their obligation except as directed to some *service* or other which they must perform for God – wherein what matters is not the intrinsic worth of their actions as much as, rather, that they are performed for God to please him through passive obedience, however morally indifferent the actions might be in themselves. It does not enter their heads that, whenever they fulfill their duties toward human beings (themselves and others), by that very fact they also conform to God's commands; hence, that in all their doings and non-doings, so far as these have reference to morality, they are *constantly in the service of God;* and that it is absolutely impossible to serve him more intimately in some other way (for they can act and exercise their influence on no other than earthly beings, not on God). Since every great lord of this world has a special need of being *honored* by his subjects, and of being *praised* through signs of submissiveness; nor can he expect, without this, as much compliance with his orders from his subjects as he needs to rule over them effectively; and, in addition, however reasonable a human being may be, he always finds an immediate pleasure in attestations of honor: so we treat duty, to the extent that it is equally God's command, as the transaction of an *affair* of God, not of humans; and thus arises the concept of a religion of *divine service* instead of the concept of a purely moral religion.

Since all religion consists in this, that in all our duties we look upon God as the lawgiver to be honored universally, the determination of religion, so far as the conformity of our conduct with it is concerned, comes down to knowing *how God wills* to be honored (and obeyed). – Now a divine legislative will commands either through laws in themselves *merely statutory* or through *purely moral* laws. As regards the latter, each individual can recognize by himself, through his own reason, the will of God which lies at the basis of his religion; for the concept of the Divinity actually originates solely from the consciousness of these laws and from reason's need to assume a power capable of procuring for them the full effect possible in this world in conformity with the moral final end. The concept of a divine will, determined merely according to purely moral laws, allows us to think of only *one* religion which is purely moral, just as of *only one*

6:104

God. If, however, we assume statutory laws of such a will, and put our religion in observing them, then cognition of these laws is possible not through our own mere reason but only through revelation. And, whether given to each individual secretly or publicly – that it may be propagated among human beings through tradition or scripture – this revelation would be a *historical* and not a *purely rational faith.* – And even assuming divine statutory laws (laws which let us recognize them as obligatory, not of themselves, but only inasmuch as they are the revealed will of God), even then pure *moral* legislation, through which God's will is originally engraved in our hearts, is not only the unavoidable condition of all true religion in general but also that which actually constitutes such religion, and for which statutory religion can contain only the means to its promotion and propagation.

So if the question How does God wish to be honored? is to be answered in a way universally valid for every human being, *each considered simply as a human being,* there is no second thought that the legislation of his will might not be simply *moral.* For a statutory legislation (which presupposes a revelation) can be regarded only as contingent, as something that cannot have reached, nor can reach, every human being, hence does not bind all human beings universally. Thus, "not they who say Lord! Lord! But they who do the will of God,"[95] those, therefore, who seek to become well-pleasing to him, not through loud praises of him (or of his envoy, as a being of divine origin) according to revealed concepts which not every human being can have, but through a good life conduct, regarding which everyone knows his will – these will be the ones who offer to him the true veneration that he desires.

If, however, we regard ourselves as duty-bound to behave not just as human beings but also as *citizens* within a divine state on earth, and to work for the existence of such an association under the name of a church, then the question How does God will to be honored in *a church* (as a congregation of God)? appears unanswerable by mere reason, but to be in need of a statutory legislation only proclaimed through revelation, hence of a historical faith which we can call "ecclesiastical" in contradistinction to pure religious faith. For in pure religious faith it all comes down to what constitutes the matter of the veneration of God, namely the observance in moral disposition of all duties as his commands. On the other hand, a church which is the union in a moral community of many human beings of equally many dispositions, needs a *public* form of obligation, some ecclesiastical form that depends on experiential conditions and is intrinsically contingent and manifold, hence cannot be recognized as duty without divine statutory laws. However, we should not therefore forthwith presume that the determination of this form is a task of the divine lawgiver; there is rather reason to assume that it is God's will that we should ourselves carry out the idea of such a community. And, though human

6:105

beings might have indeed tried out many a form of church with unhappy result, yet they ought not to cease striving after this end, if need be through renewed attempts which as much as possible avoid the mistakes of previous ones, since the task, which for them is at the same time a duty, is left entirely up to them. We therefore have no reason, in founding and informing any church, to hold its laws straightaway as divine and *statutory;* it is, rather, presumptuous to declare them such, in order to spare ourselves the trouble of improving the church's form further, or, perhaps, even an usurpation of higher authority, in order to impose a yoke upon the multitude by means of ecclesiastical statutes, under the pretense of divine authority. But it would be just as arrogant peremptorily to deny that the way a church is organized may perhaps also be a special divine dispensation, if, so far as we can see, the church is in perfect harmony with moral religion, and if, in addition, we cannot see how it could ever have made its appearance all at once without the requisite preparatory advances of the public in religious concepts. Now, in the hesitation over this task – whether God or human beings themselves should found a church – there is proof of the human propensity to a *religion of divine service* (*cultus*), and, since such a religion rests on arbitrary precepts, to faith in statutory divine laws based on the assumption that some divine legislation, not to be discovered through reason but in need of revelation, must supervene to even the best life conduct (a conduct that the human being could always adopt under the guidance of the pure moral religion); attention is thereby given to the veneration of the supreme being directly (and not by way of that compliance to his commands already prescribed to us through reason). Thus it happens that human beings will never regard either union into a church, or agreement over the form to be given to it, or likewise any *public* institution for the promotion of the moral [content] of religion, as necessary in themselves but only for the purpose of, as they say, serving their God, by means of festivities, professions of faith in revealed laws, and the observance of precepts that belong to the form of the church (which is however itself a means). Although all these observances are at bottom morally indifferent actions, yet, precisely for this reason, they are deemed to be all the more pleasing to God, since they are supposed to be carried out just for his sake. Thus in the molding of human beings into an ethical community, ecclesiastical faith naturally* precedes pure religious faith: there were *temples* (buildings consecrated to public service) before *churches* (places of assembly for instruction and inspiration in moral dispositions); *priests* (consecrated stewards in the practices of piety) before *ministers* (teachers of pure moral religion), and for the most part they still come first in the rank and value accorded to them by the crowd at large.

6:106

Now once it stands as unalterable that a statutory *ecclesiastical faith* is

---

*† Morally speaking it ought to happen the other way around.

115

not added to the pure faith of religion as its vehicle and the means for the public union of human beings in promoting it, we must also concede that the preservation of this pure faith unchanged, its universal and uniform

6:107 diffusion, and even the respect for the revelation assumed within it, can hardly be adequately provided for through *tradition*, but only through *scripture;* which, again, as a revelation to present and future generations, must be the object of the highest respect, for this is what human need requires in order to be certain of the duty to divine service. A holy book commands the greatest respect even among those (indeed, among these most of all) who do not read it, or are at least unable to form any coherent concept of religion from it; and no subtle argument can stand up to the knockdown pronouncement, *Thus it is written.* Hence also the passages in it that are to lay down a point of faith are simply called *sayings.* The appointed interpreters of such scripture are themselves, by virtue of their very occupation, consecrated persons, as it were; and history proves that never could a faith based on scripture be eradicated by even the most devastating political revolutions, whereas a faith based on tradition and ancient public observances meets its downfall as soon as the state breaks down. How fortunate,* when one such book, fallen into human hands, contains complete, besides its statutes legislating faith, also the purest moral doctrine of religion, and this doctrine can be brought into the strictest harmony with those statutes (which [in turn] contribute to its introduction). In this event, both because of the end to be attained thereby and the difficulty of explaining by natural laws the origin of the enlightenment of the human race proceeding from it, the book can command an authority equal to that of a revelation.

. .

And now something more relating to this concept of a revealed faith.

There is only *one* (true) *religion;* but there can be several kinds of

6:108 *faith.* – We can say, further, that in the various churches divided from one another because of the difference in their kinds of faith, one and the same true religion can nevertheless be met with.

It is therefore more appropriate (as it in fact is more customary) to say: This human being is of this (Jewish, Mohammedan, Christian, Catholic, Lutheran) *faith,* than: He is of this or that religion. This last expression ought in justice not to be used at all in addressing the larger public (in catechisms and sermons), for it is too learned and unintelligible for them; indeed, modern languages provide no word for it of equivalent meaning.

---

* An expression for everything wished for, or worthy of being wished for, but which we can neither foresee nor bring about through our effort according to the laws of experience; for which, therefore, if we want to name a ground, can adduce no other than a generous providence.

The ordinary human being will every time understand by it his own ecclesiastical faith, which is the one that falls within the grasp of his senses, whereas religion hides inside him and depends on moral dispositions. We do most people too much honor when we say of them that they profess this or that religion, for they know* none and demand none; statutory ecclesiastical faith is all that they understand by the word. So too the so-called religious struggles, which have so often shaken the world and spattered it with blood, have never been anything but squabbles over ecclesiastical faiths. And the oppressed have never really complained for being hindered from adhering to their religion (for no external power can do this), but for not being allowed to practice their ecclesiastical faith publicly.

Now whenever, as usually happens, a church passes itself off as the only universal one (even though it is based on faith in a particular revelation which, since it is historical, can never be demanded of everyone), whoever does not acknowledge its (particular) ecclesiastical faith is called an *unbeliever*, and is wholeheartedly hated; whoever deviates from it only in part (in nonessentials), is called an *erring believer* and is at least shunned as a source of infection. Finally, if someone declares himself for this church yet deviates from its faith in something essential (something made out to be so), especially if he propagates his errant belief, he is called a *heretic (Ketzer)** and, like a rebel, is held more punishable than an external foe and is expelled from the church through excommunication (like that which the Romans pronounced on him who crossed the Rubicon without the consent of the Senate) and given over to all the gods of hell. The correctness of belief that the teachers or heads of a church claim solely for themselves in matters of ecclesiastical faith is called *orthodoxy*, which we may perhaps divide into *despotic (brutal)* and *liberal*. – If a church which claims that its ecclesiastical faith is universally binding is to be called *catholic*, and *protestant* a church that protests against such claims of others (though it would often gladly exercise them itself, if it could), then the attentive observer will come across many a renowned example of protestant catholics and, by contrast, still more offensive examples of arch-catholic protestants: the first are human beings whose frame of mind (though this is not that of their church) is given to *self-expansion;* by comparison with these the second clearly stand out, but not at all to their advantage, with the *narrowness* of theirs.

6:109

* According to Georgius (*Alphab. Tibet.*, p. 11),⁹⁶ the Mongols call Tibet *Tangut-Chazar*, i.e. the land of the house-dwellers, in order to distinguish these from themselves, nomads who live in deserts under tents; hence the name "Chazars," and from this *Ketzer²* since the Mongols adhered to the Tibetan faith (of the Lames), which conforms to Manicheism and perhaps originated from it, and they spread this name in their incursions into Europe; hence too the names *Haeretici* and *Manichaei* were used as synonymous some time ago.⁹⁷
ʸ *kennen*
ᶻ i.e. heretic

6:109

VI.

ECCLESIASTICAL FAITH HAS THE PURE FAITH OF RELIGION FOR ITS SUPREME INTERPRETER

We have noted that, although a church sacrifices the most important mark of its truth, namely the legitimate claim to universality, whenever it bases itself upon a faith of revelation which, as historical faith, (even if more widely spread and more firmly secured for the remotest posterity through scripture) is incapable of a transmission that commands conviction universally,[98] yet, because of the natural need of all human beings to demand for even the highest concepts and grounds of reason something that *the senses can hold on to*, some confirmation from experience or the like, (a need which must also be seriously taken into account when the intention is *to introduce* a faith universally) some historical ecclesiastical faith or other, usually already at hand, must be used.

6:110 Now to unite the foundation of a moral faith (be this faith an end or merely an auxiliary means) with such an empirical faith which, to all appearances, chance has dealt to us, we require an interpretation of the revelation we happen to have, i.e. a thoroughgoing understanding of it in a sense that harmonizes with the universal practical rules of a pure religion of reason. For the theoretical element of ecclesiastical faith cannot be of moral interest to us, if it does not work toward the fulfillment of all human duties as divine commands (which constitutes the essential of every religion). This interpretation may often appear to us as forced, in view of the text (of the revelation), and be often forced in fact; yet, if the text can at all bear it, it must be preferred to a literal interpretation that either contains absolutely nothing for morality, or even works counter to its incentives.* –

---

*† To illustrate this with an example, take Psalm 59: vv. 11–16,[99] where we find a *prayer* for revenge that borders on the horrific. Michaelis (*Ethic*, Part II, p. 202)[100] approves of this prayer and adds: "The psalms are *inspired;* if they pray for revenge, then it cannot be wrong: *We should not have a holier morality than the Bible.*" I pause here at this last statement and ask whether morality must be interpreted in accordance with the Bible, or the Bible, on the contrary, in accordance with morality. – Without now considering the passage of the New Testament, "It was said to our fathers, etc., but I say to you, Love your enemies, *bless those who curse you*, etc."[101] – how this passage, which is also inspired, can hold along with the other – I shall try either to fit that passage to those of my moral principles which stand on their own (for instance, that here are understood not corporeal enemies but, symbolized by them, the invisible ones which are much more pernicious to us, namely the evil inclinations which we must wish to bring under our feet completely), or, if this will not do, I shall rather assume that this passage is to be understood, not at all in a moral sense, but in terms of the relation that the Jews considered themselves to have toward God as their political regent – as also another passage of the Bible, where it is said: "Vengeance is mine; I shall repay! saith the Lord,"[102] which is commonly interpreted as a moral warning against private revenge, though it apparently only refers to the law in force in every state that one should seek satisfaction for insults in the court of justice of the overlord, where the judge's permission to the plaintiff to propose any punishment he wishes, however harsh, is not to be taken as approval of the plaintiff's vindictiveness.

We shall also find that this is how all types of faith – ancient and new, some written down in holy books – have always been treated, and that rational and thoughtful teachers of the people have kept on interpreting them until, gradually, they brought them, as regards their essential con-   6:111
tent, in agreement with the universal principles of moral faith. The moral philosophers among the Greeks and, later, among the Romans, did exactly the same with their legends concerning the gods. They knew in the end how to interpret even the coarsest polytheism as just a symbolic representation of the properties of the one divine being; and how to invest all sorts of depraved actions, and even the wild yet beautiful fancies of their poets, with a mystical meaning that brought popular faith (which it would never have been advisable to destroy, for the result might perhaps have been an atheism even more dangerous to the state) close to a moral doctrine intelligible to all human beings and alone beneficial. Late Judaism, and Christianity too, consist of such in part highly forced interpretations, yet, [in] both [instances], directed to ends undoubtedly good and necessary to every human being. The Mohammedans know very well (as Reland shows)[103] how to inject a spiritual meaning in the description of their paradise, otherwise dedicated to every sensuality, and the Indians do the same with the interpretation of their *Vedas*,[104] at least for the more enlightened part of their people. – [105] That this, however, can be done without ever and again greatly offending against the literal meaning of the popular faith is due to the fact that, long before this faith, the predisposition to moral religion lay hidden in human reason; and, though its first raw expressions were indeed intent on just the practice of divine service and, for its sake, gave rise to those alleged revelations, yet they thereby also implanted in their poetic fabrications, though unintentionally, something of the character of their supersensible origin. – Nor can we charge such interpretations with dishonesty, provided that we do not wish to claim that the meaning we give to the symbols of a popular faith, or even to holy books, is exactly as intended by them, but leave this issue open and only assume the *possibility* that their authors may be so understood. For the final purpose of even the reading of these holy books, or the investigation of their content, is to make better human beings; whereas their historical element, which contributes nothing to this end, is something in itself quite indifferent, and one can do with it what one wills. – (Historical faith is "dead, being alone,"[106] i.e. of itself, considered as declaration, contains nothing, nor does it lead to anything that would have a moral value for us.)

Hence, though a scripture is accepted as divine revelation, its supreme   6:112
criterion will nonetheless be something like this: "Every scripture given by inspiration of God is profitable for doctrine, for reproof, for correction, etc.";[107] and, since this last – namely the moral improvement of human beings – constitutes the true end of all religion of reason, it will also

contain the supreme principle of all scriptural exegesis. This religion is "the Spirit of God, who guides us into all truth."[108] And this it is which in *instructing* us also *animates* us with basic principles for action, and relates whatever the scripture may yet contain for historical faith entirely to the rules and incentives of pure moral faith, which alone constitutes true religion in each ecclesiastical faith. All investigation and interpretation of Scripture must proceed from the principle that this spirit is to be sought in it, and "eternal life can be found therein only so far as Scripture testifies to this principle."[109]

Now placed besides this interpreter of Scripture, but subordinated to him, is another, namely the *scriptural scholar*. The authority of Scripture, as the worthiest and in the enlightened world now the only instrument of union of all human beings into one church, establishes the ecclesiastical faith which, as popular faith, cannot be ignored, since no doctrine exclusively based on reason would seem to the people to make an unalterable norm; they demand a divine revelation, hence also a historical authentication of its authority through the deduction of its origin. Now human art and wisdom cannot climb up to heaven to ascertain for itself the credentials of the mission of the first teacher but must be satisfied with signs which, the content apart, can yet be gathered from the way the faith was introduced, i.e. with human reports which we must eventually trace back to very ancient times, and in languages now dead, to evaluate their historical credibility. Hence *scriptural scholarship* is required to preserve the authority of a church based on holy Scripture, though not that of a religion (for to have universality a religion must always be based on reason), even if such scholarship establishes nothing more than that there is nothing in the Scripture's origin which would make its acceptance as immediate divine revelation impossible. And this would be enough not to disturb those who fancy that they find in this idea [of revealed Scripture] a special strengthening of their moral faith and, therefore, gladly accept it. – Yet not only the *certification* of holy Scripture, but its *exposition* as well, requires scholarship, and for the same reason. For how will the unlearned, who can read it only in translation, be certain of its meaning? Hence the expositor, who has control of the underlying language, must also have a broad acquaintance with history and critical judgment, in order to draw from the situation, the customs and beliefs (the popular religion) of an earlier time the means with which to unlock the understanding of the church community.

Religion of reason and scriptural scholarship are, therefore, the properly appointed interpreters and trustees of a sacred document. It is self-evident that they must not on any account be hindered by the secular arm in the public use of their insights and discoveries in this field, or be bound to certain dogmas; for otherwise the *laity* would be forcing the *clerics* to fall in line with their opinion which they hold, however, only because of the

6:113

instruction of the clerics. When the state takes care that there is no lack of scholars and of individuals of morally good standing to govern over the entire church body, to whose consciences it can entrust this task, it has already done all that its duty and authority entail.[110] That the lawgiver extend this [duty and authority] into the schools, and attend to their quarrels (which, so long as they are not carried on from the pulpit, leave the church-public totally undisturbed), is an unreasonable demand, which the public cannot make on him without presumption, for it is beneath his dignity.

Yet a third claimant to the office of interpreter steps forward, one who needs neither reason nor learning to recognize both the true meaning of Scripture and its divine origin, but only an inner *feeling*. Now we certainly cannot deny that "whoever follows the light of Scripture and *does* what it prescribes, will surely discover that it is of God,"[111] and that the very impulse to good actions and uprightness of life, which the human being who reads Scripture or listens to it must feel, would have to convince him of its divine nature: for this impulse is but the effect of the moral law which fills the human being with heartfelt respect, and hence deserves to   6:114
be considered also as divine command. But just as we cannot derive or convey the recognition of laws, and that they are moral, on the basis of any sort of feeling, equally so and even less can we derive or convey on the basis of a feeling sure evidence of a direct divine influence: for the same effect can have more than one cause, whereas in this case the morality alone of the law (and of the doctrine), recognized through reason, is the cause of the effect. And even on the assumption that this origin is merely a possibility, our duty is yet to construe it in this sense, if we do not wish to open wide the gates to every kind of enthusiasm, and even cause the unequivocally moral feeling to lose dignity through association with all sorts of other fanciful ones. – Feeling is private to each individual and cannot be expected of others, even when we have advance cognition of the law from which or according to which it arises; thus we cannot extol it as a touchstone for the genuineness of a revelation, since it teaches absolutely nothing but only contains the manner in which a subject is affected as regards his pleasure or displeasure, and no cognition whatever can be based on this. –

There is, therefore, no norm of ecclesiastical faith except Scripture, and no other expositor of it except the *religion of reason* and *scholarship* (which deals with the historical element of Scripture). And, of these two, the first alone is *authentic* and valid for the whole world, whereas the second is merely *doctrinal;* its aim is the transformation of the ecclesiastical faith for a given people at a given time into a definite and self-maintaining system. As regards ecclesiastical faith, there is no avoiding the fact that historical faith ultimately becomes just a faith in scholars and in their insight – a circumstance that does not, indeed, particularly redound to the honour of human nature, but which can be made good through public freedom of thought. And this freedom is all the more justified since only if scholars submit their interpretations to public scrutiny, and themselves remain always open and receptive to better insight, can they count on the community's confidence in their decisions.

VII.
THE GRADUAL TRANSITION OF ECCLESIASTICAL FAITH TOWARD THE EXCLUSIVE DOMINION OF PURE RELIGIOUS FAITH IS THE COMING OF THE KINGDOM OF GOD

The distinguishing mark of the true church is its *universality;* and the sign of this, in turn, is the church's necessity and its determinability in only one possible way. Now historical faith (which is based upon revelation as experience) has only particular validity, namely for those in contact with the history on which the faith rests, and, like all cognition based on experience, carries with it the consciousness not that the object believed in *must* be so and not otherwise but only that it *is* so; hence it carries at the same time the consciousness of its contingency. This faith can therefore indeed suffice as an ecclesiastical faith (of which there can be several); but only the pure faith of religion, based entirely on reason, can be recognized as necessary and hence as the one which exclusively marks out the *true* church. – Thus, even though (in accordance with the unavoidable limitation of human reason) a historical faith attaches itself to pure religion as its vehicle, yet, if there is consciousness that this faith is merely such and if, as the faith of a church, it carries a principle for continually coming closer to pure religious faith until finally we can dispense of that vehicle, the church in question can always be taken as the *true* one; but, since conflict over historical dogmas can never be avoided, it can be named only church *militant,* though with the prospect at the end of flowering into the unchanging and all-unifying church *triumphant!* We call the faith of every individual receptive to (worthy of) eternal happiness, a *saving* faith. This too can be but one faith, and, despite the diversity of ecclesiastical faiths, it can yet be met in any in which, tending to its goal of pure religious faith, it is practical. The faith of a religion of service is, on the contrary, a *slavish* and mercenary faith (*fides mercenaria, servilis*) and cannot be considered as saving, because it is not moral. For moral faith must be a free faith, founded on pure dispositions of the heart (*fides ingenua*).[112] The one faith fancies to please God through actions (of *cultus*) which (though laborious) yet possess no moral worth in themselves, hence are actions extracted only through fear or hope, the kind which also an evil human being can perform, whereas for that the other faith presupposes as necessary a morally good disposition.

Saving faith holds two conditions for its hope of blessedness: the one with respect to what it itself cannot bring about, namely the lawful undoing (before a judge) of actions done; the other with respect to what it can and should bring about, namely the conversion to a new life conformable to its duty. The first is faith in satisfaction (reparation for guilt, redemption, reconciliation with God); the second, faith in the ability to become well-pleasing to God in a future good conduct of life. – The two conditions add up to one faith; they belong together necessarily. The necessity of a connection cannot be seen, however, unless we assume that one faith can be derived from the other, i.e. that according to the law of morally efficient causes either the faith in absolution from the debt resting upon us will elicit a good life conduct, or the true and active disposition of a good life conduct – one to be pursued at all times – will elicit faith in that absolution.

Here now appears a remarkable antinomy of human reason with itself, the resolution of which – or, if this is not possible, at least its settlement – can alone determine whether a historical (ecclesiastical) faith must always supervene as an essential portion of saving faith over and above the pure religious one, or whether, as mere vehicle, historical faith will finally pass over, in however distant a future, into pure religious faith.

1. If it is presupposed that satisfaction has occurred for the sins of humankind, it is indeed understandable that each and every sinner would gladly bring it to bear upon himself and, if this depended simply on *faith* (it would amount to a declaration on the sinner's part of his intention that the satisfaction occur also for him), he would not for an instant suffer misgivings on that account. It is totally inconceivable, however, how a rational human being who knows himself to deserve punishment could seriously believe that he only has to believe the news of a satisfaction having been rendered for him, and (as the jurists say) accept it *utiliter,*[a]113 in order to regard his guilt as done away with, indeed, to such an extent (to its very roots) that a good life conduct, for which he has not made the least effort so far, would be even for the future the unavoidable consequence of   6:117 his faith and his acceptance of the proffered relief. No thoughtful person can bring himself to this faith, however much self-love often transforms into a hope the mere wish for a good, for which one does nothing or can do nothing, as though the object were to come on its own, lured by the mere yearning for it. One cannot think any such thing possible unless a human being considers this faith itself as heavenly instilled in him, as something, therefore, for which his reason has no need to account fur-

[a] for one's advantage

ther. If a human being is not capable of this, or if he is still too upright to affect any such confidence in him simply as a means of ingratiating himself, despite all the respect for such an overflowing satisfaction, despite every wish that it were also accessible to him, yet he cannot but regard it as only conditional, that is, consider the improvement of his life conduct, as much as lies in his power, as having to come first, before he gives even the least credit to the hope that the favor from on high will redound to his good. – If, therefore, historical cognition of this favor belongs to ecclesiastical faith, whereas the improved life conduct belongs to pure moral faith as a condition, then *the pure moral faith must take precedence over the ecclesiastical.*

2. But if humankind is corrupt by nature, how can a human being believe that on his own, try hard as he will, he can make a "new man"[114] of himself, one well-pleasing to God, when, conscious of the transgressions of which he has so far been guilty, he still stands in the power of the evil principle and finds no capacity in him sufficient to improve things in the future? If he cannot regard the justice, which he has himself aroused against himself, as reconciled through foreign satisfaction, and, through this faith, himself as reborn, as it were, and thus capable for the first time to undertake a new life conduct – which would then be the consequence of his union with the good principle – on what would he base his hope of becoming a human being well-pleasing to God? – Faith in a merit which is not his own, but through which he is reconciled with God, would therefore have to precede any striving for good works, and this contradicts the previous proposition. This conflict cannot be mediated through insight into the causal determination of the freedom of a human being, i.e. into the causes that make a human being become good or bad: in other words, it cannot be resolved theoretically, for this question totally surpasses the speculative capacity of our reason. Practically, however, where the question is not what comes first in the use of our free will physically, but morally, whence, in other words, we are to make our start, whether from faith on what God has done for our sake, or from what we ought to do in order to become worthy of it (whatever this may be), there is no hesitation in deciding for the second alternative.

For the acceptance of the first requisite for salvation, namely faith in a vicarious satisfaction, is in any case only necessary for the theoretical concept; we cannot *make* the removal of sin *comprehensible* in any other way. By contrast, the necessity of the second principle is practical and, indeed purely moral: surely we cannot hope to partake in the appropriation of a foreign satisfying merit, and thus in salvation, except by qualifying for it through our zeal in the compliance with every human duty, and this must be the effect of our own work and not, once again, a foreign influence to which we remain passive. For since the command to do our duty is unconditional, it is also necessary that the human being make the

6:118

command, as a maxim, the basis of his faith, i.e. that he begin with the improvement of his life as the supreme condition under which alone a saving faith can occur.

Ecclesiastical faith, being historical, rightly begins with the first principle. But, since it contains only the vehicle for the pure faith of religion (in which the true end lies), what in this faith (as practical) constitutes the condition, namely the maxim of *action*, must come first: the maxim of *knowledge* or theoretical faith must only bring about the consolidation and completion of that maxim of action.

In this connection it can also be remarked that, according to the first principle, faith (namely, faith in vicarious satisfaction) is accounted to the human being as duty, whereas faith in a good life conduct, such as is brought about in him through a higher influence, is accounted to him as grace. – According to the second principle the reverse holds true. For according to it, a *good life conduct* is (as supreme condition of grace) unconditional *duty*, whereas the satisfaction from on high is merely a *matter of grace*. – The first principle is accused (often not unjustly) of ritual *superstition*, which knows how to reconcile a criminal life conduct with religion; the second, of *naturalistic unbelief*, which combines indifference 6:119 or, indeed, even antagonism to all revelation with an otherwise perhaps exemplary conduct of life. – This, however, would be like cutting the knot (by means of a practical maxim) instead of disentangling it (theoretically), something which is after all permitted in religious questions. – At any rate, by way of satisfying the theoretical preoccupation, the following can be of use. – The living faith in the prototype of a humanity well-pleasing to God (the Son of God) refers, *in itself*, to a moral idea of reason, insofar as the latter serves for us not only as guideline but as incentive as well; it is, therefore, all the same whether I start out from it (as *rational* faith) or from the principle of a good life conduct. By contrast, faith in this very same prototype *according to its appearance* (faith in the God-man) is not, as *empirical* (historical) faith, one and the same as the principle of a good life conduct (which must be totally rational); and it would therefore be something quite different to wish to start with such a faith* and derive a good life conduct from it. To this extent there would be a contradiction between the two propositions above. However, in the appearance of the God-man, the true object of the saving faith is not what in the God-man falls to the senses, or can be cognized through experience, but the prototype lying in our reason which we put in him (since, from what can be gathered from his example, the God-man is found to conform to the prototype), and such a faith is all the same as the principle of a good life conduct. – Hence we do not have two principles here that differ in themselves, so that to start from the one or the other would be to enter on opposite paths, but

*† Which would have to justify the existence of such a person on historical evidence.

only one and the same practical idea from which we proceed: once, so far as this idea represents the prototype as situated in God and proceeding from him; and again, so far as it represents it as situated in us; in both cases, however, so far as it represents the prototype as the standard measure of our life conduct. And the antinomy is therefore only apparent: for only through a misunderstanding does it regard the very same idea, only taken in different relations, as two different principles. – However, if one wished to make the historical faith in the actuality of an appearance, such as has only once occurred in the world, the condition of the one saving faith, then there would indeed be two entirely different principles (the one empirical, and the other rational), and there would arise over them a true conflict of maxims, whether to proceed from the one or the other as starting point, which no reason would ever be able to settle. – [Take] the proposition: We must believe that there once was a human being (of whom reason tells us nothing) who has done enough through his holiness and merit, both for himself (with respect to his duty) and for all others (and their deficiency as regards their duty), to hope that we ourselves can become blessed in the course of a good life, though only in virtue of this faith. This proposition says something quite different from the following: We must strive with all our might after the holy intention of leading a life well-pleasing to God, in order to be able to believe that God's love for humankind (already assured to us through reason) will somehow make up, in consideration of that honest intention, for humankind's deficiency in action, provided that humankind strives to conform to his will with all its might. – What's said in the first does not lie in the power of every human being (including the unlearned). History testifies that all forms of religion have been ruled by this conflict between the two principles of faith; for all religions have had their expiations, however they have construed them. On the other hand, moral disposition has not failed, for its part, to make its demands heard. Yet the priests have at all times complained more than the moralists. They have moaned loudly (and in the form of demands on the authorities to combat the problem) over the neglect of the service of God, which was instituted to reconcile the people with heaven and ward off misfortune from the state. The moralists, by contrast, have complained about the decay of morals, which they very much blame on those means of remission of sin with which the priests have made it easy for everyone to be reconciled with the Divinity over the grossest vices. In fact, if for the repayment of debts already incurred or yet to be incurred an inexhaustible fund is already at hand, to which we only need to help ourselves to make us blameless (and, in spite of all claims made by conscience, we shall no doubt help ourselves to it first and foremost), whereas we can postpone our commitment to a good life conduct until, because of this repayment, we have first sorted ourselves out, then it is not easy to conceive other consequences for such a faith. – Yet, were this faith so portrayed, as if it

6:120

had such a peculiar force and such a mystical (or magical) influence that, however much we ought to regard it, from what we know, merely as historical, it would nonetheless be in a position of improving the whole human being radically (of making a new man[115] out of him) if he just holds on to it and to all the feelings bound with it, then such a faith would have to be regarded as itself imparted and inspired directly by heaven (with and within the historical faith), and everything, the moral constitution of humankind included, would then be reduced to an unconditional decree of God: "He hath mercy on whom he will, and whom he will he *hardeneth*,"[116]* and this, taken according to the letter, is the *salto mortale* of human reason.[117]   6:121

It is therefore a necessary consequence of the physical and, at the same time, the moral predisposition in us – the latter being the foundation and at the same time the interpreter of all religion – that in the end religion will gradually be freed of all empirical grounds of determination, of all statutes that rest on history and unite human beings provisionally for the promotion of the good through the intermediary of an ecclesiastical faith. Thus at last the pure faith of religion will rule over all, "so that God may be all in all."[118] – The integuments within which the embryo is first formed into a human being must be laid aside if the latter is to see the light of day. The leading-string of holy tradition, with its appendages, its statutes and observances, which in its time did good service, become bit by bit dispensable, yea, finally, when a human being enters upon his adolescence, turn into a fetter. So long as he (the human species) "was a child, he was as clever as a child"[119] and knew how to combine learning too, and even a philosophy helpful to the church, with propositions imposed upon him without any of his doing: "But when he becomes a man, he puts away the childish things."[120] The degrading distinction between *laity* and *clergy* ceases, and equality springs from true freedom, yet without anarchy, for each indeed obeys the law (not the statutory one) which he has prescribed for himself, yet must regard it at the same time as the will of the world ruler as revealed to him through reason, and this   6:122

---

* That [text] can, indeed, be interpreted as follows: No human being can say with certainty why this human being becomes good, that one evil (both comparatively), for we often seem to find the predisposition that makes for the distinction already at birth, and even contingencies of life over which nobody has any control are at times the decisive factor; and just as little can we say what will become of either. In this matter we must therefore entrust judgment to the All-seeing; and this is so expressed in the text as if he pronounces his decree upon them before they are born, thus prescribing to each the role that he will eventually play. For the world creator, if he is conceived in anthropopathic terms, *prevision* in the order of appearance is at the same time also *predestination*. But in the supersensible order of things in accordance with the laws of freedom, where time falls away, there is just one *all-seeing knowledge*, without the possibility of explaining why one human being behaves in this way, another according to opposite principles, and yet, at the same time, of reconciling the why with freedom of the will.

ruler invisibly binds all together, under a common government, in a state inadequately represented and prepared for in the past through the visible church. – All this is not to be expected from an external revolution, which produces its effect, very much dependent on fortuitous circumstances, in turbulence and violence: what is thus for once put in place at the establishment of a new constitution is regrettably retained for centuries to come, for it is no longer to be altered, not, at least, except through a new revolution (which is always dangerous). – The basis for the transition to the new order of things must lie in the principle of the pure religion of reason, as a revelation (though not an empirical one) permanently taking place within all human beings, and this basis, once grasped after mature reflection, will be carried to effect, inasmuch as it is to be a human work, through gradual reform; for, as regards revolutions, which can shorten the advance of the reform, they are left up to Providence and cannot be introduced according to plan without damage to freedom. –

We have reason to say, however, that "the Kingdom of God is come into us,"[121] even if only the principle of the gradual transition from ecclesiastical faith to the universal religion of reason, and so to a (divine) ethical state on earth, has put in roots universally and, somewhere, also *in public* – though the actual setting up of this state is still infinitely removed from us. For since this principle contains the basis for a continual approximation to the ultimate perfection, there lies in it (invisibly) – as in a shoot that develops and will in the future bear seeds in turn – the whole that will one day enlighten the world and rule over it. But truth and goodness (and in the natural predisposition of every human being there lies the basis both for insight into these and for heartfelt sympathy for them) do not fail, once made public, to propagate everywhere, in virtue of their natural affinity

6:123   with the moral predisposition of rational beings. The obstacles due to political and civil causes, which might interfere with their spread from time to time, serve rather to make all the more profound the union of minds with the good (which never leaves the thoughts of human beings after these have once cast their eyes upon it).*

. .

---

* Without either refusing the service of ecclesiastical faith or feuding with it, we can retain its useful influence as a vehicle yet equally deny to it – as the illusion of a duty to serve God ritually – every influence on the concept of true (viz. moral) religion. And so, in spite of the diversity of statutory forms of faith, we can establish tolerance among their adherents through the basic principles of the one religion of reason, with reference to which teachers ought to expound all the dogmas and observances of their various faiths; until, with time, by virtue of a true enlightenment (an order of law originating in moral freedom) which has gained the upper hand, the form of a degrading means of compulsion can be exchanged, with everybody's consent, for an ecclesiastical form commensurate to the dignity of a moral religion, viz. a free faith. – To reconcile ecclesiastical unity of faith with freedom in matters

Such is therefore the work of the good principle – unnoticed to human   6:124
eye yet constantly advancing – in erecting a power and a kingdom for itself
within the human race, in the form of a community according to the laws
of virtue that proclaims the victory over evil and, under its dominion,
assures the world of an eternal peace.

Division two
Historical representation of the gradual establishment of the dominion of the good principle on earth

We cannot expect to draw a *universal history* of the human race from
religion on earth (in the strictest meaning of the word); for, inasmuch as it
is based on pure moral faith, religion is not a public condition; each
human being can become conscious of the advances which he has made in
this faith only for himself. Hence we can expect a universal historical
account only of ecclesiastical faith, by comparing it, in its manifold and
mutable forms, with the one, immutable, and pure religious faith. From
this point onward, where ecclesiastical faith publicly acknowledges its
dependence on the restraining conditions of religious faith, and its necessity to conform to it, the *church universal* begins to fashion itself into an
ethical state of God and to make progress toward its fulfillment, under an
autonomous principle which is one and the same for all human beings and

---

of faith is a problem which the idea of the objective unity of the religion of reason constantly
urges us to resolve through the moral interest that we take in it, but which, if we turn for it to
human nature, we have little hope of bringing about in a visible church. The idea is one of
reason which is impossible for us to display in an intuition adequate to it but which, as
practical regulative principle, has nonetheless the objective reality required to work toward
this end of unity of the pure religion of reason. It is the same here as with the political idea of
the right of a state,[b] insofar as this right ought at the same time to be brought into line with
an international law[c] which is universal and *endowed with power*. Experience refuses to allow
us any hope in this direction. There seems to be a propensity in human nature (perhaps put
there on purpose) that makes each and every state strive, when things go its way, to subjugate
all others to itself and achieve a universal monarchy but, whenever it has reached a certain
size, to split up from within into smaller states. So too each and every church entertains the
proud pretension of becoming a universal one; as soon as it has propagated and acquires
ascendancy, however, a principle of dissolution and schism into various sects makes its
appearance.

 † If we are allowed to assume a design of providence here, the premature and hence
dangerous (since it would come before human beings have become morally better) fusion of
states into one is averted chiefly through two mightily effective causes, namely the difference
of languages and the difference of religions.

[b] *Staatsrecht*
[c] *Völkerrecht*

129

for all times. – We can see in advance that this history will be nothing but the narrative of the enduring conflict between the faith of divine service and the faith of moral religion, the first of which, as historical faith, human beings are constantly inclined to place higher, while the second has, for its part, never relinquished its claim to the preeminence that pertains to it as the only faith which improves the soul – a claim which, at the end, it will surely assert.

This history can have unity, however, only if merely restricted to that portion of the human race in which the predisposition to the unity of the universal church has already been brought close to its development. For here the question at least of the distinction between a rational and a historical faith is already being openly stated, and its resolution made a matter of the greatest moral concern; whereas the history of the dogmas of various peoples, whose faiths are in no way connected, is no guarantee of the unity of the church. Nor can the fact that at some point a certain new faith arises in one and the same people, substantially different from the previously dominant one, be counted as [indication] of this unity, even if, inherent in the previous faith, were the *occasional* causes of the new production. For we must have a principle of unity if we are to count as modifications of one and the same church the succession of different forms of faith which replace one another – and it is really with the history of that church that we are now concerned.

For this purpose, therefore, we can deal only with the history of the church which from the beginning bore within it the germ and the principles of the objective unity of the true and *universal* religious faith to which it is gradually being brought nearer. – And it is apparent, first of all, that the *Jewish* faith stands in absolutely no essential connection, i.e. in no unity of concepts, with the ecclesiastical faith whose history we want to consider, even though it immediately preceded it and provided the physical occasion for the founding of this church (the Christian).

The *Jewish faith*, as originally established, was only a collection of merely statutory laws supporting a political state; for whatever moral additions were *appended* to it, whether originally or only later, do not in any way belong to Judaism as such. Strictly speaking Judaism is not a religion at all but simply the union of a number of individuals who, since they belonged to a particular stock, established themselves into a community under purely political laws, hence not into a church;[122] Judaism was rather *meant* to be a purely secular state, so that, were it to be dismembered through adverse accidents, it would still be left with the political faith (which pertains to it by essence) that this state would be restored to it (with the advent of the Messiah). The fact that the constitution of this state was based on a theocracy (visibly, on an aristocracy of priests or leaders who boasted of instructions directly imparted to them from God), and that God's name was therefore honored in it (though only as a secular regent with absolutely no rights over, or claims upon, conscience), did not make that constitution religious. The proof that it was not to have been a religious constitution is clear. *First,* all its commands are of the kind which 6:126 even a political state can uphold and lay down as coercive laws, since they deal only with external actions. And although the Ten Commandments would have ethical validity for reason even if they had not been publicly given, yet in that legislation they are given with no claim at all on the *moral disposition* in following them (whereas Christianity later placed the chief work in this) but were rather directed simply and solely to external observance. And this is also clear from the fact that, *second,* all the consequences of fulfilling or transgressing these commandments, all rewards or punishments, are restricted to the kind which can be dispensed to all human beings in this world indifferently. And not even this is done in accordance with ethical concepts, since both rewards and punishments were to extend to a posterity which did not take any practical part in the deeds or misdeeds, something which in a political state may indeed be a clever device for fostering obedience, but would be contrary to all equity in an ethical one. Moreover, whereas no religion can be conceived without faith in a future life, Judaism as such, taken in its purity, entails absolutely no religious faith. This can be further supported by the following remark. It can hardly be doubted that, just like other peoples, even the most savage, the Jews too must have had a faith in a future life, hence had their heaven and hell, for this faith automatically imposes itself upon everyone by virtue of the universal moral predisposition in human nature. Hence it must have come about *intentionally* that the lawgiver of this people, though portrayed as God himself, did not *wish* to show the least consideration for the future life – an indication that his intention was to found only a political and not an ethical community, for to speak in a political community of rewards and punishments not visible in this life would be, on this assumption, a totally inconsequential and improper procedure. Now, although it can also hardly be doubted that the Jews subsequently produced, each for himself, some sort of religious faith which they added to the articles of their statutory faith, yet such a faith never was an integral part of the legislation of Judaism. *Third,* far from establishing an age suited to the 6:127 achievement of the *church universal,* let alone establishing it itself in its time, Judaism rather excluded the whole human race from its communion, a people especially chosen by Jehovah for himself, hostile to all other peoples and hence treated with hostility by all of them. In this connection also we should not place too much weight on the fact that this people set up, as universal ruler of the universe, a one and only God who could not be represented by any visible image. For we find in most other peoples that their doctrine of faith equally tended in this direction, and incurred the suspicion of polytheism only because of the *veneration* given to certain mighty undergods subordinated to the one God. For a God who wills only obedience to commands for which absolutely no improvement of moral disposition is required cannot truly be that moral being whose concept we find necessary for a religion. Religion is rather more likely to occur with a faith in many such mighty invisible beings, if a people were somehow to think of them as uniting, in spite of their "departmental" differences, in deeming worthy of their pleasure only those human beings who adhere to virtue with all their heart, than when faith is dedicated to but one being, who, however, makes of a mechanical cult the main work.

We cannot, therefore, begin the universal history of the Church (inasmuch as this history is to constitute a system) anywhere but from the origin of Christianity, which, as a total abandonment of the Judaism in which it originated, grounded on an entirely new principle, effected a total revolution in doctrines of faith.[123] The care that the teachers of Christianity take, and may even have taken from the very beginning, to link it to Judaism with a connecting strand, in wishing to have the new faith regarded as only a continuation of the old one which contains all its events in prefiguration, shows all too clearly that their only concern in this matter is, and was, about the most apt means of *introducing* a pure moral religion in place of an old cult to which the people were much too well habituated, without, however, directly offending against their prejudices. The subsequent discarding of the corporeal sign which served wholly to separate this people from others is itself warrant for the judgment that the new faith, not bound to the statutes of the old, nor, indeed, to any statute at all, was to contain a religion valid for the world and not for one single people.

Thus from Judaism – but from a Judaism no longer patriarchal and uncontaminated, no longer standing solely on a political constitution
6:128 (which also had already been shattered); from a Judaism already mingled, rather, with a religious faith because of the moral doctrines which had gradually gained public acceptance within it; at a juncture when much foreign (Greek) wisdom had already become available to this otherwise still ignorant people, and this wisdom presumably had had the further effect of enlightening it through concepts of virtue and, in spite of the oppressive burden of its dogmatic faith, of making it ready for revolutions which the diminution of the priests' power, due to their subjugation to the rule of a people indifferent to every foreign popular faith, occasioned – it was from a Judaism such as this that Christianity suddenly though not unprepared arose. The teacher of the Gospel announced himself as one sent from heaven while at the same time declaring, as one worthy of this mission, that servile faith (in days of divine service, in professions and practices) is inherently null; that moral faith, which alone makes human beings holy "as my father in heaven is holy"[124] and proves its genuineness by a good life-conduct, is on the contrary the only one which sanctifies. And, after he had given in his very person, through teaching and suffering even to undeserved

yet meritorious death,* an example conforming to the prototype of a humanity well-pleasing to God, he was represented as returning to the heaven from which he came. For, though he left his last will behind him by word of mouth (as in a testament), yet, as regards the power of the memory of his merit, his teaching and example, he was able to say that "he (the ideal of a humanity well-pleasing to God) would still be with his disciples, even to the end of the world."[125] To this teaching – which would indeed need confirmation through miracles if it had to do only with *historical faith* in the descent and the possibly supramundane rank of his person, but which, as part of a moral and soul-saving faith, can dispense with all such proofs of its truth – to this teaching there are nonetheless added in a holy book miracles and mysteries, and the propagation of these is itself a miracle requiring a historical faith which cannot be authenticated or secured in meaning and import except through scholarship.

Every faith which, as historical, bases itself on books, needs for guarantee a *learned public* in whom it can be controlled, as it were, through writers who were the contemporaries of the faith's first propagators yet in

6:129

---

* With which the public record of his life (which can therefore also serve universally as an example for imitation) ends. The more esoteric story of his *resurrection* and *ascension* (which, simply as ideas of reason, would signify the beginning of another life and the entrance into the seat of salvation, i.e. into the society of all the good), added as sequel and witnessed only by his intimates, cannot be used in the interest of religion within the boundaries of mere reason, whatever its historical standing. This is not just because it is a historical narrative (for so also is the story of what went before), but because, taken literally, it implies a concept which is indeed very well suited to the human sense mode of representation but is very troublesome to reason's faith concerning the future, namely the concept of the materiality of all the beings of this world – a *materialism* with respect to human *personality*, which would be possible only on the condition of one and the same *body* (psychological materialism), as well as a *materialism* with respect to *existence*[d] in general in a world, which, on this principle, could not be but *spatial* (cosmological materialism). By contrast, the hypothesis of the spirituality of the rational beings of this world, according to which the body can remain dead on earth and yet the same person still be living, or the hypothesis that the human being can attain to the seat of the blessed in spirit (in his non-sensuous[e] quality) without being transposed to some place in the infinite space surrounding the earth (which we also call heaven) – this hypothesis is more congenial to reason, not merely because it is impossible to conceive a matter endowed with thought, but, most of all, because of the contingency to which our existence after death would be exposed if we made it rest merely on the coherence of a certain clump of matter under a certain form, whereas we can conceive the permanence of a simple substance as natural to it. – On the latter presupposition (of spirituality) reason can, however, neither find an interest in dragging along, through eternity, a body which, however purified, must yet consist (if personality rests on its identity) of the same material which constitutes the body's organic basis and which, in life, the body itself never quite grew fond of; nor can it render comprehensible what this calcareous earth, of which the body consists, should be doing in heaven, i.e. in another region of the world where other matters might presumably constitute the condition of the existence and preservation of living beings.

[d] *Gegenwart*
[e] *nicht-sinnlich*

6:129

no way suspect of special collusion with them, and whose connection with our present authors has remained unbroken. The pure faith of reason, on the contrary, does not need any such documentation but is its own proof. Now at the time of the revolution in question, there already was among the people who ruled over the Jews and had spread in their very homeland (among the Romans) a learned public from whom the history of the political events of the time has been transmitted to us through an unbroken series of writers, and this people, though little concerned with the religious faiths of their non-Roman subjects, was not at all unreceptive to public miracles allegedly occurring among them; yet its writers made no mention, neither of the miracles nor of the equally public revolution which these caused (with respect to religion) among that people subjected to them, though they were contemporary witnesses. Only later, after more than one generation, did they institute research into the nature – but not into the history of the origin – of this change in faith which had hitherto remained unrecognized by them (and had occurred not without public commotion), in an effort to find it in their own annals. Hence, from its origin until the time when Christianity developed a learned public of its own, its history is obscure, and we thus have still no cognition of what effect its doctrine had upon the morality of its adherents, whether the first Christians were individuals truly improved morally or just people of ordinary cast. At any rate, from the time that Christianity itself became a learned public, or became part of the universal one, its history, so far as the beneficial effect which we rightly expect from a moral religion is concerned, has nothing in any way to recommend it. – How mystical enthusiasm in the life of hermits and monks and the exaltation of the holiness of the celibate state rendered a great number of individuals useless to the world; how the alleged miracles accompanying all this weighed down the people with the heavy chains of a blind superstition, how, with the imposition of a hierarchy upon free human beings, the terrible voice of *orthodoxy* rose from the mouth of self-appointed canonical expositors of scripture, and this voice split the Christian world into bitter parties over opinions in matters of faith (upon which, without recourse to pure reason as the expositor, no universal agreement can possibly be attained); how in the East, where the state itself, in an absurd manner, attended to the articles of faith of priests and their priestdom, instead of holding these priests within the narrow confines of a simple teacher's station (out of which they are at all times inclined to transgress into that of ruler) – how at the end, I say, this state inevitably had to become the prey of external enemies who finally put an end to the dominion of its faith; how in the West, where faith erected a throne of its own independent of secular power, the civil order was wrecked and rendered impotent, together with the sciences (which support it), by a self-proclaimed vicar of God; how the two parts of the Christian world were overcome by barbari-

6:130

6:131

134

ans, like plants and animals which, on the verge of disintegration through disease, attract destructive insects to complete the process; how, again in the West, the spiritual leader just mentioned ruled over kings and chastised them like children by means of the magic wand of his threat of excommunication, and incited them to foreign wars (the Crusades) which would depopulate another portion of the world, and to feuds among themselves, and the subjects to rebellion against those in authority over them and to bloodthirsty hatred against their otherwise-minded confreres in one and the same so-called universal Christianity; how the root of this strife, which even now is kept from violent outbreaks only through political interest, lies hidden in the fundamental principle of an ecclesiastical faith which rules despotically, and still occasions apprehension over the replaying of similar scenes: This history of Christianity (which, so far as it was to be erected on a historical faith, could not have turned out otherwise), when beheld in a single glance, like a painting, could indeed justify the outcry, *tantum religio potuit suadere malorum!,*[f] did not the fact still clearly enough shine forth from its founding that Christianity's true first purpose was none other than the introduction of a pure religious faith, over which there can be no dissension of opinions; whereas all that turmoil which has wrecked the human race, and still tears it apart, stems from this alone: because of a bad propensity in human nature, what should have served at the beginning to introduce this pure faith – i.e. to win over to the new faith, through its own prejudices, the nation which was accustomed to its old historical faith – this was subsequently made the foundation of a universal world-religion.

Should one now ask, Which period of the entire church history in our ken up to now is the best? I reply without hesitation, *The present.* I say this because one need only allow the seed of the true religious faith now being sown in Christianity – by only a few, to be sure, yet in the open – to grow unhindered, to expect from it a continuous approximation to that church, ever uniting all human beings, which constitutes the visible representation (the schema) of an invisible Kingdom of God on earth. – In matters   6:132
which ought to be moral and soul improving by nature, reason has wrested itself free from the burden of a faith constantly exposed to the arbitrariness[g] of its interpreters, and, in all the lands on our part of the world, universally among those who truly revere religion (though not everywhere openly), it has accepted, in the *first* place, the principle of reasonable *moderation* in claims concerning anything that goes by the name of revelation. To wit: Since no one can dispute the *possibility* that a scripture which, in its practical content, contains much that is godly may also be regarded (with respect to what is historical in it) as divine revelation; more-

---

[f] "Such evil deeds could religion prompt!" Lucretius, *De rerum natura,* I:101.
[g] *Willkür*

over, since the union of human beings into one religion cannot feasibly be established and given permanence without a holy book and an ecclesiastical faith based on it; since also, given the present situation of human insight, some new revelation ushered in through new miracles can hardly be expected, the most reasonable and the fairest thing to do, once a book is already in place, is to use it from then on as the basis for ecclesiastical instruction, and not to weaken its value through useless or malicious attacks, yet at the same time not to force faith in it upon any human being, as requisite for his salvation. A *second* principle is this: Since the sacred narrative is only adopted for the sake of ecclesiastical faith, and, by itself alone, it neither could, nor ought to, have any influence whatever on the reception of moral maxims but is rather given to this faith only for the vivid presentation of its true object (virtue striving toward holiness), it should at all times be taught and expounded in the interest of morality, and the point should thereby also be stressed, carefully and (since espe-

6:133   cially the ordinary human being has in him a constant propensity to slip into passive* faith) repeatedly, that true religion is not to be placed in the knowledge or the profession of what God does or has done for our salvation, but in what we must do to become worthy of it; and this can never be anything but what possesses an unquestionably *unconditional* value, hence is alone capable of making us well-pleasing to God, and every human being can at the same time be fully certain of its necessity without the slightest scriptural learning. – Now it is the duty of the rulers not to hinder the public diffusion of these principles; on the contrary, much is risked, and at one's own responsibility, when we intrude upon the way of divine providence by favoring certain historical ecclesiastical doctrines, which at best have in their favor only an appearance of truth to be established by scholars, and, through the offer or withdrawal of certain civil advantages otherwise available to everyone, by exposing the subjects'

6:134   conscience to temptation – † all of which, apart from the harm which

* One cause of this propensity lies in the principle of security, namely that the mistakes of a religion in which I was born and brought up, in which I was instructed without any choice of mine, and in which I did not alter anything through any ratiocination of mine, are not charged on my account but on that of my educators or of the teachers publicly appointed to that task – a reason too why we do not readily approve of somebody's public change of religion, to which, to be sure, yet another (and deeper) is added, namely, that with the uncertainty which we all privatively feel regarding which, among the historical faiths, is the right one, whereas moral faith is everywhere the same, we find it highly unnecessary to cause a sensation on this score.

† If a government does not wish to be regarded as doing violence to conscience because it only prohibits *the public declaration* of one's religious opinions while not hindering anyone from *thinking* in secret whatever he sees fit, then we commonly make fun of this, saying that no freedom is thereby granted by the government, since thought cannot be prevented anyway. But what the secular supreme power cannot do, the spiritual power can. It can prohibit even thought, and actually hinder it as well; indeed, it can exercise this coercion (namely the prohibition even to think otherwise than it prescribes) upon its mighty authorities themselves. –

thereby befalls a freedom which is in this case holy, can hardly produce good citizens for the state. Who, among those who conspire to hinder such a free development of the divine predispositions to the world's highest good, or even promote its hindrance, would wish, upon reflection in consultation with conscience, to answer for all the evil which can arise from such violent interventions and hamper, perhaps for a long time to come, or indeed even set back the advance in goodness envisaged by the world's government, even though no human power or institution could ever abolish it entirely?

As regards its guidance by Providence, the Kingdom of Heaven is finally represented in this history not only as coming nearer, in an approach delayed indeed at certain times yet never entirely interrupted, but as being ushered in as well. Now the Kingdom of Heaven can be interpreted as a symbolic representation aimed merely at stimulating greater hope and courage and effort in achieving it, if to this narrative there is attached a prophecy (just as in the Sibylline books)[126] of the consummation of this great cosmic revolution, in the image of a visible Kingdom of God on earth (under the governance of his representative and vicar, who has again come down [from heaven]), and of the happiness which is to be enjoyed here on earth under him after the separation and expulsion of the rebels who once again make an attempt at resistance; together with the total extirpation of these rebels, and of their leader (as in the Apocalypse),[127] so that the *end of the world* constitutes the conclusion of the story. The teacher of the Gospel manifested the Kingdom of God on earth to his disciples only from its glorious, edifying, and moral side, namely in terms of the merit of being citizens of a divine state; and he instructed them as to what they had to do, not only that they attain to it themselves, but that they be united in it with others of like mind, and if possible with

---

For because of their propensity to a servile faith of divine worship, to which they are spontaneously inclined not only to give the greatest importance, above moral faith (which is the service of God above all through the observance of their duties), but also the only importance, one that compensates for any other deficiency, it is always easy for the custodians of orthodoxy, as the shepherds of souls, to instill into their flock such a pious terror of the slightest deviation from certain propositions of faith based on history, indeed the terror of any investigation, that they will not trust themselves to allow a doubt to arise even in thought alone regarding these propositions imposed on them, since this would amount to lending an ear to the evil spirit. True, to be free of this coercion one needs only *to will* (and this is not the case with the coercion to public confessions imposed by a sovereign); but it is precisely this willing on which a bar is being applied internally. Yet, though this true coercion of conscience is bad enough (since it leads to inner hypocrisy), it is not as bad as the restriction of external freedom of faith, because, through the advancement of moral insight and of our awareness of freedom, from which alone true respect of duty can arise, internal coercion must gradually disappear on its own, whereas external coercion hinders all spontaneous advances in the ethical communion of the believers, which constitutes the essence of the true church, and totally subjects its form to political ordinances.   6:134

137

the whole human race. But as regards happiness, which constitutes the other part of the human being's unavoidable desire, he told them from the
6:135 beginning that they could not count on it during their life on earth. He prepared them instead to be ready for the greatest tribulations and sacrifices; yet (since total renunciation of the physical element of happiness cannot be expected of a human being, so long as he exists) he added: "Rejoice and be exceeding glad: for great is your reward in Heaven."[128] The addition to the history of the church that deals with its future final destiny represents it, however, as finally *triumphant*, i.e. as crowned with happiness here on earth, after having overcome all obstacles. – The separation of the good from the evil, which would not have been conducive to the church's end in the course of its advance to perfection (since the mingling of the two was necessary precisely for this reason, in part to sharpen the virtue of the good, and in part to turn the other away from their evil through the example of the good), is represented as the final consequence of the establishment of the divine state after its completion. And here yet a last proof of the stability of this state, regarded as power, is added: its victory over all external foes, who are also considered [as assembled] in one state (the state of hell), whereby all earthly life then comes to an end, as "the last enemy (of good human beings), death, is destroyed,"[129] and immortality commences on both sides, to the salvation of the one, and the damnation of the other; the very form of a church is dissolved; the vicar on earth enters the same class as the human beings who are now elevated to him as citizens of Heaven, and so God is all in all.[130]*

This representation in a historical narrative of the future world, which is not itself history, is a beautiful ideal of the moral world-epoch brought about by the introduction of the true universal religion and *foreseen*[h] in
6:136 faith in its completion – one which we do not *see directly*[i] in the manner of an empirical completion but *have a glimpse of*[j] in the continuous advance and approximation toward the highest possible good on earth (in this there is nothing mystical but everything proceeds naturally in a moral

* This expression (if we set aside its element of mystery, which transcends the bounds of possible experience and only belongs to the sacred *history* of mankind, hence does not concern us practically) can be so understood: historical faith, which, as ecclesiastical, needs a holy book to guide human beings but, precisely for this reason, hinders the church's unity and universality, will itself cease and pass over into a pure religious faith which illumines the whole world equally; and we should diligently work for it even now, through the continuous development of the pure religion of reason out of its present still indispensable shell.
† Not that it "will cease" (for it might always be useful and necessary, perhaps, as vehicle) but that "it can cease"; whereby is intended only the intrinsic firmness of pure moral faith.
ʰ *ausgesehenen*
ⁱ *absehen*
ʲ *hinaussehen*

way), i.e. we can make preparation for it. The appearance of the Antichrist, the millennium, the announcement of the proximity of the end of the world, all take on their proper symbolic meaning before reason. And the last of them, represented (like the end of life, whether far or near) as an event which we cannot see in advance, expresses very well the necessity for us always to be ready for it, yet (if we ascribe to this symbol its intellectual meaning) in fact always to consider ourselves as actually the chosen citizens of a divine (ethical) state. "When, therefore, cometh the Kingdom of God?" – "The Kingdom of God cometh not in visible form. Neither shall they say: Lo here; or lo there! *For behold, the Kingdom of God is within you!*" (Luke, 17, 21–22).*

---

*† A kingdom of God is here represented not according to a particular covenant ([it is] not a messianic kingdom) but according to a *moral* one (available to cognition through mere reason). A messianic kingdom (*regnum divinum pactitium*)[k] would have to draw its proof from history, and there it is divided into the *messianic* kingdom of the *old* and of the *new* covenant. Now it is worthy of notice that the worshippers of the former (the Jews) have preserved their identity though dispersed throughout the world, whereas the adherents of other religions have normally assimilated their faith with that of the people among whom they scattered. This phenomenon strikes many as being so remarkable[l] that, in their judgment, it certainly could not have been possible by nature but only as an extraordinary event designed for a divine purpose. – But a people in possession of a written religion (sacred books) never assimilates in faith with a people which (like the Roman Empire, i.e. the whole civilized world at the time) has nothing of the kind but only has customs; it rather sooner or later makes proselytes. Hence the Jews too, after the Babylonian captivity (when, as it appears, their sacred books were read publicly for the first time), were no longer accused of their propensity to run after false gods, at the very time when the Alexandrian culture, which must have had an influence on them too, could have made it easy for them to give these gods a systematic form. So too the Parsees, followers of the religion of Zoroaster, have until now retained their faith in spite of their dispersion, because their *dustoors*[m] possessed the Zendavesta. Those Hindus, on the other hand, who under the name of "Gypsies" have scattered far and wide, have not avoided the mixture of foreign faith, since they came from the scum of the population (the Pariahs, to whom it is even forbidden to read their sacred books). However, what the Jews would not have achieved on their own, the Christian and later the Mohammedan religion, but the Christian especially, did for them, since these religions presuppose the Jewish faith and the sacred books pertaining to it (although the Mohammedan religion claims that they have been distorted). For the Jews could always rediscover their ancient documents among the Christians (who had issued from them) if in their wanderings, where the skill to read them and hence the desire to possess them may have repeatedly died out, they just retained memory of having at one time possessed them. Hence we do not run across Jews outside the lands indicated, if we except the few on the coast of Malabar and perhaps one community in China (and of these the first were able to be in continual business relation with their fellow believers in Arabia), although there is no doubt that they must have spread in those rich lands as well but, because of the lack of any affinity between their faith and the local, ended up forgetting theirs completely. At any rate, it is quite awkward to base edifying considerations upon this preservation of the Jewish people and their religion in circumstances so disadvantageous to them, for both parties

6:137

[k] a divine kingdom secured by covenant

[l] *wundersam*

[m] high priests

General remark

Investigation into all forms of faith that relate to religion invariably runs across a *mystery* behind their inner nature, i.e. something *holy*, which can indeed be *cognized*[n] by every individual, yet cannot be *professed*[o] publicly, i.e. cannot be communicated universally. – As something *holy* it must be a moral object, hence an object of reason and one capable of being sufficiently recognized[p] internally for practical use; yet, as something *mysterious*, not for theoretical use, for then it would have to be communicable to everyone and hence also capable of being externally and publicly professed.

Now faith in something which, however, we yet regard as a holy mystery can either be looked upon as *divinely dispensed* or as a *pure faith of reason.* Unless impelled by the most extreme need to accept the first kind, we shall make it a maxim to abide by the second. – Feelings are not cognitions; they are not, therefore, the marks of a mystery; and, since mystery relates to reason yet is not something that can be imparted universally, each individual will have to look for it (if there is any such thing) in his own reason.

It is impossible to determine, *a priori* and objectively, whether there are such mysteries or not. Hence we shall have to look directly into the inner, the subjective, part of our moral predisposition in order to see whether any can be found in us. We shall not, however, be allowed to count among the holy mysteries the *grounds* of morality, which are inscrutable to us, but only what is given to us in cognition yet is not susceptible of public disclosure; for morality allows of open communication, even though its cause is not given to us. Thus freedom – a property which is made manifest to the human being through the determination of his power of choice by the unconditional moral law – is no mystery, since cognition of it can be *communicated* to everyone; the ground of this property, which is inscrutable to us, is however a mystery, since it is *not given* to us in cognition. This very freedom, however, when applied to the final object of practical reason

believe that they find confirmation in it. One sees in the preservation of the people to which it belongs, and of its ancient faith that has remained unadulterated in spite of the dispersion among so many peoples, the proof of a special beneficent providence which is saving this people for a future kingdom on earth; the other sees in it nothing but the admonishing ruins of a devastated state which stands in the way of the Kingdom of Heaven to come but which a particular providence still sustains, partly to preserve in memory the old prophecy of a messiah issuing from this people, and partly to make of it an example of punitive justice, because, in its stiffneckedness, that people wanted to make a political and not a moral concept of this messiah.

[n] *gekannt*
[o] *bekannt*
[p] *erkannt*

(the realization of the final moral end), is alone what inevitably leads us to holy mysteries. – *

Since by himself the human being cannot realize the idea of the su-   6:139
preme good inseparably bound up with the pure moral disposition, either with respect to the happiness which is part of that good or with respect to the union of the human beings necessary to the fulfillment of the end, and yet there is also in him the duty to promote the idea, he finds himself driven to believe in the coöperation or the management of a moral ruler of the world, through which alone this end is possible. And here there opens up before him the abyss of a mystery regarding what God may do, whether *anything* at all is to be attributed to him and *what* this something might be in particular, whereas the only thing that a human being learns from a duty is what he himself must do to become worthy of that fulfillment, of which he has no cognition or at least no possibility of comprehension.

This idea of a moral ruler of the world is a task for our practical reason. Our concern is not so much to know what he is in himself (his nature) but what he is for us as moral beings; even though for the sake of this relation we must think the divine nature by assuming it to have the full perfection required for the execution of his will (e.g. as the will of an immutable, omniscient, all-powerful, etc. being). And apart from this relation we can cognize nothing about him.

Now, in accordance with this need of practical reason, the universal true religious faith is faith in God (1) as the almighty creator of heaven

---

* The *cause* of the universal gravity of all matter in the world is equally unknown to us, so much so that we can even see that we shall never have cognition of it, since its very concept presupposes a first motive force unconditionally residing within it. Yet gravity is not a mystery; it can be made manifest to everyone, since its *law* is sufficiently cognized. When Newton represents it as if it were the divine presence in appearance (*omnipraesentia phaenomenon*),[q] this is not an attempt to explain it (for the existence of God in space involves a contradiction) but a sublime analogy in which the mere union of corporeal beings into a cosmic whole is being visualized, in that an incorporeal cause is put underneath them – and so too would fare the attempt to comprehend the self-sufficient principle of the union of rational beings in the world into an ethical state, and to explain this union from that principle. We recognize only the duty that draws us to it; the possibility of the intended effect in obeying this duty lies outside the bounds of all our insight. – There are mysteries that are   6:139
hidden things of nature (*arcana*), and there are mysteries of politics (things kept secret, *secreta*); yet we *can* still become acquainted[r] with either, inasmuch as they rest on empirical causes. With respect to that which is universal human duty to have cognition of (namely anything moral) there can be no mystery; but with respect to that which God alone can do, for which to do anything ourselves would exceed our capacity and hence also our duty, there we can have a genuine, i.e. a holy, mystery of religion (*mysterium*). And it might perhaps be useful only to know and to understand that there is such a mystery rather than to have insight into it.

[q] phenomenal omnipresence
[r] *können . . . uns bekannt werden*

and earth, i.e. morally as *holy* lawgiver; (2) as the preserver of the human race, as its *benevolent* ruler and moral guardian; (3) as the administrator of his own holy laws, i.e. as *just* judge.

6:140   This faith really contains no mystery, since it expresses solely God's moral bearing toward the human race. It is also by nature available to all human reason and is therefore to be met with in the religion of most civilized peoples.* It is also inherent in the concept of a people regarded as a community, where such threefold superior power (*pouvoir*) is always to be thought, except that the people is here represented as ethical, and hence the threefold quality of the moral head of the human race, which in a juridico-civil state must of necessity be distributed among three different subjects, † can be thought as united in one and the same being.

6:141   But since this faith, which purified the moral relation of human beings to the highest being from harmful anthropomorphism on behalf of universal religion and brought it up to measure with the true morality of a people of God, was first set forth in a certain doctrine of faith (the Christian one) and made public to the world only in it, its promulgation can well be called

---

* In the sacred prophetic story of the "last things," the *judge of the world* (really he who will take as his own under his dominion those who belong to the kingdom of the good principle, and will separate them out) is represented and spoken of not as God but as the Son of man.[131] This seems to indicate that *humanity itself,* conscious of its limitation and fragility, will pronounce the sentence in this selection. And this is a generosity which does not, however, violate justice. – In contrast, when represented in his Divinity (the Holy Spirit), i.e. as he speaks to our conscience with the voice of the holy law which we ourselves recognize and in terms of our own reckoning, the judge of human beings can be thought of only as passing judgment according to the rigor of the law, for we ourselves know absolutely nothing of how much can be credited in our behalf to the account of our frailty but have only our trespasses before our eyes, together with the consciousness of our freedom and of the violation of our duty for which we are wholly to be blamed, and hence have no ground for assuming generosity in the judgment passed on us.

† It is hard to give a reason why so many ancient peoples hit upon this idea, unless it is that the idea lies in human reason universally whenever we want to think of the governance of a people and (on the analogy of this) of world governance. The religion of Zoroaster had these three divine persons, Ormuzd, Mithra, and Ahriman,[132] the Hindu religion had Brahma, Vishnu, and Shiva[133] – but with only this difference, that the religion of Zoroaster represents its third person as the creator not just of *evil* as punishment but also of the *moral evil* itself for which humans are being punished, whereas the Hindu religion represents it only as judging and punishing. The religion of Egypt had its Ptha, Kneph, and Neith,[134] of whom, so far as the obscurity of the reports from those ancient times allow us to surmise, the first was to represent spirit, distinguished from matter, as *world-creator;* the second, a generosity which sustains and *rules;* the third, a wisdom which limits this generosity, *i.e. justice.* The Goths

6:141 revered their Odin (father of all), their Freya (also Freyer, goodness), and Thor, the judging (punishing) God. Even the Jews seem to have pursued these ideas in the final period of their hierarchical constitution. For in the charge of the Pharisees that Christ had called himself a *Son of God,* they do not seem to put any special weight of blame on the doctrine that God has a son, but only on Christ's claim to be the Son of God.[135]

the revelation of something which had hitherto remained a mystery for human beings through their own fault.

This revelation says, *first*, that we should represent the supreme law-giver, neither as *merciful* and hence *forbearing* (indulgent) toward human weakness, nor as *despotic* and ruling merely according to his unlimited right; and his laws not as arbitrary, totally unrelated to our concepts of morality, but as directed at the holiness of the human being. *Second*, we must place his goodness, not in an unconditional *benevolence* toward his creatures, but in that he first sees to their moral constitution through which they are *well-pleasing* to him, and only then makes up for their incapacity to satisfy this requirement on their own. *Third*, his justice cannot be represented as *generous* and *condoning* (for this implies a contradiction), and even less as dispensed by the lawgiver in his quality of holiness (for before it no human being is justified), but only as restricting his generosity to the condition that human beings abide by the holy law, to the extent that as *sons of men*[136] they can measure up to it. – In a word, God wills to be served as morally qualified in three specifically different ways, for which the designation of different (not physically, but morally) personalities of one and the same being is not a bad expression. And this creed of faith at the same time expresses the whole of pure moral religion which, without this distinction of personalities, would run the danger of degenerating into an anthropomorphic servile faith, because of the human propensity to think of the Divinity as a human authority[s] (who does not usually 6:142 separate in his rule [the parts of] this threefold quality but rather often mixes or interchanges them).

But, if this very faith (in a divine Trinity) were to be regarded not just as the representation of a practical idea, but as a faith that ought to represent what God is in himself, it would be a mystery surpassing all human concepts, hence unsuited to a revelation humanly comprehensible, and could only be declared in this respect as mystery. Faith in it as an extension of theoretical cognition of the divine nature would only be the profession of a creed of ecclesiastical faith totally unintelligible to human beings or, if they think that they understand it, the profession of an anthropomorphic creed, and not the least would thereby be accomplished for moral improvement. – Only what we can indeed thoroughly understand and penetrate in a practical context, but which surpasses all our concepts for theoretical purposes (for the determination of the nature of the object in itself), is mystery (in one context) and can yet (in another) be revealed. Of this kind is the above mentioned mystery, which can be divided into three mysteries revealed to us through our own reason:

1. The mystery of the *call* (of human beings to be citizens of an ethical

[s] *Oberhaupt*

state). – We can form a concept of the universal and *unconditional* subjection of human beings to the divine legislation only insofar as we also consider ourselves his *creatures;* just so can God be considered the ultimate source of all natural laws only because he is the creator of natural things. It is, however, totally incomprehensible to our reason how beings can be *created* to use their powers freely, for according to the principle of causality we cannot attribute any other inner ground of action to a being, which we assume to have been produced, except that which the producing cause has placed in it. And, since through this ground (hence through an external cause) the being's every action is determined as well, the being itself cannot be free. So through our rational insight we cannot reconcile the divine and holy legislation, which only applies to free beings, with the concept of the creation of these beings, but must simply presuppose the latter as already existing free beings who are determined to citizenship in 6:143 the divine state, not in virtue of their creation, but because of a purely moral necessitation, only possible according to the laws of freedom, i.e. through a call. So the call to this end is morally quite clear; for speculation, however, the possibility of beings who are thus called is an impenetrable mystery.

2. The mystery of *satisfaction.* The human being, so far as we have cognition of him, is corrupted and of himself not in the least adequate to that holy law. However, if the goodness of God has called him as it were into being, i.e. has invited him to a particular kind of existence (to be a member of the Kingdom of Heaven), he must also have a means of compensating, from the fullness of his own holiness, for the human being's inadequacy with respect to it. But this goes against the spontaneity (presupposed in every moral good or evil which a human being might have within himself), according to which the required goodness must stem from a human being himself, not from someone else, if it is to be imputable to him. – Inasmuch as reason can see, therefore, no one can stand in for another by virtue of the superabundance of his own good conduct and his merit; and if we must *assume* any such thing, this can be only for moral purposes, since for ratiocination it is an unfathomable mystery.

3. The mystery of *election.* Even if we admit such a vicarious satisfaction as possible, a morally believing acceptance of it is itself a determination of the will toward the good that already presupposes in the human being a disposition well-pleasing to God – one which the human being, in his natural corruption, cannot however bring about on his own within himself. But that a heavenly *grace* should work in him to grant this assistance to one human being, yet denies it to another, not according to the merit of works but through some unconditional *decree,* and elects one part of our race to salvation, the other to eternal reprobation: this again does not yield the concept of a divine justice but must at best be deferred to a wisdom whose rule is an absolute mystery to us.

Now regarding these mysteries, so far as they touch the moral life-history of every human being – namely how does it happen that there is a moral good or evil in the world at all, and (if evil is in every human being and at all times) how is it that good will still originates from it and is restored in a human being; or why, when *this* happens in some, are others however excluded from it – regarding this God has revealed nothing to us, nor can he reveal anything, for we would not *understand* it.* It would be as if from the human being, through his freedom, we wanted to *explain* and *make comprehensible* to us what happens; regarding this God has indeed revealed his will through the moral law in us but has left the *causes* whereby a free action occurs or does not occur on earth in the same obscurity in which everything must remain for human investigation; all this ought to be conceived, as history, according to the law of cause and effect yet also from freedom.† Regarding the objective rule of our conduct, however, all that we need is sufficiently revealed (through reason and Scripture), and this revelation is equally understandable to every human being.

6:144

That the human being is called to a good life conduct through the moral law; that, through an indelible respect for this law which lies in him, he also finds in himself encouragement to trust in this good spirit and to hope that, however it may come about, he will be able to satisfy this spirit; finally, that, comparing this expectation with the rigorous command of the law, he must constantly test himself as if summoned to accounts before a judge – reason, heart, and conscience all teach this and drive us to it. It is presumptuous to require that more be made manifest to us, and if this were to happen, we must not regard it as a universal human need.

6:145

But, although that great mystery which encompasses in one single formula all those we have mentioned can be made comprehensible to

---

*† We normally have no misgivings in asking novices in religion to believe in mysteries, since the fact that we do not *comprehend* them, i.e. that we have no insight into the possibility of their object, could just as little justify our refusal to accept them as it could the refusal to accept (say) the capacity of organic matter to procreate – a capacity which likewise no one comprehends yet, though it is and will remain a mystery for us, no one can refuse to accept. We do, however, *understand* what this expression means, and have an empirical concept of its object together with the consciousness that it contains no contradiction. – Now we can with right require of every mystery proposed for belief that we *understand* what is meant by it. And this does not happen just because we understand *one by one* the words with which the mystery is enunciated, i.e. by attaching a meaning to each separately, but because, when combined together in one concept, the words still allow a meaning and do not, on the contrary, thereby escape all thought. – It is unthinkable that God could make this cognition come to us through *inspiration*, if we for our part do not fail earnestly to wish for it, for such cognition could simply not take hold in us, since the nature of our understanding is incapable of it.
†† Hence in a practical context (whenever duty is at issue), we understand perfectly well what freedom is; for theoretical purposes, however, as regards the causality of freedom (and equally its nature) we cannot even formulate without contradiction the wish to understand it.

every human being through his reason, as an idea necessary in practice, yet we can say that, to become the moral foundation of religion, and particularly of a public one, it was revealed at the time when it was *publicly* taught for the first time, and was made into the symbol of a totally new religious epoch. *Solemn formulas* normally contain a language of their own, sometimes mystical and not understood by everyone, intended only for those who belong to a particular society (a brotherhood or community), a language which properly (out of respect) ought to be used only for a ceremonial act (as, for instance, when someone is to be initiated in an exclusive society as member). The highest goal of the moral perfection of finite creatures, never completely attainable by human beings, is, however, the love of the Law.

In conformity with this idea, "God is love"[137] would be a principle of faith in religion: In God we can *revere* the loving one (whose love is that of moral *approbation* of human beings so far as they conform to his holy laws), the Father; in God also, so far as he displays himself in his all-encompassing idea, which is the prototype of the humanity generated and beloved by him, we can *revere* his *Son;* and, finally, so far as he makes his approbation depend upon the agreement of human beings with the condi-

6:146   tion of his love of approbation, the *Holy Spirit;** but we cannot truly *call*

---

* This Spirit, through whom the love of God as author of salvation (really, our correspond-ing love proportionate to his) is united to the fear of God as lawgiver, i.e. the conditioned with the condition, and which can therefore be represented "as proceeding from both,"[138] besides "leading to all truth (observance of duty),"[139] is at the same time the true Judge of human beings (at the bar of conscience). For "judging" can be taken in a twofold sense: as concerning either merit and the lack of merit, or guilt and nonguilt. God, considered as *love* (in his Son), judges human beings insofar as a merit can yet accrue to them over and above

6:146   their guilt, and here his verdict is: *worthy* or *unworthy*. He separates out as his own those to whom such merit can still be imputed. The rest go away emptyhanded. On the other hand, the sentence of the judge according to *justice* (of the judge properly so called, under the name of Holy Spirit) upon those to whom no merit can accrue, is: *guilty* or *not guilty*, i.e. damnation or absolution. – In the first instance the *judging* means the *separating out* of the meritorious from the unmeritorious, the two sides both competing for the one prize (salvation). But by *merit* we do not understand here a moral advantage before the law (for with respect to the latter no surplus of observance to duty can accrue to us over and above what is due), but only in comparison to other human beings, relative to their moral disposition. *Worthiness* has moreover always only negative meaning (not-unworthiness), that is, moral receptivity to such goodness. – Hence he who judges under the first qualification (as *brabeuta*)' pronounces a judgment of election between *two* persons (or parties) competing for the same prize (salva-tion); while he who judges under the second (the judge in the proper sense) passes sentence upon *one and the same* person before a court (conscience) that decides between prosecution and defense. – Now if it is assumed that, although all human beings are indeed guilty of sin, to some there can nonetheless accrue a merit, then the pronouncement of the judge pro-ceeds *from love*, a lack of which can lead only to *a judgment of rejection* and its inevitable consequence of a *judgment of condemnation* (since the human being is now handed over to the *just* judge). – It is thus, in my opinion, that the apparently contradictory propositions, "The
' an arbiter of games (Greek)

upon him in this multiform personality (for this would imply a diversity of beings, whereas God is always only a single object), though we can indeed in the name of that object which he himself loves and reveres above all else, and with which it is both a wish and a duty to enter in moral union.[142] For the rest, the theoretical profession of faith in the divine nature under this threefold quality belongs to the mere classical formula of an ecclesiastical faith, to distinguish it from other forms derived from historical sources – a formula to which few human beings are in a position of attaching a clear and distinct concept (one not exposed to misunderstanding); its examination pertains rather to teachers in their relation to one another (as philosophical and erudite expositors of a holy book), that they may agree on its meaning, not all of which is suited to the general capacity of comprehension or to the needs of the time, while mere literal faith hurts rather than improves the true religious disposition.

6:147

Son will come again to judge the quick and the dead,"[140] but also, "God sent not his Son into the world to condemn the world; but that the world through him might be saved" (John 3:7), can be reconciled; and they can agree with the other where it is said, "He that believeth not in him is condemned *already*" (John 3:18), namely by the Spirit, of whom it is said, "He will judge the world because of sin and righteousness."[141] – The anxious solicitude over such distinctions as we are instituting here in the domain of mere reason, strictly for reason's sake, might well be regarded as useless and burdensome subtlety; and so they would be indeed, if they were directed to an inquiry into the divine nature. But since in their religious affairs human beings are constantly inclined to turn to the divine goodness on account of their faults without, however, being able to circumvent his justice, and yet a *generous judge* in one and the same person is a contradiction, it is obvious that their concepts on this subject must be very wavering and inherently inconsistent even from a practical point of view, hence their justification and exact determination of great practical importance.

The philosophical doctrine of religion
Part four

Part four
Concerning service and counterfeit service[u]
under the dominion of the good principle,
or,
Of religion and priestcraft

It is already a beginning of the dominion of the good principle and a sign "that the Kingdom of God is at hand,"[143] even if only the principles of its constitution begin to become *public;* for in the world of the understanding something is already there when the causes, which alone can bring it to pass, have taken root generally, even though the complete development of its appearance in the world of the senses is postponed to an unseen distance. We have seen that to unite in an ethical community is a duty of a special kind (*officium sui generis*), and that, though we each obey our private duty, we might indeed thereby derive an *accidental agreement* of all in a common good, without any special organization being necessary for it, yet that such a universal agreement is not to be hoped for, unless a special business is made of resisting the attacks of the evil principle (which human beings themselves otherwise tempt each other to serve as tools) by the union of all with one another for one and the same end, and the establishment of one community under moral laws, as a federated and therefore stronger force. – We have also seen that such a community, **as a Kingdom of God,** can be undertaken by human beings only through *religion,* and, finally, that in order for religion to be public (a requisite for a community), this *Kingdom* is represented in the visible form of a *church,* 6:152 the founding of which therefore devolves on human beings as a work which is entrusted to them and can be required of them.

To erect a church as a community under religious laws, however, seems to require more wisdom (of insight as well as of good disposition) than human beings can be thought capable of; it seems that the moral goodness especially, which is aimed at through such an organization, must for this purpose be *presupposed* in them already. Nonsensical is in fact even

[u] Counterfeit service = *Afterdienst*

the expression that *human beings* should *found* a Kingdom of God (as we might well say of them that they can establish the kingdom of a human monarch); God must himself be the author of his Kingdom. Since we do not know, however, what God may directly do to display in actuality the idea of his Kingdom, in which to be citizens and subjects we discover the moral vocation within us, yet know very well what we must do to make ourselves fit to be members of it, this idea, whether aroused and made *public* in the human race through reason or through Scripture, still binds us to the formation of a church, of which God himself is in the last instance the author of the *constitution* as founder, whereas human beings, as members and free citizens of this kingdom, are in all instances the authors of the *organization;* thus those among them who manage the public affairs of the church in accordance with this organization will constitute the church's *administration*, as ecclesiastical servants, while the rest will make up a fellowship, the *congregation*, subject to their laws.

Now, since a pure religion of reason, as a public religious faith, admits only the mere idea of a church (that is, an invisible church), and since only the visible one, founded on laws, is in need of and susceptible to an organization by human beings, it follows that service under the dominion of the good principle in the invisible church cannot be considered as ecclesiastical service, and that the religion of reason does not have legal servants who act as the *officials* of an ethical community; the members of this community receive their orders from the highest lawgiver individually, without intermediary. But, since with respect to our duties (which, taken collectively, we must at the same time look upon as divine commands) we nevertheless are at all times at the service of God, the *pure religion of reason* will have all right-thinking human beings as its *servants* (yet without being *officials*); but to this extent they cannot be called servants of a church (that is, of a visible one, which alone is at issue here). – However, since every church erected on statutory laws can be the true church only to the extent that it contains within itself a principle of constantly coming closer to the pure faith of religion (which, when operative,[v] is what truly constitutes religion in every faith) and of eventually being able to dispense with ecclesiastical faith (in its historical aspect), we shall nonetheless be able to posit in these laws, and among the officials of the church founded on them, a *service* of the church (*cultus*), provided that these officials direct their teaching and order to that final end (a public religious faith). By contrast the servants of a church who do not take this end into consideration but rather declare the maxim of constant approximation to it as damnable, while dependence on the historical and statutory part of the church's faith as alone salvific, can justly be accused of *counterfeit service* of the church or the ethical community under the dominion of the good principle (which is represented through the church). – By a

6:153

---

[v] *praktisch*

"counterfeit service" (*cultus spurius*) is meant the persuasion that we are serving someone with deeds which, in fact, go counter to his intention. This comes about in a community when that which has value only as means for satisfying the will of a superior, is given out to be, and is substituted for, what would make us well-pleasing to him *directly*, and the superior's intention is thereby frustrated.

First part
Concerning the service of God in a religion in general

Religion is (subjectively considered) the recognition of all our duties as divine commands.* That religion, in which I must first know that something is a divine command in order that I recognize it as my duty, is *revealed* religion (or a religion which requires a revelation); by contrast, that religion in which I must first know that something is duty before I can acknowledge it as a divine command is *natural religion.* Anyone who de-

6:154

---

* With this definition some erroneous interpretations of the concept of a religion in general are obviated. *First,* so far as theoretical cognition and profession of faith are concerned, no assertoric knowledge is required in religion (even of the existence of God), since with our lack of insight into supersensible objects any such profession can well be hypocritically feigned; speculatively, what is required is rather only a *problematic* assumption (hypothesis) concerning the supreme cause of things, whereas with respect to the object toward which our morally legislative reason bids us work, what is presupposed is an *assertoric* faith, practical and hence free, that promises a result for the final aim of religion; and this faith needs only *the idea of God* which must occur to every morally earnest (and therefore religious) pursuit of the good, without pretending to be able to secure objective reality for it through theoretical cognition. Subjectively, the *minimum* of cognition (it is possible that there is a God) must alone suffice for what can be made the duty of every human being. *Second,* this definition of a religion in general obviates the erroneous representation of religion as an aggregate of *particular* duties immediately relating to God, and thereby prevents that we take on (as human beings are inclined to do anyway) *works of courtly service* over and above the ethico-civil duties of humanity (of human beings to human beings) and subsequently seek to make up for the very deficiency in the latter by means of the former. There are no particular duties toward God in a universal religion; for God cannot receive anything from us; we cannot act on him or for him. Should we want to transform our guilt-inspired awe before him into a particular duty, we would forget that such an awe is not a particular act of religion but the religious disposition which universally accompanies all our actions done in conformity to duty. Even when it is said: "One ought to obey God before human beings," this only means that whenever statutory commands, regarding which human beings can be both legislators and judges, conflict with duties which reason prescribes unconditionally – and God alone can judge whether they are observed or transgressed – the former must yield precedence to the latter. Would we, on the contrary, understand by that in which God must be obeyed before human beings the statutory commands of God as alleged by a church, the principle would then easily become the often heard war-cry of hypocritical and ambitious clerics inciting revolt against their civil authority. For anything permissible, which civil authority commands, is *certainly* a duty; whereas, whether something which is indeed permissible in itself yet cognizable by us only through divine relation is truly commanded by God, this is (at least for the most part) highly uncertain.

6:154

153

clares natural religion as alone morally necessary, i.e. a duty, can also be called *rationalist* (in matters of faith). If he denies the reality of any supernatural divine revelation, he is called *naturalist;* should he, however, allow

6:155 this revelation, yet claim that to take cognizance of it and accept it as actual is not necessarily required for religion, then he can be named *pure rationalist;* but, if he holds that faith in divine revelation is necessary to universal religion, then he can be called pure *supernaturalist* in matters of faith.

By virtue of his very title, the rationalist must of his own accord hold himself within the limits of human insight. Hence he will never deny in the manner of a naturalist, nor will he ever contest either the intrinsic possibility of revelation in general or the necessity of a revelation as divine means for the introduction of true religion; for no human being can determine anything through reason regarding these matters. The point of dispute can therefore concern only the reciprocal claims of the pure rationalist and the supernaturalist in matters of faith, or what either accepts as necessary and sufficient, or only as accidental, to the one and only true religion.

If religion is divided not according to its first origin and inner possibility (for then it divides into natural and revealed) but simply according to the characteristic that renders it capable of *external communication*, it can be of two different kinds. It is either the *natural religion*, of which (once it is there) every human being can be convinced through his reason; or it is a *learned religion*, of which one can convince others only by means of erudition (in and through which the others have to be guided). – This distinction is very important, for from the origin of a religion alone we cannot draw any conclusion regarding its suitability or unsuitability to be a universal religion of humanity, but we can on the basis of its constitution as universally communicable, or not; the first property constitutes, however, the essential characteristic of the religion which ought to bind every human being.

Accordingly a religion can be *natural*, yet also *revealed*, if it is so constituted that human beings *could and ought to have* arrived at it on their own through the mere use of their reason, even though they *would* not have come to it as early or as extensively as is required, hence a revelation of it at a given time and a given place might be wise and very advantageous to the human

6:156 race, for then, once the thereby introduced religion is at hand and has been made publicly known, everyone can henceforth convince himself of its truth by himself and his own reason. In this case the religion is *objectively* a natural one, though *subjectively* one-revealed; hence it truly deserves also the first title. For that there once was such a supernatural revelation might well subsequently be entirely forgotten without the religion in question losing the least thereby, either in comprehensibility or certainty, or in its power over minds. It is otherwise, however, with a religion which on account of its intrinsic constitution cannot be considered but as revealed. If it were not preserved in a totally secure tradition or in holy books as records, it would disappear from the world; and a supernatural revelation would have to come about, either one publicly repeated from time to time or one continuously enduring within each human being, without which the spread and propagation of any such faith would not be possible.

But every religion in part at least, even a revealed religion, must also contain certain principles of natural relgion. For revelation can be added in thought to the concept of a *religion* only through· reason, since this very concept is one of pure reason, being derived from an obligation under the will of a *moral* lawgiver. We too shall therefore consider a revealed religion as yet *natural*, on the one hand, but on the other hand, as *learned* religion; we shall test it and be able to sort out what, and how much, it is entitled to from the one source or the other.

We cannot however do this, if our intention is to talk about a revealed religion (or at least one presumed to be so), without selecting some examples from history, for to be understood we would still have to think up instances as examples, and the possibility of these instances could otherwise be contested to us. But we cannot do better than adopt, as medium for the elucidations of our ideas of a revealed religion in general, some book which contains [instances] of that sort, especially a book inextricably interwoven with teachings that are ethical and hence related to reason, and then hold it before us, one among a variety of books dealing with religion and virtue accredited to a revelation, as an example of the practice, useful in itself, without thereby wanting to intrude into the business of those to whom is entrusted the interpretation of this very book as an aggregate of positive doctrines of revelation, or to challenge their exegesis based on scholarship. The practice is, on the contrary, advantageous to scholarship, since the latter proceeds toward one and the same end as the philosophers, namely the moral good; [they aim,] through their own rational grounds, to bring scholarship to precisely where it itself expects to arrive by another road. – In our case this book can be the New Testament, as the source of the Christian doctrine of faith. In keeping with our intent, we now wish to expound the Christian religion in two sections – first, as natural religion, and then, second, as learned religion – with reference to its content and the principles found in it. 6:157

FIRST SECTION
OF THE FIRST PART
THE CHRISTIAN RELIGION AS
NATURAL RELIGION

Natural religion, as morality (with reference to the freedom of the subject), combined with the concept of that which can actualize its ultimate end (the concept of *God* as moral originator of the world), and referred to a duration of the human being proportionate to the entirety of this end (immortality), is a pure practical concept of reason which, despite its infinite fruitfulness, yet presupposes only so little a capacity for theoretical reason that, practically, we can sufficiently convince every human being of it and everyone can expect its effect at least, as duty. This religion possesses the great prerequisite of the true church, namely the qualification for universality, inasmuch as by universality we mean validity for every human being (*universitas vel omnitudo distributiva*),*ᵂ* i.e. communality of insight.*ˣ* To propagate and preserve itself as world religion in this sense, it requires indeed a staff ministering (*ministerium*) to the purely invisible church, but no officials (*officiales*), i.e. teachers but no dignitaries, for by virtue of the rational religion of single individuals no church in the sense of a universal union (*omnitudo collectiva*)*ʸ* is yet in place, nor is any such church really contemplated through that idea. – But since such a communality of insight could not of itself preserve itself, nor, without taking on the form of a visible church, [could it] propagate itself to its [full] universality, but [could] only [do so] if a collective universality, or the union of the believers in one (visible) church according to principles of a pure religion of reason, is added to it, yet this church would not originate from that communality of insight of itself, nor, were it to be established, would it be brought by its free adherents (as was shown above) to a permanent state as a *community* of believers (because none of these enlightened individuals believes himself in need of fellowship in such a church for his religious convictions) unless certain statutory ordinances – which, however, have standing (authority) as law – are added to the natural laws which reason alone can recognize, what constitutes a special duty of human beings and a means to their higher end is still lacking, namely their permanent union in a visible church; but the said authority, to be the founder of such a church, presupposes a fact*ᶻ* and not just a concept of pure reason.

6:158

If we now assume a teacher of whom the story (or, at least, a general opinion which is not in principle disputable) has it that he was the first to advocate a pure and compelling religion, one within the grasp of the whole world (i.e. a natural religion) and of which the doctrines, as preserved for us, we can therefore test on our own; [that he did so] publicly and even in defiance of a dominant ecclesiastical faith, oppressive and devoid of moral scope (a faith whose cult can serve as example of the type of faith, essentially statutory, that at the time was the norm in the world); if we find that he made this universal religion of reason the supreme and indispensable condition of each and every religious faith, and then added certain statutes to it containing forms and observances intended to serve as means for the establishment of a church founded upon those principles: then, de-

---

ᵂ universality or distributive totality
ˣ *allgemeine Einhelligkeit*
ʸ collective totality
ᶻ *Factum*

spite the accidentality and arbitrariness^a of what he ordained to this end, we cannot deny to the said church the name of the true universal church, nor can we deny to him the authority due to one who called human beings to union in this church, which he did without wishing to add to their fatih with new and onerous ordinances, or to turn actions first instituted by him into special holy practices, obligatory in themselves as constitutive elements of religion.

After this description one will not fail to recognize the person who can be revered, not indeed as the *founder* of the *religion* which, free from every dogma, is inscribed in the heart of all human beings (for there is nothing arbitrary in the origin of this religion), but as the founder of the first true *church*. – For accreditation of his dignity as of divine mission, we shall adduce some of his teachings as indubitable documents of a religion in general, let their historical status be what it may (for in the idea itself is already present the sufficient ground for accepting them); they can surely be none other than pure doctrines of reason, for these alone are teachings that carry their own proof and on which, therefore, the accreditation of any other must principally rest. 6:159

First, he maintains that not the observance of external civil or statutory ecclesiastical duties but only the pure moral disposition of the heart can make a human being well-pleasing to God (Matthew, 5.20–48); that sins in thought are regarded in the eyes of God as equivalent to deed (5.28)[144] and that holiness is above all the goal for which the human being should strive (5.48);[145] that, for example, to hate in one's heart is tantamount to killing (5.22);[146] that an injustice brought upon a neighbor can be made good only through satisfaction rendered to the neighbor himself, not through acts of divine service (5.24),[147] and that, on the point of truthfulness, the civil instrument for extracting it,* the oath, detracts from respect for truth itself (5.34–37);[148] – that the natural but evil propensity of the 6:160

---

* It is not easy to understand why religious teachers hold as so insignificant this clear prohibition against a means of forcing confession before a civil tribunal which is based upon mere superstition, not upon conscientiousness. For that we are here counting most on the efficacy of superstition can be recognized from the fact that a human being whom we do not trust to tell the truth in a solemn declaration, on the truthfulness of which rests the judgment of human justice (the one sacred thing in the world), we yet believe will be persuaded to do so through a formula which does not contain anything over and above that declaration itself except the invocation of divine punishments upon himself (punishments which he cannot escape anyway, because of his lie), as if it depended on him whether or not he renders account to this supreme tribunal. – In the cited passage of Scripture, this kind of attestation is presented as an *absurd* presumption – wanting to make actual, as though through magic words, things that are not within our power. – It is easy to see, however, that the wise teacher, who here says that whatever goes beyond Yea, Yea, and Nay, Nay, in the attestation of truth comes of evil, had in view the bad effect that oaths bring in their train, namely that the greater importance attributed to them almost sanctions the common lie.
^{a} *des Willkürlichen*

human heart ought to be completely reversed, that the sweet feeling of revenge must be transformed into tolerance (5.39.40)[149] and the hatred of one's enemies into beneficence (5.44).[150] Thus he says, he does intend to satisfy the Jewish law in full (5.17),[151] whence it is obvious that not scholarship but pure religion of reason must be its interpreter, for, taken according to the letter, the law allows the very opposite of all this. – Furthermore, with his signposts of the strait gate and narrow way he does not leave unnoticed the misinterpretation of the law which human beings allow themselves in order to evade their true moral duty and make up for it by fulfilling the ecclesiastical duty (7.13).[152]* He nevertheless requires of these pure dispositions that they should also be demonstrated in *deeds* (5.16),[154] and, by contrast, he rebuffs the crafty hope of those who, through invocation and praise of the supreme lawgiver in the person of his envoy, would make up for their lack of deeds and ingratiate themselves into his favor (7.21).[155] And he wants these works to be performed also in public, as an example for imitation (5.16),[156] in an attitude of cheerfulness, not as actions extorted from slaves (6.16),[157] in such a way that, from a small beginning in the communication and propagation of such dispositions, religion will gradually grow into a kingdom of God through its inner power, like a seed in good soil or a ferment of goodness (13.31,32,33).[158] – Finally, he sums up all duties (1) into one *universal* rule (which includes the internal as well as the external moral relation of human beings), namely, Do your duty from no other incentive except the unmediated appreciation of duty itself, i.e. love God (the Legislator of all duties) above all else; (2) and into a *particular* rule, one namely that concerns the human being's external relation to other human beings as universal duty, Love

6:161 every one as yourself, i.e. promote his welfare from an unmediated goodwill, one not derived from selfish incentives. And these commands are not merely laws of virtue but precepts of *holiness* which we ought to strive after, yet in view of them the striving itself is called *virtue*. – He therefore rebuffs every hope of those who would wait quite passively for this moral goodness, with hands in their lap, as if it were a heavenly gift from above. And he confronts anyone who leaves unused the natural disposition to goodness that lies in human nature (as a capital entrusted to him), in lazy confidence that surely a higher moral influence will somehow make up for his lack in moral constitution and perfection, with the threat that even the good which he might have done by natural predisposition may not come about in him because of this neglect (25.29).[159]

Concerning the expectation, very natural to the human being, that as

---

* The *strait gate* and the narrow way, which leads to life, is that of a good life-conduct; the *wide gate* and the broad way frequented by the many is the *church*.[153] Not as if it were up to the church and its dogmas whether the human being is lost, but because the *entrance* into it and the profession of its statutes or the celebration of its rites are regarded as the manner in which God truly wants to be served.

regards happiness his lot will be proportionate to his moral conduct, especially in view of the many sacrifices of happiness that must be undertaken for the sake of moral conduct, this teacher promises (5.11,12)[160] a reward for such sacrifices in a future world, but, in accordance with the different dispositions behind moral conduct, of a different kind for those who did their duty *for the sake of the reward* (or also for release from a deserved punishment) than for those better human beings who performed it for its own sake. When one ruled by self-interest – the God of this world – only refines it by the use of reason and extends it outside the narrow bounds of the present without renouncing it, he is represented as one who takes it upon himself to defraud his master and wins from him sacrifices on behalf of duty (Luke, 16.3 – 9).[161] For if it occurs to him that eventually, perhaps soon, he must abandon this world, and that he can take nothing with him of what he possesses to the next, he may well decide to write off his account what he or his master, self-interest, could legitimately require of needy human beings here on earth, and thereby procure for himself as it were transfer bills payable in another world; in this, as regards the incentives of such beneficent actions, he indeed acts *prudently* rather than *morally*, yet in conformity with the moral law, at least according to its letter, and he can legitimately hope that for this too he will not remain unrewarded in the future.* Compare with this what is said of beneficence toward the needy motivated simply by duty (Matt., 25.35– 40),[162] where the judge of the world declares as the true elects to his kingdom those who extended help to the needy without it even entering their minds that what they were doing was also worthy of recompense, or that they were perhaps binding heaven to a recompense, so to speak, precisely because they were acting without attention to it, and we can then clearly see that when the teacher of the Gospel speaks of a recompense in the world to come, he did not mean thereby to make this recompense an incentive of actions but only (as an uplifting representation of the consummation of divine goodness and wisdom in the guidance of the human race) an object of the purest admiration and greatest moral approval for a reason which passes judgment upon human destiny as a whole.

6:162

Here we then have a complete religion, which can be proposed to all human beings comprehensibly and convincingly through their own rea-

---

* We know nothing about the future, nor ought we to look for more than what stands in rational connection with the incentives of morality and their end. Here belongs the belief that there is no good action which will not also have its good consequence in the world to come for him who performs it; that, therefore, however reprehensible a human being might find himself at the end of his life, he must not on that account allow himself to stop short of doing at least *one* more good action which is in his power; and that, in doing it, he has cause to hope that, in proportion as he now harbors a purely good intention, it will yet be of greater worth to him than those deedless absolutions which are supposed to make up for the lack of good actions without contributing anything to the lessening of the guilt.

6:162

son; one, moreover, whose possibility and even necessity as a prototype for us to follow (so far as human beings are capable of it) has been made visible in an example, without either the truth of those teachings or the authority and the worth of the teacher requiring any other authentication (for which scholarship or miracles, which are not matters for everyone, would be required). The appeals which we here find to older (Mosaic) legislation and prefiguration, as though these were to serve the teacher as authentication, were not given in support of the truth of the teachings [as objects of] thought, but only for their introduction among people who, without exception and blindly, clung to the old. And this must always be more difficult among human beings whose heads, filled with statutory dogmas of faith, have been made almost incapable of receiving the religion of reason than when this religion is to be brought to the reason of
6:163 unlearned yet also unspoiled human beings. Hence no one should be disconcerted to find an exposition, which accommodated itself to the prejudices of the times, now enigmatic and in need of careful interpretation; though it everywhere lets a religious doctrine shine forth, and often even points to it explicitly, which must be comprehensible to every human being and must convince without expenditure of learning.

SECOND SECTION
THE CHRISTIAN RELIGION AS A LEARNED RELIGION

Inasmuch as a religion propounds as necessary dogmas of faith of which we cannot have cognition through reason as such but which must yet be transmitted unadulterated (according to the essential content) to all human beings for all future times, it must be regarded (if we do not wish to assume a continuous miracle of revelation) as a sacred possession entrusted to the care of the *learned*. For although this religion, accompanied by miracles and deeds, could *at the beginning* find entry everywhere, even with respect to things not validated by reason, yet the report itself of these wonders, as well as of the doctrines dependent on them for their validation, would *in the passage of time* necessitate a written, documented, and unchanging instruction to posterity.

The acceptance of the principles of a religion is preeminently called *faith* (*fides sacra*).[b] We shall have to consider the Christian faith, therefore, on the one hand as pure *rational faith*, and on the other as *revealed faith* (*fides statutaria*).[c] The first may be considered as a faith freely accepted by everyone (*fides elicita*),[d] the second as a commanded faith (*fides imperata*).[e]

[b] sacred faith
[c] statutory faith
[d] elicited faith
[e] commanded faith

Of the evil that lies in the human heart and of which nobody is free; of the impossibility of ever retaining ourselves justified before God on the basis of our life-conduct and yet of the necessity of such a valid justification before him; of the futility of substituting ecclesiastical observances and pious servile works for the lack of righteousness and yet of the inescapable obligation to become a new man: [of all this] everyone can be convinced through his reason, and to be convinced of it is part of religion.[163]

But from the point where Christian doctrine is built upon facts[f] and not   6:164 upon mere concepts of reason, it is no longer called simply the Christian *religion,* but the Christian *faith,* which has been made the foundation of a church. The service of a church consecrated to such a faith has therefore two sides. On the one side, it is the service that must be rendered to the church in accordance with its historical faith; on the other side, it is the service due to it according to the practical and moral faith of reason. Neither side can stand in the Christian church on its own, separated from the other: the second not from the first, because the Christian faith is a religious faith; and the first not from the second because it is a learned faith.

The Christian faith, as a *learned* faith, rests on history, and, to the extent that erudition (objectively) is at its base, it is not in itself a *free* faith or one derived from insight into theoretically sufficient grounds of demon-stration (*fides elicita*). Were it a pure faith of reason, it would still have to be regarded as a free faith even though the moral laws upon which it is based as faith in a divine legislator command unconditionally – in the way it was also represented in the first section. Indeed, if only this believing were not made into a duty, even as historical faith it could be a theoretically free faith, if all human beings were learned. If, however, it is to be valid for all human beings, even the unlearned, it is a faith not merely commanded but one which obeys the command blindly (*fides servilis*),[g] i.e., it does not investigate whether the command is actually divine.

In Christian revealed doctrine, however, we cannot by any means begin with an *unconditional faith* in revealed propositions (of themselves hidden to reason) and then have erudite cognition follow behind, somewhat like a mere defense against an enemy attacking the rear train; for then the Christian faith would not just be *fides imperata* but *fides servilis* as well. Hence it must always be taught at least as *fides historica elicita,*[h] i.e. *erudi-tion* would have to constitute in it, as a revealed doctrine of faith, not the rearguard but the vanguard, the small number of scriptural scholars (the clerics), who also cannot totally dispense with profane learning, dragging behind them the long train of the unlearned (the laity) who are on their   6:165 own uninformed about Scripture (among whom even the civil authorities

---

[f] *Facta*

[g] slavish faith

[h] elicited historical faith

belong). – If this is not however to happen, universal human reason must be recognized and honored as supreme commanding principle in a natural religion within the Christian doctrine of faith; whereas the doctrine of revelation, upon which a church is founded and which stands in need of scholars as interpreters and preservers, must be cherished and cultivated as a mere means, though a most precious one, for giving meaning, diffusion, and continuity to natural religion even among the ignorant.

This is the true *service* of the church under the dominion of the good principle; but that service in which revealed faith is to come ahead of religion is a *counterfeit service* through which the moral order is totally reversed, and what is mere means is unconditionally commanded (as an end). Faith in propositions, of which the unlearned cannot be made sure either through reason or Scripture (inasmuch as the latter would have first to be authenticated), would then be made into an absolute duty (*fides imperata*) and, as slavish service, it would be elevated, together with other observances connected with it, to the rank of saving faith, though it has no morally determining ground of actions. – A church founded upon this last principle does not have true *servants* (*ministri*), like those of the first constitution, but commanding high *officials* (*officiales*), and these, although (as in a Protestant church) they do not display themselves in hierarchical splendor as spiritual officials clothed with external power but even protest in words against any such thing, in fact wish to be regarded as the exclusive chosen interpreters of a holy Scripture, having robbed the pure religion of reason of its due dignity as at all times its highest interpreter, and having commanded scriptural scholarship for use solely in the interests of ecclesiastical faith. Thus they transform *service* of the church (*ministerium*) into a *domination* of its members (*imperium*), even though, to hide this presumptuousness, they make use of the modest title of the former. The maintenance of this domination, however, which to reason would have been easy, costs the church dearly in outlay of great erudition. For, "blind with respect to nature, it scrambles to gather the whole antiquity above its head and buries itself under it."[164] – The course which things take, once brought to this pass, is as follows:

First, the procedure prudently followed by the first propagators of Christ's doctrine to procure for it introduction among their people is taken to be a part of religion itself, valid for all times and all peoples, so that we ought to believe that *every Christian must be a Jew, whose Messias has come;* it is not however altogether coherent to say that a Christian is not really bound by any law of Judaism (as statutory) yet must accept the entire holy book of this people on faith as divine revelation given to all human beings.* – But the authenticity of this book at once poses a big difficulty

6:166

*† Mendelssohn very ingeniously makes use of this weak point of the customary picture of Christianity to preempt any suggestion of religious conversion made to a son of Israel. For, as

(and this authenticity is far from being established by the fact that passages in it, indeed the entire history narrated there, is used in the books of the Christians for just this end). Prior to the beginning of Christianity, and even before its considerable advance, Judaism had yet to penetrate among the *learned public*, i.e. it was yet to be known to the learned contemporaries of other peoples, its history yet to be controlled so to speak, and its sacred book thus brought to historical credibility because of its antiquity. And, even if this were all sorted out, it does not suffice to be acquainted with[i] the book in translation and transmit it to posterity in this form. The security of the ecclesiastical faith based on it rather requires that there should be learned individuals knowledgeable in the Hebrew language (so far as this is possible for a language of which we have only one single book) at all times and among all peoples. And it ought not to be merely a concern of historical science, but one on which hangs the salvation of humankind, that there should be individuals sufficiently knowledgeable in this language to secure the true religion for the world.

6:167

The Christian religion suffers indeed from a similar fate, [namely] that although its sacred events occurred openly under the very eyes of a learned people yet its history was already more than one generation past before it penetrated among its learned public; hence the authentication of those events must do without the corroboration of contemporaries. Yet Christianity has the great advantage over Judaism of being represented as coming *from the mouth of the first teacher* not as a statutory but as a moral religion. And since it thereby treads in the closest proximity to reason, it was capable through reason to propagate with the greatest assuredness by itself, even without historical scholarship, at all times and among all peoples. But the first founders of *congregations* found it yet necessary to intertwine the history of Judaism with it, and this, granted the founders' situation at the time, was the sound thing to do, though only sound

---

he said, since the faith of the Jews is, according to the admission of the Christians, the lower floor upon which Christianity rests as the floor above, any such suggestion would be tantamount to asking someone to demolish the ground floor in order to feel at home on the second.[165] His true opinion, however, shines through quite clearly. He means to say: first remove Judaism from your *religion* (though in the historical teaching of faith it may always remain as an antiquity) and we shall be able to take your proposal under advisement. (In fact nothing would then be left over, except pure moral religion unencumbered by statutes.) Our burden will not be lightened in the least by throwing off the yoke of external observances, if another is imposed in its place, namely the yoke of a profession of faith in sacred history, which, for the conscientious, is an even more onerous burden. – In any case, the sacred books of this people will no doubt always be preserved and attended to, though not for the sake of religion, yet for scholarship. For the history of no other people dates with any pretension of credibility as far back as this – back to epochs of prehistory within which we can fit all the profane history known to us (even to the beginning of the world). And so the great blank which profane history necessarily leaves open is filled by sacred history.
[i] *kennen*

Judaism is part of Christianity at certain period in history [handwritten annotation]

perhaps with respect to that situation; and so, that history has come down to us together with the founders' sacred legacy. These founders of the *church*, however, took up those fortuitous means of advocacy into the essential articles of faith themselves, and either augmented them with tradition and interpretations, which acquired legal force from the councils, or authenticated them through scholarship. And there still is no foreseeing how many alterations still lie ahead of faith because of this scholarship, or its extreme opposite, the inner light to which every layman can lay claim. And this cannot be avoided so long as we seek religion not within us but from the outside.

Second part
Concerning the counterfeit service of God in a statutory religion

6:168

The one and true religion contains nothing but laws, i.e. practical principles, of whose unconditional necessity we can become conscious and which we therefore recognize as revealed through pure reason (not empirically). Only for the sake of a church, of which there can be different and equally good forms, can there be statutes, i.e. ordinances held to be divine, though to our purely moral judgment they are arbitrary and contingent. Now to deem this statutory faith (which is in any case restricted to one people and cannot contain the universal world religion) essential to the service of God in general, and to make it the supreme condition of divine good pleasure toward human beings, is a *delusion of religion*,* and acting upon it constitutes counterfeit service, i.e. a pretension of honoring God through which we act directly contrary to the true service required by him. *no interpretation of gods will in Judaism because no prophet – a counterpart* [handwritten annotation]

---

* Delusion is the mistake of regarding the mere representation of a thing as equivalent to the thing itself. For a rich miser, for instance, the delusion of *parsimony* is to regard the representation of being able to make use of his riches at will as sufficient substitute for never using them. The delusion of *honor* posits praise in others, which is at bottom only the external representation of their esteem (which internally they perhaps do not entertain at all), the value that ought to be attributed to the esteem itself; to this delusion also belongs, therefore, the obsession for titles and decorations, since these are only external representations of preeminence over others. *Madness*[j] too is so called because it is the habit of taking a mere representation (of the imagination) for the presence of the thing itself, and to value it as such. – Now the consciousness of possessing a means to a certain end (before we have availed ourselves of it) is the possession of this end in representation only; hence to be satisfied with this consciousness, as though it could count as possession of the end, is a *practical delusion*, which is all that is at issue here.

[j] *Wahnsinn*; cf. *Wahn* = delusion

§ I

CONCERNING THE UNIVERSAL SUBJECTIVE
GROUND OF RELIGIOUS DELUSION

Anthropomorphism, which is hardly to be avoided by human beings in their theoretical representation of God and his being, but is also harmless enough (provided that it does not influence concepts of duty), is highly dangerous with respect to our practical relation to his will and to our very morality; for, since *we are making a God for ourselves,** we create him in the way we believe that we can most easily win him over to our advantage, and   6:169 ourselves be dispensed from the arduous and uninterrupted effort of affecting the innermost part of our moral disposition. The principle that the human being usually coins to justify this behavior is that in everything we do solely for the sake of pleasing God (provided that it does not run directly counter to morality, though not contributing to it in the least) we demonstrate to God our willingness to serve him as his obedient and, because obedient, well-pleasing subjects: therefore, we are also serving him *(in potentia).*[l] – There need not always be sacrifices for the human being to believe that he is rendering this service to God: festivals too, or even public games, as among the Greeks and Romans, have often had to serve, and still serve, to make the Divinity favorable to a people, or also to individuals, in keeping with their delusion. Yet sacrifices (penances, castigations, pilgrimages, etc.) have always been regarded as more powerful, more likely to work on the favor of heaven, and more apt to remove sin, since they more forcefully serve to indicate unbounded (though not moral) subjection to the will of heaven. The more useless such self-inflicted torments are, the less aimed at the universal moral improvement of the human being, the holier they seem to be. For, just because they have absolutely no use in the world, and yet cost effort, they seem to be aimed solely at attesting devotion to God. – Although, it is said, God has in no respect been served through the deed, he nonetheless sees good will

---

*† Although it certainly sounds questionable, it is in no way reprehensible to say that every   6:169 human being *makes a God* for himself, indeed, he must make one according to moral concepts (attended by the infinitely great properties that belong to the faculty of exhibiting an object in the world commensurate to these concepts) in order to honor in him *the one who made him.* For in whatever manner a being has been made known[k] to him by somebody else, and described as God, indeed, even if such a being might appear to him in person (if this is possible), a human being must yet confront this representation with his ideal first, in order to judge whether he is authorized to hold and revere this being as Divinity. Hence, on the basis of revelation alone, without that concept being *previously* laid down in its purity at its foundation as touchstone, there can be no religion, and all reverence for God would be *idolatry.*[166]
[k] *bekannt*
[l] potentially

in it, a heart which is indeed too weak to obey his moral commands but makes up for this lack by its demonstrated eagerness to obey. Visible here is the propensity to a form of conduct which has no moral value in itself, except perhaps as a means of elevating the sensible faculty of representation for the purpose of harmonizing it with the ideas of the end, or of repressing it in case it works counter to these ideas.* Yet in our mind we attribute to this conduct the value of the end itself, or, what amounts to the same thing, we attribute to the mind's readiness to take on attitudes of dedication to God (called *devotion*) the value of these attitudes themselves. And this way of doing things is, therefore, a mere delusion of religion, which can assume all kinds of forms, in some appearing closer to the moral form than in others, yet in all not merely an unpremeditated deception but a maxim by which we attribute intrinsic value to the means rather than the end. And, because of this maxim, the delusion is equally absurd in all its forms, and, as a hidden inclination to deceit, equally to be condemned.

§ 2

THE MORAL PRINCIPLE OF RELIGION OPPOSED TO THE DELUSION OF RELIGION

To begin with I accept the following proposition as a principle requiring no proof: *Apart from a good life-conduct, anything which the human being supposes that he can do to become well-pleasing to God is mere religious delusion and counterfeit service of God.* – I say, anything that *the human being* believes that he can do, for we are not thereby denying that, beyond all that *we* can do, there might yet be something in the mysteries of the supreme wisdom which only God can do to make us human beings well-pleasing to him.

---

* For those who believe[167] that in the critique of pure reason they are faced by intrinsic contradictions whenever they stumble upon the distinctions between the sensible and the intelligible, I here remark that, whenever mention is made of sensuous[m] means to promote the intellectual side (of the purely moral disposition), or of the obstacles which these means put in its way, the influence of these two so unlike principles must never be thought as *direct*. For, as beings of the senses, we can have effect only with respect to the *appearances of the intellectual principle*, i.e. with respect to the determination of our physical powers through the *power of free choice* as exhibited in actions, whether in opposition to the law or in its favor, so that cause and effect are represented as in fact of like kind. But as regards what transcends the senses (the subjective principle of morality in us which lies hidden in the incomprehensible property of freedom), for example the pure religious disposition, we have no insight into anything in it which touches upon the relation in the human being of cause to effect apart from its law (though this is enough by itself); i.e. we cannot *explain* to ourselves the possibility of actions as events in the world of the senses from a human being's moral constitution as [something] imputable to them, precisely because these actions are free, whereas the grounds of explanation of any event must be drawn from the world of the senses.
[m] *sinnlich*

But if the church should proclaim such a mystery as in some sense revealed, then the opinion that to *believe* in this revelation, as related to us in sacred history, and to *profess* it (whether internally or externally) is something which in itself can make us well-pleasing to God, is itself a dangerous religious delusion. For this faith, as the inner profession of what a human being firmly holds to be true, is a *deed* so patently extracted through fear that a sincere human being might sooner agree to any other condition than to this one; for in all other compulsory works he would only be doing something superfluous at most, whereas here, by making a declaration of whose truth he is not convinced, something contrary to his conscience. That confession, therefore, regarding which he persuades himself that of itself (as the acceptance of a good offered to him) it can make him well-pleasing to God, is something which he fancies himself capable of rendering over and above his good life-conduct in obedience to the moral laws which are to be practiced in the world, inasmuch as with his service he turns directly to God.

In the *first* place, reason does not leave us altogether without comfort with respect to the lack of a righteousness of our own (which is valid before God). Reason says that whoever does, in a disposition of true devotion to duty, as much as lies within his power to satisfy his obligation (at least in a steady approximation toward complete conformity to the law), can legitimately hope that what lies outside his power will be supplemented by the supreme wisdom *in some way or other* (which can render permanent the disposition to this steady approximation), without reason thereby presuming to determine the way or know in what it consists, for God's way can perhaps be so mysterious that, at best, he could reveal it to us in a symbolic representation in which the practical import alone is comprehensible to us, whereas, theoretically, we could not in the least grasp what this relation of God to the human being is in itself, or attach concepts to it, even if God wanted to reveal such a mystery to us. – Suppose now that a certain church were to claim that it knows precisely the way in which God makes up for that moral lack in the human race, and were at the same time to sentence to eternal damnation all human beings who do not know in any natural way that means of justification of which 6:172 reason has no cognition, and hence also to fail to elevate it to a principle of religion and to profess it as such: Who is the unbeliever in this case? he who has confidence, without knowing how what he hopes for will come to pass; or he who must know precisely the way human beings are released from evil or, failing this, give up all hope of this redemption? – At bottom the latter does not set much store by the knowledge of this mystery (for his reason already teaches him that it is totally useless for him to know something about which he can do nothing) but only wants to know it so that he can make for himself (even if it happens only inwardly) a divine service of the belief, of the acceptance, the profession, and the glorifica-

167

tion of all that is revealed, and this divine service might win for him the favor of heaven prior to any expenditure of his own powers toward a good life-conduct, hence quite gratuitously, and would indeed elicit this conduct in a totally supernatural fashion, or, where he may have perhaps gone against it, would at least make up for the transgression.

Second: if the human being strays even slightly from the above maxim, there are *no bounds* left for the counterfeit service of God (superstition),["] for everything is arbitrary past that maxim (provided that it does not contradict morality directly). From a sacrifice by lip service, which costs him the least, to the sacrifice of natural goods, which might otherwise better be used to the advantage of humanity, yea, even to the immolation of his own person by losing himself to the world (in the ranks of hermits, fakirs or monks), he offers everything to God, except his moral disposition; and when he says that he brings his heart too to him, he does not mean by this the disposition of a life-conduct well-pleasing to him but a heartfelt wish that his sacrifice may be accepted as payment in place of this disposition (*natio gratis anhelans, multa agendo nihil agens.* Phaedrus).[168]

Finally, when once we go over to the maxim of a service presumed to be of itself well-pleasing to God and also, if need be, conciliatory, yet not purely moral, there is no essential difference among the ways of serving him as it were mechanically which would give one way an advantage over another. In worth (or rather worthlessness) they are all the same, and it would be mere affectation to regard oneself as privileged, because of a *more refined* deviation from the one intellectual principle of genuine respect of God, over those who allow themselves to become guilty of an assumedly coarser debasement to sensuality. Whether the devout individual makes his statutory visit at *church* or undertakes a pilgrimage to the sanctuaries in Loretto or Palestine; whether he takes his formulas of prayer to the heavenly authority with his *lips*, or by means of a *prayer-wheel*, like the Tibetan (who believes that his wishes, even if set out in writing, will reach their end just as well, only provided that they be *set in motion* by some thing or another, by the wind, for instance, if written on flags, or by the hand, if enclosed in a canister as though in a slinging device),[169] or whatever the surrogate for the moral service of God might be, it is all the same and of equal worth. – Differences of external form here count equally for nothing but everything depends, rather, upon the acceptance or the forsaking of the one single principle of becoming well-pleasing to God – [upon] whether [we do it] through moral disposition alone, so far as the latter manifests its vitality in actions which are its appearance, or through pious play-acting and nothing-doing.* But is there not also perhaps a dizzying *delusion of virtue*, rising

6:173

---

* It is a psychological phenomenon that the adherents to a confession in which there is somewhat less of the statutory to believe, feel themselves as it were ennobled thereby and
["] *die Superstition*

above the bounds of human capacity, and might it not well be reckoned, together with groveling delusion of religion, in the general class of self-deceptions? No. The disposition of virtue has to do with something *actual*, which is in itself well-pleasing to God and conforms to what is best for the world. True, a delusionary sense of superiority may attach itself to it – the delusion of regarding oneself adequate to the idea of one's holy duty. But this is only accidental. And to place the highest value in that disposition is not a delusion, as it is, for instance, to place it in the ecclesiastical exercises of devotion, but an absolutely efficacious contribution to the world's highest good.

It is furthermore customary (at least in the church) to call *nature* what can be done by the human being on the strength of the principle of virtue, and *grace* what only serves to supplement the deficiency of all his moral capacity and, since adequacy in this respect is also duty for us, can be only wished or also hoped and prayed for; to regard the two as together effective causes of a disposition sufficient to a conduct of life well-pleasing to God; and not merely to distinguish the two but, rather, to set them well against one another. 6:174

The persuasion that we can distinguish the effects of grace from those of nature (virtue), or even to produce these effects in us, is *enthusiasm;* for nowhere in experience can we recognize a supersensible object, even less exert influence upon it to bring it down to us, though there do occur from time to time in the mind movements that work toward morality but which we cannot explain, and about which are forced to admit our ignorance: "The wind bloweth where it listeth. . . . but thou canst not tell whence it cometh, etc."[170] To want to *perceive* heavenly influences is a kind of madness in which, no doubt, there can also be method (since those alleged inner revelations must always attach themselves to moral, and hence rational, ideas), but which nonetheless always remains a self-deception detrimental to religion. To believe that grace may have its effects, and that perhaps there must be such effects to supplement the imperfection of our striving for virtue, is all that we can say on the subject; for the rest, we are not capable of determining anything concerning their distinguishing marks and even less of doing something toward their production.

The delusion that through religious acts of cult we can achieve anything in the way of justification before God is religious *superstition*, just as the delusion of wanting to bring this about by striving for a supposed

---

more enlightened, though they have still retained enough of statutory faith that, from their fancied pinnacle of purity, they should not look down with contempt (as they in fact do) upon their brothers in ecclesiastical delusion. The reason for this is that, however little, they do thereby find themselves somewhat nearer to pure moral religion, though they yet depend on the delusion wanting to supplement it through pious observances in which reason is only less passive.

contact with God is religious *enthusiasm*. – It is superstitious delusion to want to become well-pleasing to God through actions that any human being can do without even needing to be a good human being (e.g. by the profession of statutory articles of faith, the observance of ecclesiastical practice and discipline, etc.). And it is called superstitious because it is a choosing of merely natural (not moral) means which on their own can have absolutely no effect on something which is not nature (i.e. the ethical good). – But a delusion is called enthusiastic when the imagined means themselves, being supersensible, are not within the human being's power, even without considering the unattainability of the supersensible end intended through them; for this feeling of the immediate presence of the highest being, and the distinguising of it from any other, even from the moral feeling, would constitute the receptivity of an intuition for which there is no sense [faculty] in human nature. – Since superstitious delusion contains means in themselves suitable to many individuals, and possible to them as well, at least to counteract the obstacles that stand in the way of a disposition well-pleasing to God, it is to this extent yet related to reason and only accidentally reprehensible, i.e. only inasmuch as it transforms what can only be a means into an object immediately well-pleasing to God. Enthusiastic religious delusion is, on the contrary, the moral death of the reason without which there can be no religion, because, like all morality in general, religion must be founded on principles.

Thus the principle in an ecclesiastical faith which rectifies or prevents every religious delusion is this: ecclesiastical faith must contain within itself, besides the statutory articles which it yet cannot quite dispense with, another principle as well, of bringing about the religion of good life conduct as its true goal, in order at some future time to be able to dispense with statutory articles altogether.

§ 3

CONCERNING PRIESTCRAFT* AS A REGIME
IN THE COUNTERFEIT SERVICE
OF THE GOOD PRINCIPLE

The veneration of mighty invisible beings, which was wrung from the helpless human being because of the fear naturally rooted in the con-

---

*† This name,° which designates only the authority of a spiritual father (πάππα), takes on the sense of a reproach only through the related concept of the spiritual despotism found in all ecclesiastical forms, however unpretentious and popular they declare themselves. Hence in comparing sects I do not want in any way to be understood as meaning to disparage the usages and ordinances of one as contrasted to any other. They all deserve equal respect, so far as their forms are attempts by poor mortals to give sensible representation to the Kingdom of God on earth, but equal blame as well, when (in a visible church) they mistake the form of the representation of this idea for the thing itself.

° *Pfaffenthum*

sciousness of his powerlessness, did not immediately begin with a religion but with the servile worship of God (or idols) which, whenever it received a certain public and legal form, became a *temple service;* and it became an *ecclesiastical service* only after the moral culture of human beings gradually came to be associated with these laws: at the foundation of both lies a historical faith, until we finally begin to regard them as provisional, and we begin to see in them the symbolic representation and the means of further-ance of a pure faith of religion.

Between a *shaman* of the Tunguses and the European prelate who rules over both church and state, or (if, instead of the heads and leaders, we only want to look at the faithful and their ways of representation) between the wholly sensuous[p] *Wogulite,* who in the morning lays the paw of a bear skin over his head with the short prayer, "Strike me not dead!"[171] and the subli-mated *Puritan* and Independent[172] in Connecticut, there certainly is a tre-mendous distance in the *style* of faith, but not in the *principle;* for, as regards the latter, they all equally belong to one and the same class, namely of those who place their service of God in something (faith in certain statutory articles, or the observance of certain arbitrary practices) which cannot by itself constitute a better human being. Only those whose intention is to find this service solely in the disposition to good life-conduct distinguish them-selves from those others by crossing over into an entirely different principle, one exalted[q] far above the other, namely the principle whereby they profess themselves members of a (invisible) church which encompasses all right-thinking people within itself and alone, in virtue of its essential composi-tion, can be the true church universal.

The one aim which they all have in common is to steer to their advan-tage the invisible power which presides over human destiny; they are of different minds only over how to go about it. If they hold that power to be an intelligent being and, therefore, attribute to him a will from which they await their lot, their effort can then be directed only to the choice of the manner in which, as beings subject to his will, they can become pleasing to him through their doings or nondoings. If they think of him as a moral being, then their own reason will easily persuade them that the condition of earning his favor must be their morally good life-conduct, especially the pure disposition which is the subjective principle of the latter. Yet it is possible that the highest being may perhaps wish, in addition, to be served in a manner which we cannot recognize through mere reason, namely through actions in which, on their own, we cannot indeed detect anything moral but which we arbitrarily take upon ourselves nonetheless, either because commanded by him, or else in order to attest our submissiveness to him, and which, in either mode of procedure, if they constitute a whole

6:177

[p] *sinnlichen*
[q] *erhabenen*

of systematically ordered activities, would thus establish a *service* of God in general. – Now if the two are to be joined, then either we must accept each as a direct way of pleasing God or take one of them as only the instrument of the other, which is the true service of God. It is self-evident that the moral service of God (*officium liberum*)^r pleases him directly. We could not however recognize it as the supreme condition of all that is pleasing in the human being (as already stipulated also by the concept of morality) if it were possible to regard the services of wages (*officium mercenarium*)^s as well-pleasing to God *on its own;* for nobody would then know which service is to be given precedence in any given case, in order to direct our judgment regarding our duties accordingly, or how the two supplement one another. Hence actions which have no moral value in themselves will have to be accepted as well-pleasing to God only to the extent that they serve as means in the furtherance of what, with respect to them, is good unmediatedly (for morality), i.e., *for the sake of the moral service of God.*

Now the human being who makes use of actions that in themselves contain nothing well-pleasing to God as means nevertheless for gaining God's unmediated favor, and therewith the fulfillment of his wishes, is under the delusion of possessing an art of achieving a supernatural effect through entirely natural means. Attempts of this sort are normally called *sorcery,* a word for which we however wish to substitute the otherwise familiar word *fetishism* (for "sorcery" carries with it the attendant concept of commerce with the evil principle, whereas the attempts at issue can also conceivably be undertaken through misunderstanding, with good moral intent). However, the thought of a supernatural effect on the part of a human being could occur to anybody only on the supposition that he

6:178 works upon God and makes use of him as a means to produce an effect in the world for which his own powers alone, yea, even his insight into whether the effect is well-pleasing to God, do not suffice. And this entails an absurdity in its very conception.

But if, in addition to what makes him the object of divine favor directly (through the active disposition to a good life-conduct), a human being seeks also by means of certain formalities to make himself *worthy* of a supplement to his impotence through supernatural assistance, and to this purpose his only intention is to make himself *receptive* to the attainment of the object of his morally good wish through observances which have indeed no unmediated value yet serve as means to the furtherance of that moral disposition, then, to be sure, he is counting on something *supernatural* to supplement his natural impotence, yet not something which is an *effect* of the *human being* (through influence upon the divine will) but

^r free service
^s mercenary service

something *received,* which he can hope for but not produce himself. – But if actions, which, so far as we can see, do not contain in themselves anything moral and well-pleasing to God are nevertheless intended by him to serve him as means, indeed as conditions by which to expect support for his wishes from God directly, he must then be under a delusion, namely that, although he possesses neither the physical faculty nor the moral receptivity for the supernatural, he can nevertheless bring it about through actions which are *natural,* though not in themselves at all related to morality (actions which require no disposition well-pleasing to God for their exercise, and which can therefore be performed by the most wicked human being just as well as by the best), through formulas of invocation, through professions of a servile faith, through ecclesiastical observances, and the like, and that he can thus *conjure up* as it were God's support; for between merely physical means and a morally efficacious cause there is no connection at all according to a law, of which reason can form a thought, and according to which the moral cause can be represented as determinable to certain effects through the physical means.

Whoever therefore gives precedence to the observance of statutory laws, requiring a revelation as necessary to religion, not indeed merely as a means to the moral disposition but as the objective condition for becoming well-pleasing to God directly, and whoever places the striving for a good life-conduct behind the historical faith (whereas the latter, as something which can only be well-pleasing to God *conditionally,* ought to be directed to the former, which alone pleases God *absolutely*) – whoever does this transforms the service of God into mere *fetishism;* he engages in a counterfeit service, which sets back all the work leading to true religion. So much depends, when we wish to join two good things, on the order in which we combine them! – But it is in this distinction that true *enlightenment* consists; through it does the service of God for the first time become a free and hence moral cult. If, however, the human being departs from it, the yoke of a (statutory) law will be imposed on him instead of the freedom of the children of God, and this yoke, since it is an unconditional coercion to believe in something of which we can have cognition only historically and hence cannot carry conviction with everyone, can be much more burdensome* to conscientious human beings than the whole business of

6:179

* "That yoke is easy, and the burden is light"[173] where the duty incumbent upon every human being can be regarded as imposed upon him by himself and through his own reason, and to this extent he takes it upon himself freely. Only moral laws, as divine commands, are however of this kind, and of them alone the founder of the pure church could say: "My commands are not grievous,"[174] for these commands do not weigh down, because everyone sees the necessity of following them on his own; hence nothing is here being forced upon him; whereas ordinances despotically imposed upon us by command, of which we cannot see any use though imposed for our best interests (yet not through our own reason), are like vexations (drudgery) to which we subject ourselves only because forced to. In themselves,

piously ordained observances could ever be, for the celebration of these observances is enough to be in harmony with an established ecclesiastical community without anyone needing to profess either inwardly or outwardly that he believes them to be part of an order *founded by God*, for it is by this profession that conscience is really harassed.

Priestcraft is therefore the constitution of a church to the extent that a *fetish-service* is the rule; and this always obtains wherever statutory commands, rules of faith and observances, rather than principles of morality, make up the groundwork and the essence of the church. Now there are indeed many ecclesiastical forms in which the fetishism is so manifold and mechanical that it appears to drive out nearly all of morality, hence also religion, and to usurp their place, and thus borders very closely on paganism. Here, however, where worth or the lack thereof rests on the nature of one principle which binds above all others, there is no question of a more or less. If that principle imposes humble submission to a constitution as compulsory service and not rather the free homage due to the moral law *in general*, then, however few the imposed observances, let them but be declared as unconditionally necessary and it is enough for a fetish-faith through which the masses are ruled and robbed of their moral freedom through obedience to a church (not to religion). The constitution of this church (hierarchy) can be monarchical or aristocratic or democratic: this is merely a matter of organization; its constitution still is and remains under any of these forms always despotic. Where articles of faith are included in the constitutional law, a *clergy* rules which believes that it can actually dispense with reason, and ultimately with scriptural scholarship itself, because, since it is the single authoritative guardian and interpreter of the will of the invisible lawgiver, it has the exclusive authority to administer the prescriptions of faith; hence, thus equipped with this absolute power, it need not convince but *only give orders*. – Now, since apart from this clergy all that is left is the *laity* (the head of the political commonwealth not excepted), the church finally rules the state, not indeed through force, but through influence over minds, and also, in addition, through pretense of the benefit which the state could allegedly derive from the unconditional obedience to which a spiritual discipline has habituated the very *thinking* of the people. Thus the habit of hypocrisy undermines, unnoticed, the integrity and loyalty of the subjects; sharpens them in the simulation of service also in civil duties, and, like all wrongly accepted principles, brings about exactly the opposite of what was intended.

∴

however, regarded in the purity of their source, the actions commanded to us through those moral laws are precisely the ones which the human being finds the hardest. We would gladly undertake the most burdensome of pious drudgery in their stead, if it were only possible to offer this in payment for them.

This is, however, the inevitable consequence of at first sight an apparently harmless transposition of the principles of the one saving religious faith, for the issue was to which of the two one should concede priority of place as supreme condition (to which the other is subordinated). It is fair, it is reasonable, to assume that not just the "wise after the flesh,"[175] the learned or skilled at ratiocination, are called to this enlightenment concerning their true well-being – for the whole human race should be capable of this faith – but that rather "the foolish things of the world,"[176] even the ignorant or those most limited conceptually, must be able to lay claim to such instruction and inner conviction. Now it might indeed seem that a historical faith is precisely of this sort, especially if the concepts which it needs for expressing its message are entirely anthropological and quite suited to the senses. For what is easier than to grab and to partake with others of a narrative made so accessible to the senses and so simple, or to repeat the words of mysteries when there is absolutely no necessity to attach any meaning to them! And how easily does this sort of thing find access everywhere, especially in conjunction with the promise of a great advantage, and how deeply rooted does faith in truth of such a narrative become when the latter bases itself, moreover, upon a document long recognized as authentic, and faith in it is thus certainly suited even to the commonest human capacities! Now though news of such an event, as well as the faith in rules of conduct based on it, are not intended solely or primarily for the learned or the wise of the world, these latter are yet not excluded from them. And thus arise so many doubts, partly concerning the truth of the event, partly the sense in which its exposition is to be taken, that to accept faith in it, subjected as it would be to so many (however well intentioned) controversies, as the supreme condition of a universal and exclusively saving faith, would be the most absurd thing conceivable. – There is, on the other hand, a practical cognition which, though resting solely upon reason and not in need of any historical doctrine, yet lies as close to every human being, even the simplest, as though it had been literally inscribed in his heart – a law, which we need only name in order immediately to agree with everybody else about its authority, and which carries with it *unconditional* binding force in everyone's consciousness, namely the law of morality. And, what is more, this cognition either already leads of itself alone to faith in God, or at least determines the concept of him as that of a moral legislator, thus guiding toward a pure religious faith which is not only within the grasp of every human being but also in the highest degree worthy of respect. Indeed, it leads so naturally to this that, if one wanted to make the experiment, he would find that this faith can be elicited from every human being, upon questioning, in its entirety, without any of it having ever been taught to him. It is, therefore, not only an act of prudence to begin with this faith, and to let a historical faith consistent with it follow after it, but also duty to make it the

6:181

6:182

supreme condition under which alone we can hope to partake of whatever salvation a historical faith might ever promise, in such a way indeed that we can and may concede validity to the latter as universally binding only according to the interpretation given to it by pure religious faith (because it contains universally valid doctrine), whereas the moral believer still is always open to historical faith to the extent that he finds it beneficial to the vitality of his pure religious disposition; only in this way does this historical faith have a pure moral worth: because it is free and not coerced through any threat (for then it can never be sincere).

But even when the service of God in a church is preeminently directed to the pure moral veneration of God according to the laws prescribed to humanity in general, we can yet ask whether, in the church in question, the *doctrine of divine blessedness* alone or the pure *doctrine of virtue* as well, each separately, should make up the content of the religious instruction. The first of these designations, namely the *doctrine of divine blessedness*, perhaps best expresses the meaning of the word *religio* (as understood nowadays) in an objective sense.

Divine blessedness comprises two determinations of the moral disposition in relation to God. The *fear* of God is this disposition in obedience to his commands from *imposed* duty (the duty of a subject), i.e. from respect for the law. The *love* of God is instead [obedience] from one's own *free choice* and from pleasure in the law (from the duty of a child). Both contain, therefore, over and above morality, the concept of a supersensible being endowed with the properties required for the attainment of the highest good which is aimed at through morality but transcends our faculties. And the concept of the *nature* of this being, whenever we go beyond the moral relation of his idea to us, is always in danger of being thought by us anthropomorphically and hence in a manner often directly prejudicial 6:183   to our ethical principles. Its idea cannot therefore stand on its own in speculative reason but bases its very origin, and more still its force, entirely on its reference to our self-subsistent determination to duty. Now, which is more natural in the first instruction of youth, or also in the ministration of the pulpit: to expound the doctrine of virtue ahead of the doctrine of divine blessedness, or that of divine blessedness ahead of the doctrine of virtue (perhaps even without mentioning the latter at all)? The two obviously stand in necessary connection with each other. This is not however possible, since they are not *of one kind*, except [in this way]: one must be conceived and expounded as end and the other merely as means. But the doctrine of virtue stands on its own (even without the concept of God); the doctrine of divine blessedness contains the concept of an object which we represent to ourselves, with reference to our morality, as a cause supplementing our incapacity with respect to the final moral end. Hence divine blessedness cannot of itself constitute the final end of moral striving but can only serve as a means of strengthening what in itself makes for

a better human being, [i.e.] virtuous disposition; and this it does by holding out to this striving and guaranteeing for it (as striving after goodness,
even after holiness) the expectation of the final end for which it is itself
powerless. The concept of virtue, by contrast, is derived from the soul of
the human being. It is already within him in full, though undeveloped,
and, unlike the concept of religion, is not in need of ratiocination through
inferences. In the purity of this concept; in the awakening to consciousness of a capacity otherwise never surmised by us, of being able to become
master over the greatest obstacles within us; in the dignity of the humanity
which the human being must respect in his own person and personal
vocation, and which he strives to achieve – there is in this something that
so uplifts the soul, and so leads it to the very Deity, which is worthy of
adoration only in virtue of his holiness and as the legislator of virtue, that
the human being, even when still far removed from allowing this concept
the power of influencing his maxims, is yet not unwiling to be supported
by it. For through this idea he already feels himself to a degree ennobled,
whereas the concept of a world ruler, who makes of this duty a command-
ment for us, still lies far removed from him, and, were he to begin with it,
he would run the risk of dashing his courage (which is an essential compo-
nent of virtue) and of transforming divine blessedness into a fawning
slavish subjection to the commands of a despotic might. The courage to
stand on one's own feet is itself strengthened through the doctrine of   6:184
atonement which follows from it. For this doctrine represents what cannot
be altered as wiped out, and opens up for us the path to a new conduct of
life; whereas, when the doctrine is made to come first, the futile endeavor to
render undone what has been done (expiation), the fear concerning the
imputation of expiation, the representation of our total incapacity for the
good, and the anxiety lest we slip back into evil, must take the courage
away from the human being,* and must reduce him to a state of groaning

---

* The different kinds of faith among peoples gradually impart to the latter a character which
also distinguishes them externally in their civic bond, and is later attributed to them as
though it were a generalized temperamental trait. Thus in its first establishment Judaism
drew upon itself the charge of *misanthropy*, for a people was to cut itself off from all other
peoples and avoid intermingling with them by means of every conceivable – and in some
cases painful – observance. Mohammedanism is distinguished by its *pride*, because it finds
confirmation of its faith in victories and in the subjugation of many peoples rather than in
miracles, and because its devotional practices are all of a fierce kind. †The Hindu faith gives
its adherents the character of *pusillanimity*, for reasons directly opposite to those just
mentioned. – Now surely it is not because of the inner nature of the Christian faith, but
because of the manner in which people's minds are introduced to it, that a similar charge can
be brought against it with respect to those who are the most serious about it but who, starting
with human corruption and despairing of all virtue, place their religious principle solely in
piety (by which is understood the principle of conducting oneself passively in view of the
divine blessedness expected through a power from above). For these [individuals] never
place any reliance in themselves but constantly look about them in constant anxiety for a

6:185 moral passivity where nothing great and good is undertaken but instead everything is expected from wishing for it. – As regards moral disposition, everything depends upon the highest concept to which the human being subordinates his duties. If reverence for God comes first, and the human being therefore subordinates virtue to it, then this object [of reverence] is an *idol*, i.e. it is thought as a being whom we may hope to please not through morally upright conduct in this world but through adoration and ingratiation; religion is then idolatry. Thus divine blessedness is not a surrogate for virtue, a way of avoiding it, but its completion, for the sake of crowning it with the hope of the final success of all our good ends.

§ 4
CONCERNING THE GUIDING THREAD OF
CONSCIENCE IN MATTERS OF FAITH

The question here is not, how conscience is to be guided (for conscience does not need any guide; to have a conscience suffices), but how conscience itself can serve as guiding thread in the most perplexing moral decisions. –

Conscience is a consciousness which is of itself' a duty. But how can we think such a consciousness, when the consciousness of all our representations seems to be necessary only for logical purposes, hence only conditionally, whenever we want to clarify our representation; hence cannot be unconditional duty?

It is a moral principle, requiring no proof, that we *ought to venture*

---

supernatural assistance, and even think that in this self-contempt (which is not humility) they possess a means of obtaining favor. The outward expression of this (in pietism or false piety) is indeed a sign of a *slavish* cast of mind.

† This remarkable phenomenon (of an ignorant though intelligent people's pride in its faith) may also have its origin from the fancy of its founder that he alone had once again restored in the world the concept of God's unity and of his supersensible nature – a concept which would have indeed ennobled his people by freeing it from the subjugation to images and the anarchy of polytheism if he could with justice credit himself with this contribution. – Concerning the characteristic of the third class of religious fellowship, which is based upon a badly understood humility, the abatement of self-conceit in the evaluation of one's own moral worth through confrontation with the holiness of the law should not bring about contempt for oneself but rather the resolution to bring ourselves ever nearer to conformity to

6:185 that law according to this noble predisposition in us. Virtue, which truly consists in the courage for this, has instead been relegated to paganism as a name already suspect of self-conceit, and in opposition to it the grovelling courting of favor is being extolled. – *False devotion (bigotterie, devotio spuria)* is the habit of placing the exercise of piety, not in actions well-pleasing to God (in the fulfillment of human duties) but in direct commerce with God through manifestations of awe; this exercise must thus be counted as *compulsory service (opus operatum)*, except that to superstition it adds also the delusion of allegedly supersensible (heavenly) feelings.

' *für sich selbst*

178

nothing where there is danger that it might be wrong (quod dubitas, ne feceris!" 6:186
Pliny).[177] So the *consciousness* that an action *which I want to undertake* is
right, is unconditional duty. Now it is understanding, not conscience,
which judges whether an action is in general right or wrong. And it is not
absolutely necessary to know, of all possible actions, whether they are
right or wrong. With respect to the action that *I* want to undertake,
however, I must not only judge, and be of the opinion, that it is right; I
must also be *certain* that it is. And this is a requirement of conscience to
which is opposed *probabilism*, i.e., the principle that the mere opinion that
an action may well be right is itself sufficient for undertaking it. – [178]
Conscience could also be defined as *the moral faculty of judgment, passing
judgment upon itself*, except that this definition would be much in need of
prior clarification of the concepts contained in it. Conscience does not
pass judgment upon actions as cases that stand under the law, for this is
what reason does so far as it is subjectively practical (whence the *casus
conscientiæ* and casuistry, as a kind of dialectic of conscience). Rather, here
reason judges itself, whether it has actually undertaken, with all diligence,
that examination of actions (whether they are right or wrong), and it calls
upon the human being himself to witness *for* or *against* himself whether
this has taken place or not.

Take, for instance, an inquisitor who clings fast to the exclusiveness
of his statutory faith even to the point, if need be, of martyrdom, and
who has to pass judgment upon a so-called heretic (otherwise a good
citizen) charged with unbelief. Now I ask: if he condemns him to death,
whether we can say that he has passed judgment according to his conscience (though erroneous), or whether we can rather accuse him of
plain *lack of conscience;* whether he simply erred or consciously did wrong;
since we can always tell him outright that in such a situation he could
not have been entirely certain that he was not perhaps doing wrong. He
was indeed presumably firm in the belief that a supernaturally revealed
divine will (perhaps according to the saying, *compellite intrare*)[v][179] permitted him, if not even made a duty for him, to extirpate supposed unbelief
together with the unbelievers. But was he really as strongly convinced of
such a revealed doctrine, and also of its meaning, as is required for
daring to destroy a human being on its basis? That to take a human
being's life because of his religious faith is wrong is certain, unless (to 6:187
allow the most extreme possibility) a divine will, made known to the
inquisitor in some extraordinary way, has decreed otherwise. But that
God has ever manifested this awful will is a matter of historical documentation and never apodictically certain. After all, the revelation reached
the inquisitor only through the intermediary of human beings and their

" do not do what you are doubtful about
ᵛ compel them to come in

IMMANUEL KANT

interpretation, and even if it were to appear to him to have come from God himself (like the command issued to Abraham to slaughter his own son like a sheep),[180] yet it is at least possible that on this point error has prevailed. But then the inquisitor would risk the danger of dong something which would be to the highest degree wrong, and on this score he acts unconscientiously. – Now such is the situation with every historical or phenomenal faith, namely that the *possibility* is always there of coming across an error; consequently it is unconscientious to act upon it, granted this possibility that what it requires or permits is perhaps wrong, i.e. at the risk of violating a human duty in itself certain.

More still: even if an action commanded by such a positive (allegedly) revealed law were in itself allowed, the question yet arises whether, in accordance with their presumed conviction, spiritual authorities or teachers may impose it upon the people to profess it as an *article of faith* (on penalty of forfeiting their status). Since conviction in this matter has no other grounds of proof except historical ones, and in the judgment of the people (if they just subject themselves to the least test) there always is the absolute possibility that an error has crept into these [proofs] or in their classical interpretation, the cleric would be compelling the people to profess as true, at least inwardly, as though it were a matter of their belief in God, i.e. as if in his presence, something which they however do not know with certainty to be such; for instance, to recognize the allocation of a certain day for the periodic public promotion of divine blessedness as part of a religion directly commanded by God; or to profess firm belief in a mystery which they do not even understand. Here the people's spiritual authority would himself be acting against his conscience, by forcing upon others a belief in something of which he cannot himself be ever wholly convinced; therefore he should consider well what he is doing, for he must answer for all the abuse arising from such servile faith. – Thus there can perhaps be truth in what is believed, yet at the same time untruthfulness in the belief (or even in the purely inward profession of it), and this is in itself damnable.

6:188   Although, as noted above,[181] human beings who have made but the slightest beginning in freedom of thought,* for they previously were un-

* I admit that I am not comfortable with this way of speaking, which even clever men are wont to use: "A certain people (intent on establishing civil freedom) is not ripe for freedom"; "The bondmen of a landed proprietor are not yet ripe for freedom"; and so too, "People are in general not yet ripe for freedom of belief." For on this assumption freedom will never come, since we cannot *ripen* to it if we are not already established in it (we must be free in order to be able to make use of our powers purposively in freedom). To be sure, the first attempts will be crude, and in general also bound to greater hardships and dangers than when still under the command but also the care of others; yet we do not ripen to freedom otherwise than through our *own* attempts (and we must be free to be allowed to make them). I raise no objections if those in power, being constrained by the circumstances of the time, put

180

der a slavish yoke of faith (e.g. the Protestants), immediately consider
themselves ennobled as it were the less they need to believe (of what is
positive and belongs to priestly precepts), the very reverse holds of those
who have not been capable of, or have not willed, any attempt of this kind;
for this is their principle: It is advisable to believe too much rather than
too little. For what we do over and above what we owe does at least no
harm and might even perhaps help. – Upon this delusion, which makes of
dishonesty in religious professions a fundamental principle (to which it is
all the easier to commit oneself, since religion makes good every mistake,
consequently also that of dishonesty) is based the so-called security
maxim in matters of fatih (*argumentum a tuto*):*ᵐ* If what I profess regarding
God is true, I have hit the mark; if not true but not something in itself
otherwise forbidden, I have merely believed it superfluously, and though
this was of course not necessary, I have only burdened myself perhaps
with an inconvenience which is no crime. The danger arising from the
dishonesty of his pretension – *the violation of conscience* in proclaiming as
certain, even before God, something of which he is yet conscious that, its   6:189
nature being what it is, cannot be asserted with unconditional confidence – this *the hypocrite regards as a mere nothing.* – The genuine maxim
of safety, alone consistent with religion, is exactly the reverse: Whatever,
as means or condition of blessedness, can be made [object of] my cognition not through my own reason but only through revelation, and can be
introduced into my profession solely through the intermediary of a historical faith, for the rest does not however contradict the pure principles of
morality – this I cannot indeed believe and assert as certain, but just as
little can I reject it as certainly false. At the same time, without determining anything in this regard, I count on the fact that whatever saving
content it may have, it will come to good for me only so far as I do not
render myself unworthy of it through a defect of the moral disposition in a
good life-conduct. In this maxim is true moral safety, namely safety before
conscience (and more cannot be required of a human being); by contrast,
the greatest danger and unsafety attend the supposedly prudential device
of craftily avoiding the detrimental consequences which might befall me
from withholding profession, for by holding out for both parties I spoil my
standing with both. –

Let the author of a creed or the teacher of a church, indeed; let every

---

off relinquishing these three bonds far, very far, into the future. But to make it a principle
that those who are once subjected to them are essentially not suited to freedom, and that one
is justified in keeping them from it for all time, this is an intrusion into the prerogatives of
Divinity itself, which created human beings for freedom. It certainly is more convenient to
rule in state, household, and church, if one succeeds in imposing such a principle. But is it
also more just?

ᵐ argument from security

human being, so far as he inwardly stands by the conviction that certain propositions are divinely revealed, ask himself: Do you really dare to avow the truth of these propositions in the sight of him who scrutinizes the heart, and at the risk of relinquishing all that is valuable and holy to you? I would have to have a very unfavorable conception of human nature (which is, after all, at least not altogether incapable of good) not to suppose that

6:190   even the boldest teacher of the faith must quake at the question.* But if this is so, how does it accord with conscientiousness to insist nevertheless on such a declaration of faith, which admits of no restriction, and to pass off the presumptuousness of such avowals even as a duty and service to God, when the freedom of human beings which is absolutely required for everything moral (such as the adoption of a religion) is thereby being totally trampled under foot, and no place is even left for the good will which says: "Lord, I believe; help thou mine unbelief!"[181]†

General remark

Whatever good the human being can do on his own, according to the laws of freedom, as compared with the faculty available to him only through supernatural help, can be called *nature*, in distinction from *grace*. Not that by the former expression we understand a physical property distinct from freedom; rather, we use it only because we at least have cognition of the *laws* of this faculty (the laws of *virtue*) and, on the *analogy of nature*, reason

---

*† The very man who has the temerity to say: He who does not believe in this or that historical doctrine as a precious truth, *that one is damned*, would also have to be ready to say: If what I am now relating to you is not true, *let me be damned!* – Were there anyone capable of such a dreadful declaration, I should advise dealing with him according to the Persian proverb concerning a *hadji:* If someone has been in Mecca once (as a pilgrim), leave the house where he dwells with you; if he has been there twice, leave the street where he resides; and if he has been there three times, then leave the city, or even the land, where he lives![182]

†† *Oh sincerity!* You Astræa,[184] who have fled from the earth to heaven, how are you (the foundation of conscience, and hence of all inner religion) to be drawn down from there to us again? I can admit, though it is much to be deplored, that straightforwardness (saying the *whole* known truth) is not to be found in human nature. But we must be able to demand *sincerity* (that *everything said* be said with truthfulness) of every human being, and if in our nature there were no predisposition to it, whose cultivation is only being neglected, the human race would have to be in its own eyes an object of deepest contempt. This required quality of the mind is one, however, exposed to many temptations, and costs many a sacrifice, and hence also calls for moral strength, i.e. virtue (which must be earned), yet must be guarded and cultivated earlier than any other, for the opposite propensity is the hardest to extirpate if it is just allowed to take root. – Now contrast with it our manner of upbringing, especially in matters of religion or, better, doctrines of faith, where fidelity of memory in answering questions concerning them, without regard for fidelity of profession (which is never put to the test), is accepted as already sufficient to make a believer of him who does not understand even what he professes as holy, and one will no longer wonder at the lack of sincerity that produces nothing but inward hypocrites.

thus possesses a visible and comprehensible clue to it. On the other hand, whether, if and when, or how much, *grace* has effect on us – this remains totally hidden to us, and in this matter, as in general in all things supernatural (to which morality, as *holiness*, belongs), reason is bereft of any information of the laws according to which it might occur.

The concept of a supernatural intervention into our moral though deficient faculty, and even into our not totally purified or at least weak disposition, to satisfy our duty in full – this is a transcendent concept, merely an idea of whose reality no experience can assure us. – But even to accept it as idea for a purely practical intent is very risky and hard to reconcile with reason; for what is to be accredited to us as morally good conduct must take place not through foreign influence but only through the use of our own powers. Yet its impossibility (that the two may not occur side by side) cannot be proven either, since freedom itself, though not containing anything supernatural in its concept, remains just as incomprehensible to us according to its possibility as the supernatural [something] we might want to assume as surrogate for the independent yet deficient determination of freedom.

But since we are at least acquainted with^x the (moral) *laws* of freedom according to which the latter is to be determined, whereas of a supernatural assistance – whether a certain moral strength perceivable in us in fact comes from it, or also on what occasions, and under what conditions this is to be expected – we can have not the least cognition,^{y} so apart from the general presupposition that grace will work in us what nature cannot if we have just made use of that nature (i.e., of our own forces) according to possibility, we cannot make any further use of this idea at all, neither for determining how (over and above the constant striving for a good life-conduct) we might draw down upon us the cooperation of this grace, nor on what occasions we might expect it. – This ideal totally escapes us; and it is, moreover, salutary to keep ourselves at a respectful distance from it, as from a sacred thing, lest, under the delusion that we do miracles ourselves, or that we perceive miracles in us, we render ourselves unfit for all use of reason, or let ourselves be tempted into a state of inertia where in passive idleness we expect from above what we ought to be seeking within us.

Now *means* are all the intermediate causes which the human being *has* 6:192 *within his power*, whereby to effect a certain intent. But there is no other means (nor can there be any) by which to become worthy of heavenly assistance, except the earnest endeavor to improve his moral nature in all possible ways, thereby making himself capable of receiving a nature fully fit – as is not in his power – for divine approval, since the expected divine

---

^{x} *kennen*
^{y} *erkennen*

assistance itself has only his morality for its aim. That the impure human being would not seek this assistance here but rather in certain sensuous practices[z] (which certainly are within his power but cannot on their own make him a better human being, yet this is what in some supernatural way they are to effect) was indeed already to be expected *a priori,* and so it also happens in fact. The concept of a so-called *means of grace,* though self-contradictory (according to what has just been said), still serves here as a means of self-deception, which is as common as it is detrimental to true religion.

The true (moral) service of God, which the faithful must render as subjects belonging to his kingdom but no less also as its citizens (under laws of freedom), is itself just as invisible as the kingdom, i.e. it is a *service of the heart* (in spirit and truth), and can consist only in the disposition of obedience to all true duties as divine commands, not in actions determined exclusively for God. Yet for the human being the invisible needs to be represented through something visible (sensible), indeed what is more, it must be accompanied by the visible for the sake of praxis[a] and, though intellectual, made as it were an object of intuition (according to a certain analogy); and although this is only a means of making intuitive for ourselves our duty in the service of God – to be sure an indispensable means yet at the same time one subject to the danger of misconstruction – yet, through a *delusion* which creeps upon us, it is easily taken for the *service of God* itself and is also commonly given this name.

This alleged service of God, when brought back to its spirit and its true meaning, namely, to a disposition ordained to the kingdom of God within us and outside us, can be divided, even by reason, into four observances of duty; and certain formalities, which do not stand in necessary connection 6:193 with them, have however been appointed to correspond to them, because these formalities have from antiquity been found to be good sensible intermediaries that serve as schemata for the duties, thus awakening and sustaining our attention to the true service of God. They are based, one and all, upon the aim of promoting the moral good: (1) of establishing *this good firmly within us,* and repeatedly to awaken in our heart the disposition for it (private prayer); (2) of *propagating* it *externally* through public assembly on days legally consecrated thereto, in order that religious doctrines and wishes (together with dispositions of the same kind) be loudly proclaimed and thereby fully shared (church-going); (3) of *transmitting* it to posterity through the reception of new members joining the fellowship of faith, it being a duty also to instruct them in this faith (in the Christian religion, *baptism*); (4) of *maintaining this fellowship* through repeated public formalities which stabilize the union of its members into an ethical body –

---

[z] *sinnlichen Veranstaltungen*
[a] *des Praktischen*

this, according to the principle of the mutual equality of the members' rights and their sharing in all the fruits of moral goodness (communion).

Every beginning in religious matters, when not undertaken in a purely moral spirit but as a means *in itself* capable of propitiating God and thus, through him, of satisfying all our wishes, is a *fetish-faith*. This is the persuasion that what cannot effect a certain thing, either according to *nature* or the moral laws of reason, will through it alone nonetheless effect the thing wished for, if only we firmly believe that it will indeed effect it, and we accompany our belief with certain formalities. Even where the conviction has already taken hold that everything in these matters depends on the moral good, which can originate only in action, the sensuous[b] human being still searches for an escape route by which to circumvent that arduous condition; namely that if only he observes *the custom* (the formalities), God will surely accept that for the act itself, and this would of course have to be called an instance of God's superabundant grace, were it not rather a grace dreamed up in slothful trust, or itself perhaps an instance of hypocritical trust. Thus in every type of public faith the human being has devised certain practices for himself, as *means of grace*, even though such practices are not related in all faiths, as in the Christian, to practical concepts and to dispositions conformable to them. (For instance, of the five great commands of the Mohammedan faith – washing, praying, fasting, almsgiving, and the pilgrimage to Mecca – almsgiving alone would deserve to be excepted, if it occurred from a truly virtuous and at the same time religious disposition to human duty, and would thus also truly deserve to be regarded as a means of grace; but in fact, since in this faith alsmgiving can well coexist with the extortion from others of things which are offered to God in the person of the poor, it does not deserve to be thus exempted.)   6:194

Specifically there can be three kinds of *delusory faith* in overstepping the boundaries of our reason with respect to the supernatural (which according to the laws of reason is neither an object of theoretical or practical use). *First*, the belief that we have cognition of something through experience which we in fact cannot accept as happening according to objective laws of experience (faith *in miracles*). *Second*, the delusion that we must include among our concepts of reason, as necessary to what is morally best for us, that of which we ourselves can form no concept through reason (faith *in mysteries*). *Third*, the delusion that through the use of purely natural means we can bring about an effect which is a mystery to us, namely the influence of God upon our morality (faith in *means of grace*). – We have already dealt with the first two of these forms of fictitious faith in the General Remarks at the end of the two immediately preceding parts of this work. It still remains for us, therefore, to treat of the means of grace (which are further distinguished from the *effects of*

[b] *sinnlich*

grace,* i.e. supernatural moral influences to which we are merely passively related; to pretend to experience these influences is, however, an enthusiastic delusion pertaining merely to feeling).

1. *Praying,* conceived as an *inner ritual* service of God and hence as a means of grace, is a superstitious delusion (a fetish-making); for it only is the *declaring of a wish* to a being who has no need of any declaration regarding the inner disposition of the wisher, through which nothing is therefore accomplished nor is any of the duties incumbent on us as commands of God discharged; hence God is not really served. A sincere

6:195 wish to please God in all our doings and nondoings, i.e. the disposition, accompanying all our actions, to pursue these as though they occurred in the service of God, is the *spirit of prayer,* and this can and ought to be in us "without ceasing."[185] But to clothe† this wish in words and formulas

---

*† See General Remark at the end of *Part One.*

† In that wish, which is the spirit of prayer, the human being only seeks to work upon himself (to give life to his dispositions by means of the *idea of God*), whereas in the other, where he declares himself in words, hence externally, he seeks to work *upon* God. In the first sense prayer can be offered with perfect sincerity, even though a human being does not pretend to be capable of asserting God's existence as wholly certain; in the second form, as an *address,* a human being assumes that this supreme object is present in person, or at least he poses (even inwardly) as though he were convinced of its presence, reckoning that, suppose this is not so, his posing can at least do no harm but might rather gain him favor; hence sincerity cannot be found in as perfect a form in this latter (verbal) prayer as it can in the former (the pure spirit of prayer). – Anyone will find the truth of this last remark confirmed if he imagines a pious and well-meaning individual, but one otherwise limited with respect to these purified religious concepts, being caught unawares by somebody else, I do not say praying aloud, but gesturing in a way which indicates praying. Everyone will naturally expect, without my saying so, that this individual will fall into confusion or embarrassment, as though caught in a situation of which he should be ashamed. But why? Because a human being found talking to himself immediately gives rise to the suspicion that he is having a slight fit of madness; and so we would also judge him (not altogether unjustly) if, though alone, we find him occupied in practices or gestures that we expect only of one who sees somebody else before him, whereas this is not the case in the adduced example. – The teacher of the gospel, however, has superbly expressed the spirit of prayer in a formula that at once renders prayer dispensable and by the same token itself as well (as a verbal formula). One finds nothing in it but the resolution to good life-conduct which, combined with the consciousness of our frailty, carries with it the standing wish to be a worthy member in the Kingdom of God; hence contains no actual request for something that God in his wisdom might perhaps refuse but a wish instead which, if earnest (efficacious), will itself bring about its objective (to become a human being well-pleasing to God). Even the wish for the means of preserving our existence for one day (the wish for bread), since it is explicitly not directed to the continuance of that existence but is only the effect of a merely felt animal need, is more an admission of what *nature wills* in us than a specially considered request for what the human being *wills* – the kind which would be for bread for another day, which is clearly enough excluded here. –

6:196 Only the kind of prayer made in moral disposition (animated only through the idea of God), since as the spirit of prayer it itself brings about its object (to be well-pleasing to God), can be made in *faith,* by which we mean no more than the assurance in us that the prayer *can be answered;* but nothing in us except morality is of this kind. For even if the request did not go

(though it be only inwardly) can, at best, only carry with it the value of a means for the continual stimulation of that disposition within us; it can- 6:196 not, however, have any direct reference to divine satisfaction, and just because of this it also cannot be duty for everyone. For a means can be 6:197

further than today's bread, nobody can yet be assured that it can be answered, i.e. that its being granted to the petitioner is necessarily bound to God's wisdom; it might perhaps better conform to this wisdom that a human being be allowed to die on this day for lack of bread. It is, further, an absurd and at the same time impudent delusion to have a try at whether, through the insistent intrusiveness of our prayer, God might not be diverted from the plan of his wisdom (to our present advantage). We cannot therefore be sure that any prayer which does not have a moral object, can be answered, i.e. we cannot pray for anything *in faith*. Indeed, even though the object may be moral yet possible only through supernatural influence (or at least such as we only expect from this source, since we have no wish to exert ourselves about it, as for example a change of heart, the putting on of the new man,[186] called rebirth), it is nonetheless so uncertain whether God will find it conformable to his wisdom to make up for our (self-incurred) deficiency supernaturally, that we rather have cause to expect the contrary. Even in this respect a human being cannot therefore pray in faith. – From this we can clarify what might be the meaning of a faith which works miracles (a faith which would still be associated with inner prayer). Since God can lend a human being no power to produce effects supernaturally (since that is a contradiction); since, on his part, according to the concepts that he forms for himself of the good ends possible in this world, a human being cannot determine how divine wisdom judges in these matters and hence cannot, by means of the wish that he nurtures in and by himself, make use of the divine power for his purposes, it follows that a gift of miracles, specifically one which is up to the human being himself whether he has it or not ("If ye had faith as a grain of mustard-seed, etc."),[187] is not, taken literally, in any way to be thought of. Such a faith, therefore, if it has to have any meaning at all, is simply an idea of the preponderance that the moral constitution of the human being, if a human being were to possess it in the full perfection pleasing to God (which he however never reaches), would have over all other moving causes which God in his supreme wisdom might have; hence a ground for being confident that, if we were or would ever become *all* that we should be and (in continued approximation) can be, nature would have to obey our wishes which, however, would in this case never be unwise.

As regards the *edification* which is the purpose of churchgoing, here too public prayer is not a means of grace but a moral solemnity, whether it be celebrated with the communal singing of the hymn of faith, or with the *address* formally directed to God through the mouth of the clergyman in the name of the whole congregation and embracing within itself every moral con- 6:197 cern of human beings. This address, since it makes these concerns visible as a public issue, where the wish of each human being should be represented as united with the wishes of all toward one and the same end (the ushering in of the Kingdom of God), not only can elevate emotions to the point of moral exaltation (whereas private prayers, since they are absolved without this sublime idea, gradually lose their influence upon the mind through habituation) but also possesses a stronger rational basis than the other*f* for clothing the moral wish, which constitutes the spirit of prayer, in the guise of a formal address, yet without any thought of evoking the presence of the supreme being, or some special power of this rhetorical figure, as means of grace. For there is a special purpose here, namely, all the more to excite the moral incentives of each individual through an external solemnity which portrays the *union of all human beings* in the shared desire for the Kingdom of God; and this cannot more appropriately be accomplished than by addressing the head of this kingdom as though he were especially present in that place.

f die erstere, i.e. private prayer

187

prescribed only to one who *needs* it for certain ends, yet hardly everyone finds this means necessary (to converse within oneself and in fact *with oneself,* though allegedly all the more comprehensibly *with God*). It is rather necessary to endeavor that, through progressive purification and elevation of the moral disposition, the spirit of prayer alone should be sufficiently stimulated within us, and that its letter (at least so far as we are concerned) should finally fall away. For the letter, like everything which is trained at a given end indirectly, rather weakens the effect of the moral idea (which, subjectively regarded, is called *devotion*). Thus the consideration of the profound wisdom of divine creation in the smallest things and of its majesty in the great whole, such as was indeed already available to human beings in the past but in more recent times has widened into the highest admiration – this consideration not only has such a power as to transport the mind into that sinking mood, called *adoration,* in which the human being is as it were nothing in his own eyes, but is also, with respect to the human moral determination, such a soul-elevating power, that in comparison words, even if they were those of King David in prayer (and David knew little of all those marvels), would have to vanish as empty sound, because the feeling arising from such a vision of the hand of God is inexpressible. – [188] Human beings are moreover prone, when disposed to religion, to transform anything in fact only connected with their per-

6:198 sonal moral improvement into a courtly service in which the expressions of humiliation and glorification are, as a rule, all the less morally felt the more verbose they are. Hence it is all the more necessary, especially in the earliest practice of prayer imposed upon children who still are in need of the letter, carefully to impress that speech (even when inwardly uttered; indeed, even the attempts to attune the mind to the comprehension of the idea of God, which is to come closer to an intuition) has here no value in itself, but the only chore is rather the enlivening of the disposition to a life-conduct well-pleasing to God, and to this [end] speech serves only as an instrument of the imagination. For otherwise all those devout attestations of awe risk producing nothing but hypocritical veneration of God instead of a practical service of him which, as such, does not consist in mere feelings.

2. *Church-going,* thought of as the solemn *general external worship of God* in a church, inasmuch as it is a sensuous[d] display to the community of believers, is not only a means valuable to each *individual* for his own *edification** but also a duty obligating them *collectively*, as citizens of a

---

* If we are looking for a meaning appropriate to this term, none is likely to be found other than that by it we understand the *moral consequence of devotion upon a subject.* Now this consequence does not consist in emotion (which as such is already comprised in the concept of devotion), though most of those who think themselves devoted (and for this reason are
[d] *sinnlich*

divine state which is to be represented here on earth; provided, that this 6:199
church does not contain formalities that might lead to idolatry and can
thus burden the conscience, e.g. certain forms of adoration of God per-
sonified as infinite goodness under the name of a human being, for such
sensuous^j portrayal of God is contrary to the command of reason: "*Thou
shalt not make unto thee any graven image*, etc."[191] But to wish to use it as in
itself a *means of grace*, as though God were directly served by it and had
attached special *graces* to the celebration of these solemnities (which are
mere sensuous^k representations of the *universality* of religion), is a delusion which might indeed suit the mentality of a good *citizen* in a *political
community*, and external propriety, yet not only contributes nothing to the
quality of the citizen as *citizen in the Kingdom of God* but rather debases it
and serves to hide under a deceptive veneer, from the eyes of others and
even from his own, the bad moral content of his disposition.

3. The one-time solemn *initiation* into the church-community, i.e. the
first reception *of a member into a church* (in the Christian church through
baptism), is a solemnity rich in meaning which imposes grave obligations
either upon the initiate, if he is himself in a position to profess his faith, or
upon the witnesses who take upon themselves the care of his education in it;
it has something holy for its end (the formation of a human being as a citizen
in a divine state) but is not, in itself, a holy action performed by others
effecting holiness and receptivity for divine grace in this subject, hence not
a *means of grace*, however extravagant in the early Greek Church was its
reputation of being capable of washing away all sins at once – a delusion
that openly betrayed its ties to an almost more than pagan superstition.

4. The oft-repeated solemn ritual of *renewal, continuation*, and *propagation of this church-community* under the laws of *equality* (*communion*), which

---

also called *sanctimonious*)^e put it entirely there; hence the word *edification* must signify the
consequence that devotion has upon the actual improvement of the human being. But this
improvement will not obtain unless the human being systematically sets to work, lays firm
principles deep in his heart in accordance with well-understood concepts, erects thereupon
dispositions appropriate to the relative importance of the duties connected with these principles, strengthens them and secures them against the attack of the inclinations and, as it were,
builds up^f a new man as a *temple of God*.[189] One can easily see that this construction can
progress but slowly; yet it must at least be possible to see that something has been *performed*.
But human beings believe themselves to be duly *edified^g* (through listening or reading or
singing) while absolutely nothing has been *built*,^{h} indeed, when hand has yet to be put to the
work, presumably because they hope that that moral edifice^i will rise up of itself, like the
walls of Thebes, to the music of sighs and of ardent wishes.[190]

^{e} *Andächtler;* cf. *Andächtig* = devoted
^{f} *erbaut*
^{g} *erbaut*
^{h} *gebaut*
^{i} *Gebäude*
^{j} *sinnlich*
^{k} *sinnlich*

after the example of the founder of such a church (and at the same time in memory of him) may well assume the form of a ritual communal partaking at the same table, has in it something great which expands people's narrow, selfish and intolerant cast of mind, especially in religious matters, to

6:200 the idea of a cosmopolitan *moral community*, and it is a good means of enlivening a community to the moral disposition of brotherly love which it represents. But to boast that God has attached special graces to the celebration of this solemn ritual, and to incorporate among the articles of faith the proposition that the ritual, though a purely ecclesiastical action, is in addition a *means of grace* – this is a delusion of religion which cannot but work counter to the spirit of religion – *Priestcraft* would thus be, in general, the dominion which the clergy has usurped over minds by pretending to have exclusive possession of the means of grace.

∙ ∙

All such artificially induced self-deceptions in religious matters have a common ground. Of the divine moral properties – holiness, mercy, and justice – the human being normally appeals directly to the second in order to avoid the forbidding condition of conforming to the requirements of the first. It is arduous to be a good *servant* (here one always hears only talk of duties); hence the human being would rather be a *favorite*, for much is then forgiven him, or, where duty has been too grossly offended against, everything is again made good through the intercession of some one else who is favored in the highest degree, while he still remains the undisciplined servant[1] he always was. But, in order to satisfy himself with some show of likelihood that this plan of his is workable, he usually transfers his conception of a human being (his faults included) over to the Divinity; and so, just as among the best *rulers of our race* legislative rigor, benevolent grace and scrupulous justice do not work their moral effect upon the actions of the subject separately and each on its own (as they should), but they rather tend to *blend* together in the mind of the human sovereign as he renders his decisions, hence one need only try to get the better of one of these properties, [namely] the fallible wisdom of the human will, to bring the other into compliance: so too does the human being hope to achieve the same thing with God by appealing exclusively to his *grace*. (For this reason the separation in thought of the properties of God, or rather of his relations to the human being, through the idea of a threefold personality, on whose analogy that separation is apparently to be thought, was

6:201 important also for religion, in order to make each relation knowable as distinct.) To this end the human being busies himself with every formality he can think of, to give sign of how much he *respects* the divine commands, in order that it will not be necessary for him to *observe* them. And, that his

[1] *der lose Knecht*

ineffective wishes may also serve to compensate for the disobedience of these commands, he cries out, "Lord! Lord!" in order that it will not be necessary for him to "do the will of his heavenly Father."[192] And so, he construes a concept of the solemn rituals surrounding the use of certain means for enlivening truly practical dispositions as though they were means of grace in themselves; he even makes out the belief that that's what they are as itself an essential element of religion (the common man: even the whole of religion) and leaves it up to the all-gracious Providence to make a better human being of him, while he busies himself with *piety* (which is a passive respect of the divine law) rather than with *virtue* (which is the deployment of one's forces in the observance of the duty which he respects), though in fact it is this virtue, *combined with piety*, which alone can constitute the idea we understand by the word *divine blessedness* (true *religious disposition*). – If the delusion of this supposed favorite of heaven reaches heights of enthusiasm, to the point of imagining that he feels the special effects of faith within him (or even has the impertinence of trusting in a supposed hidden *familiarity* with God), virtue finally becomes loathsome to him and an object of contempt. No wonder, then, that the complaint is to be heard publicly, that religion still contributes all too little to the improvement of human beings, and that the inner light ("under a bushel")[193] of these chosen individuals fails also to shine forth outwardly, through good works. And indeed, by comparison with other naturally honest human beings who carry their religion without fuss, not as substitute for but as a furtherance of the virtuous disposition which manifests its efficacy in a good life-conduct, it fails to shine forth *pre-eminently* (as we could well demand in view of their pretensions). Yet the teacher of the Gospel has himself put into our hands these external evidences of external experience as a touchstone by which we can recognize human beings, and each of them can recognize himself, by their fruits. But thus far we cannot see how those who, in their opinion, have been exceptionally favored (the elect) might in the slightest outdo the naturally honest human beings, who can be relied upon in daily affairs, in business and in need; on the contrary, taken as a whole, they can hardly withstand comparison with him, 6:202 which proves that the right way to advance is not from grace to virtue but rather from virtue to grace.

The end of all things

The end of all things

It is a common expression, used chiefly in pious language, to speak of a person who is dying as going *out of time into eternity*.

This expression would in fact say nothing if *eternity* is understood here to mean a time proceeding to infinity; for then the person would indeed never get outside time but would always progress only from one time into another. Thus what must be meant is an *end of all time* along with the person's uninterrupted duration; but this duration (considering its existence as a magnitude) as a magnitude (*duratio Noumenon*) wholly incomparable with time, of which we are obviously able to form no concept (except a merely negative one). This thought has something horrifying about it because it leads us as it were to the edge of an abyss: for anyone who sinks into it no return is possible ("But in that earnest place/ Him who holds nothing back/ Eternity holds fast in its strong arms." Haller);[1] and yet there is something attractive there too: for one cannot cease turning his terrified gaze back to it again and again (*nequeunt expleri corda tuendo*. Virgil).[a] It is frighteningly *sublime* partly because it is obscure, for the imagination works harder in darkness than it does in bright light. Yet in the end it must also be woven in a wondrous way into universal human reason, because it is encountered among all reasoning peoples at all times, clothed in one way or another. – Now when we pursue the transition from time into eternity (whether or not this idea, considered theoretically as extending cognition, has objective reality), as reason does in a moral regard, then we come up against the *end of all things* as temporal beings and as objects of possible experience – which end, however, in the moral order of ends, is at the same time the beginning of a duration of just those same beings as *supersensible*, and consequently as not standing under conditions of time; thus that duration and its state will be capable of no determination of its nature[b] other than a moral one.

Days are as it were the children of time, because the following day, with what it contains, is an offspring of the previous one. Now just as the last child of its parents is called the youngest child, so the German language likes to call the last day (the point in time which closes all time) the

8:328

---

[a] "They cannot satisfy their hearts with gazing" (Virgil, *Aeneid* 8:265).
[b] *Beschaffenheit*

youngest day.[c] The last day thus still belongs to time, for on it something or other *happens* (and not to eternity, where nothing happens any more, because that would belong to the progress of time): namely, the settling of accounts for human beings, based on their conduct in their whole lifetime. It is a *judgment day;* thus the judgment of grace or damnation by the world's judge is therefore the real[d] end of all things in time, and at the same time the beginning of the (blessed or cursed) eternity, in which the lot that has fallen to each remains just as it was in the moment of its pronouncement (of the sentence). Thus the last day also contains in itself simultaneously the *last judgment.* – Now if among the *last things* there should yet be counted the end of the world as it appears in its present shape, namely the falling of the stars from heaven, considered as a vault, and the collapse of this heaven itself (or its disappearance, as a scroll when it is rolled up),[2] both being consumed in flames, with the creation of a new earth and a new heaven as the seat of the blessed and of hell as that of the damned,[3] then that judgment day would obviously not be the last day; instead, different days would follow upon it, one after another. Yet since the idea of an end of all things takes its origin from reasonings not about the *physical* but rather about the moral course of things in the world, and is occasioned only by it, while the latter alone can be referred to the supersensible (which is to be understood only morally) – and it is the same with the idea of eternity – so consequently the representation of those last things which are supposed to come *after* the last day are to be regarded only as a way of making sensible this latter together with its moral consequences, which are otherwise not theoretically comprehensible to us.

But it is to be noted that from the most ancient times there have been two systems pertaining to the future eternity: one is that of the *unitists,*[e] awarding eternal blessedness to all human beings (after they have been purified by a longer or shorter penance), while the other is the system of 8:329 the *dualists,** which awards blessedness to *some* who have been elected,

---

* In the ancient Persian religion (of Zoroaster), such a system was grounded on the assumption of an eternal struggle between two original beings, the good principle Ormuzd and the evil Ahriman. – It is strange that in the naming of these two original beings the language of two lands distant from each other, and still farther removed from the present seat of the German language, is German. I remember reading in Sonnerat that in Ava (the land of the Burmese) the good principle[f] is called "Godeman"[g] (which appears also to lie in the name *Darius Codomannus;* and the word "Ahriman" sounds very similar to [the German for] "wicked man"[h] – present day Persian also contains a lot of originally German words; so it

[c] *Jüngster Tag* is the German term for what we call (the biblical) "judgment day"; this term will be translated henceforth as "last day."

[d] *eigentliche*

[e] *Unitarier*

[f] *Princip*

[g] "Godeman" sounds similar to the German *"guter Mann"*

[h] *arge Mann*

but eternal damnation to all *the rest*. For there would probably be no room for a system according to which all were predestined[i] to be *damned*, because then there would be no ground which could justify their being created at all; but the *annihilation* of all would indicate a defective wisdom, one which is dissatisfied with its own work and knows no other way of remedying the flaws except to destroy it. – Just the same difficulty stands in the way of the dualists as the obstacle to thinking the eternal damnation of everyone; for why, one could ask, were even a few created – Why even a single individual? – if he is supposed to exist only to be rejected for eternity? For that is worse than never having been at all.

Indeed, as far as we have insight into it, as far as we can investigate it ourselves, the dualistic system (but only under *one* supremely good original being) has – for the *practical* aims of every human being judging himself (though not for being warranted to judge others) – a preponderant ground for it: for as far as he is acquainted with himself, reason leaves him no other prospect for eternity than that which his conscience opens up for him at the end of this life on the basis of the course of his life as he has led it up to then. But this ground, as a judgment of mere reason, is far from sufficient for making this into a *dogma*, hence a theoretical proposition which is valid in itself (objectively). For what human being knows[j] himself or others through and through? Who knows enough to decide whether if we subtract from the causes of a presumably well-led course of life everything which is called the merit of fortune – such as an innately kind temperament, the naturally greater strength of his higher powers (of the understanding and reason, to tame his drives), besides that also his opportunity, the times when contingency fortunately saved him from many temptations which struck another – who knows if he separates all these from his actual character (from which he must necessarily subtract them if he is to evaluate it properly, since as gifts of fortune he cannot ascribe them to his own merit) – who will then decide, I say, whether before the all-seeing eye of a world-judge one human being has any superiority over another regarding his inner moral worth? And, on the basis of this superficial self-knowledge,[k] might it not perhaps be absurd self-conceit to pronounce any judgment at all to one's own advantage concerning one's own moral worth or that of others (or of the fates they deserve)? – Hence the unitist's system, as much as the dualist's, considered as dogma, seems to transcend completely the speculative faculty of human reason; and everything brings us back to limiting those ideas of reason

8:330

---

might be a task for those who do research into antiquity to use the guiding thread of *linguistic* affinity to inquire into the origin of the present day *religious* conceptions of many peoples. (See Sonnerat's *Travels*, Book 4, Chapter 2, B.)⁴

[i] *bestimmt*

[j] *kennt*

[k] *Selbsterkenntnis*

197

absolutely to the conditions of their practical use only. For we see nothing before us now that could teach us about our fate in a future world except the judgment of our own conscience, i.e. what our present moral state, as far as we are acquainted with it, lets us judge rationally concerning it: namely, that those principles*l* we have found ruling in ourselves during the course of our life (whether they be good or evil) will continue after death, without our having the slightest ground to assume that they will alter in that future. Hence for eternity we would have to anticipate for ourselves the consequences suiting that merit or guilt under the dominion of the good or evil principle; in this respect, consequently, it is wise to act *as if* another life – and the moral state in which we end this one, along with its consequences in entering on that other life – is unalterable. Thus from a practical point of view,*m* the system to be assumed will have to be the dualistic one – especially since the unitistic system appears to lull us too much into an indifferent sense of security – yet we might not try to make out which of the two systems deserves superiority from a theoretical and merely speculative point of view.

But why do human beings expect *an end* of the world *at all?* And if this is conceded to them, why must it be a terrible end (for the greatest part of the human race)? . . . The ground of the first point appears to lie in the fact that reason says to them that the duration of the world has worth only insofar as the rational beings in it conform to the final end of their existence; if, however, this is not supposed to be achieved, then creation itself appears purposeless to them, like a play having no resolution and affording no cognition of any rational aim. The latter point is grounded on our opinion about the corrupt nature*n* of the human race,* which corrup-

8:331

---

* In all ages self-styled sages (or philosophers), without paying enough attention to the worth of the disposition to good in human nature, have exhausted themselves in repellent, partly disgusting parables, which represent our earthly world, the dwelling place of humanity, as contemptible: (1) As an inn (caravansarai), as that dervish regards it, where everyone arriving there on his life's journey must be prepared to be driven out soon by his successor; (2) as a *penitentiary* – an opinion to which the Brahmanists, Tibetans and other sages of the Orient (and even Plato) are attached – a place of chastisement and purification for fallen spirits driven out of heaven, who are now human or animal souls; (3) as a *madhouse*, where each not only annihilates his own intents, but where each adds every thinkable sorrow to the other, and moreover holds the skill and power to do this to be the greatest honor; finally (4), as a *cloaca*, where all the excrement from the other worlds has been deposited. The latter notion is in a certain way original, and for it we have a Persian wit to thank; he transposed paradise, the dwelling place of the first human couple, into heaven, where there was a garden with ample trees richly provided with splendid fruits, whose digested residue, after the couple's enjoyment of them, vanished through an unnoticed evaporation; the exception was a single tree in the middle of the garden, which bore a fruit which was delicious but did not dry up in this way. As it now happened, our first parents now lusted after it, despite the prohibition

l Principien

m Absicht

n Beschaffenheit

198

tion is great to the point of hopelessness; this makes for an end, and indeed a terrible one, the only end (for the greatest part of humanity) that accords with highest wisdom and justice, employing any respectable standard. – Hence the _omens of the last day_ (for where the imagination has been excited by great expectations, how can there fail to be signs and miracles?) are all of a terrible kind. Some see them in increasing injustice, oppression of the poor by the arrogant indulgence of the rich, and the general loss of fidelity and faith; or in bloody wars igniting all over the earth, and so forth; in a word, in the moral fall and the rapid advance of all vices together with their accompanying ills, such as earlier times – they think – have never seen. Others, by contrast, [find them] in unusual alterations in nature – in earthquakes, storms and floods, or comets and atmospheric signs.

8:332

   In fact it is not without cause that human beings feel their existence a burden, even if they themselves are the cause. The ground of this appears to me to lie in this. – In the progress of the human race the culture of talents, skill and taste (with their consequence, luxury) naturally runs ahead of the development of morality; and this state is precisely the most burdensome and dangerous for morality just as it is for physical well-being, because the needs grow stronger than the means to satisfy them. But the moral disposition of humanity – which (like Horace's _poene pede claudo_)[o] always limps behind, tripping itself up in its hasty course and often stumbling – will (as, under a wise world governor, one may hope) one day overtake it; and thus, even according to the experimental proofs of the superior morals of our age as compared with all previous ones, one should nourish the hope that the last day might sooner come on the scene with Elijah's ascension[5] than with the like descent of Korah's troops into hell,[6] and bring with it the end of all things on earth. Yet this heroic faith in virtue does not seem, subjectively, to have such a generally powerful influence for converting people's minds as a scene accompanied by terrors, which is thought of as preceding the last things.

· ·

Note. Here we have to do (or are playing) merely with ideas created by reason itself, whose objects (if they have any) lie wholly beyond our field of vision; although they are transcendent for speculative cognition, they

---

against tasting it, and so there was no other way to keep heaven from being polluted except to take the advice of one of the angels who pointed out to them the distant earth, with the words: "There is the toilet of the whole universe," and then carried them there in order to relieve themselves, but then flew back to heaven leaving them behind. That is how the human race is supposed to have arisen on earth.

[o] "Punishment with a lame foot"; the line actually reads: _Raro antecedentem scelestum/ Deseruit pede Poena claudo_ ("Rarely does punishment fail to catch the guilty, though it runs with a lame foot"), Horace, _Odes_ 3.2.32.

8:333

are not to be taken as empty, but with a practical intent they are made available to us by lawgiving reason itself, yet not in order to brood over their objects as to what they are in themselves and in their nature, but rather how we have to think of them in behalf of moral principles directed toward the final end of all things (through which, though otherwise they would be entirely empty, acquire objective practical reality): hence we have a *free* field before us, this product of our own reason, the universal concept of an end of all things, to divide it up and to classify what stands under it according to the relation it has to our faculty of cognition.

Accordingly, the whole will be brought about, divided up and represented under three divisions: (1) the *natural** end of all things according to the order of divine wisdom's moral ends, which we therefore (with a practical intent) can *very well understand;* (2) their *mystical* (supernatural) end in the order of efficient causes, of which we *understand nothing,* and (3) the *contranatural* (perverse) end of all things, which comes from us when we *misunderstand* the final end; the first of these has already been discussed, and what follows now is the remaining two.

· ·

In the *Apocalypse* (10:5–6): "An angel lifts his hand up to heaven and swears by the one who lives from eternity to eternity who has created heaven, etc.: *that henceforth time shall be no more.*"[7]

If one does not assume that this angel "with his voice of seven thunders" (v. 3) wanted to cry nonsense, then he must have meant that henceforth there shall be no *alteration;* for if there were still alteration in the world, then time would also exist, because alteration can take place only in time and is not thinkable without presupposing it.

8:334

Now here is represented an end of all things as objects of sense – of which we cannot form any concept at all, because we will inevitably entangle ourselves in contradictions as soon as we try to take a single step beyond the sensible world into the intelligible; that happens here since the moment which constitutes the end of the first world is also supposed to be the beginning of the other one, hence the former is brought into the same temporal series with the latter, which contradicts itself.

But we also say that we think of a duration as *infinite* (as an eternity) not because we have any determinate concept of its magnitude – for that is impossible, since time is wholly lacking as a measure – but rather because that concept – since where there is time, *no end* can come about – is merely a negative one of eternal duration, by which we come not one step

* *Natural* (*formaliter*) means what follows necessarily according to laws of a certain order of whatever sort, hence also the moral order (hence not always the physical order). Opposed to it is the *nonnatural*, which can be either supernatural or contranatural. What is necessary from *natural causes* is also represented as materially natural (physically necessary).

further in our cognition, but we will have said only that reason in its (practical) intent toward its final end can never have done enough on the path of constant alterations; and if reason attempts this with the principle[p] of rest and immutability of the state of beings in the world, the result is equally unsatisfactory in respect of its *theoretical* use; on the contrary, it would fall into total thoughtlessness, and nothing would remain for it but to think as the final end an alteration, proceeding to infinity (in time) in a constant progression, in which the *disposition* (which is not a phenomenon, like the former, but something supersensible, hence not alterable with time) remains the same and is persisting. The rule for the practical use of reason in accord with this idea thus says no more than that we must take our maxims as if, in all alterations from good to better going into infinity, our moral condition, regarding its disposition (the *homo Noumenon,* "whose change takes place in heaven") were not subject to any temporal change at all.

But that at some point a time will arrive in which all alteration (and with it, time itself) ceases – this is a representation which outrages the imagination. For then the whole of nature will be rigid and as it were petrified: the last thought, the last feeling in the thinking subject will then stop and remain forever the same without any change. For a being which can become conscious of its existence and the magnitude of this existence (as duration) only in time, such a life – if it can even be called a life – appears equivalent to annihilation, because in order to think itself into such a state it still has to think something in general, but *thinking* contains a reflecting, which can occur only in time. – Hence the inhabitants of the other world will be represented, according to their different dwelling places (heaven or hell), as striking up always the same song, their "Alleluia!," or else eternally the same wailing tones ([Rev.] 19:1–6; 20:15): by which is indicated the total lack of all change in their state.

Likewise this idea, however far it surpasses our power to grasp it, is very closely related to reason in its practical reference. Even assuming a person's moral-physical state here in life at its best – namely as a constant progression and approach to the highest good (marked out for him as a goal) –, he still (even with a consciousness of the unalterability of his disposition) cannot combine it with the prospect of *satisfaction* in an eternally enduring alteration of his state (the moral as well as the physical). For the state in which he now is will always remain an ill compared with a better one which he always stands ready to enter; and the representation of an infinite progression toward the final end is nevertheless at the same time a prospect[q] on an infinite series of ills which, even though they may be outweighed by a greater good, do not allow for the possibility of

8:335

[p] *Princip*
[q] *Prospect*

201

contentment; for he can think that only by supposing that the *final end* will at sometime be *attained*.

Now the person who broods on this will fall into *mysticism* (for reason, because it is not easily satisfied with its immanent, i.e. practical use, but gladly ventures into the transcendent, also has its mysteries), where reason does not understand either itself or what it wants, but prefers to indulge in enthusiasm rather than – as seems fitting for an intellectual inhabitant of a sensible world – to limit itself within the bounds of the latter. From this comes the monstrous system of Lao-kiun[8] concerning the *highest good*, that it consists in *nothing*, i.e. in the consciousness of *feeling* oneself swallowed up in the abyss of the Godhead by flowing together with it, and hence by the annihilation of one's personality; in order to have a presentiment of this state Chinese philosophers, sitting in dark rooms with their eyes closed, exert themselves to think and sense their own nothingness. Hence the *pantheism* (of the Tibetans and other oriental peoples); and in consequence from its philosophical sublimation *Spinozism* is begotten, which is closely akin to the very ancient *system of emanation* of human souls from the Godhead (and their final reabsorption into it). All this because people would like at last to have an *eternal tranquillity* in which to rejoice, constituting for them a supposedly blessed end of all things; but really' this is a concept in which the understanding is simultaneously exhausted and all thinking itself has an end.

8:336

· ·

The end of all things which go through the hands of human beings, even when their purposes are good, is *folly*, i.e. the use of means to their ends which are directly opposed to these ends. *Wisdom*, that is, practical reason using means commensurate to the final end of all things – the highest good – in full accord with the corresponding rules of measure, dwells in God alone; and the only thing which could perhaps be called human wisdom is acting in a way which is not visibly contrary to the idea of that [divine] wisdom. But this assurance against folly, which the human being may hope to attain only through attempts and frequent alteration of his plans, is rather a "gem which the best person can only follow after, even though he *may* never *apprehend* it";' but he may never let the self-indulgent persuasion befall him – still less may he proceed according to it – that he *has grasped* it. – Hence too the projects – altering from age to age and often absurd – of finding suitable means to make *religion in a whole people pure and at the same time powerful*, so that one can well cry out: Poor mortals, with you nothing is constant except inconstancy![9]

' *eigentlich*

' cf. Philippians 3:12: "Not as though I had already attained, either were already perfect, but I follow after, if that I may apprehend that for which I also am apprehended of Christ Jesus."

If, meanwhile, these attempts have for once finally prospered far enough that the community is susceptible and inclined to give a hearing not merely to the received pious doctrines but also to a practical reason which has been illuminated by them (which is also absolutely necessary for a religion); if the sages (of a human sort) among the people – not through an undertaking among themselves (as a clergy) but as fellow citizens – draw up projects and for the most part agree – which proves in a way that is above suspicion that they are dealing with the truth – and if the people at large also takes an interest in it (even if not in every detail) through a need, generally felt and not based on authority, directed to the necessary cultivation of its moral disposition: then nothing seems to be more advisable than to let those sages go ahead and pursue their course, since for once, as regards the *idea* they are following, they are on a good path; but as regards the success of the means they have chosen to the best final end, since this – as it may turn out in the course of nature – always remains uncertain, it is advisable always to leave it to *providence*. For however incredulous one may be, one must – where it is absolutely impossible to foresee with certainty the success of certain means taken according to all human wisdom (which, if they are to deserve their name, must proceed solely toward morality) – believe in a practical way in a concurrence of divine wisdom with the course of nature, unless one would rather just give up one's final end. – Of course it will be objected: It has often been said that the present plan is the best, one must stay with it from now on, that is the state of things for eternity. "Whoever (according to this concept) is good, he is good for always, and whoever (opposed to him) is evil, is evil for ever" (Rev. 22:11): just as if eternity, and with it the end of all things, might now have already made its entrance; – and likewise since then new plans, among which the newest are often only the restoration of an old one, have always been trotted out; and henceforth too there will be no lack of *more ultimate* projects.

8:337

I am so very conscious of my incapacity to make a new and fortunate attempt here that I, who obviously possess no great power of invention, would rather advise that we leave matters as they last stood, and as for nearly a generation they have proven themselves tolerably good in their consequences. But since this may not be the opinion of men who are either of great or else of enterprising spirit, let me modestly note not so much what they would have to do as what they will have to take care that they will be up against, because otherwise they would act against their own intention (even if that were of the best).

Christianity has, besides the greatest respect that the holiness of its laws irresistibly instills, something about it which is *worthy of love*. (Here I mean not the worthiness of love of the person who obtained it for us with great sacrifices, but that of the cause itself: namely, the moral constitution which he founded, for the former [worthiness] may be inferred only from

203

the latter.) Respect is without doubt what is primary, because without it no true love can occur, even though one can harbor great respect for a person without love. But if it is a matter not merely of the representation of duty
8:338 but also of following duty, if one asks about the *subjective* ground of actions from which, if one may presuppose it, the first thing we may expect is what a person *will do* – and not a matter merely of the *objective* ground of *what he ought to do* – then love, as a free assumption of the will of another into one's maxims, is an indispensable complement to the imperfection of human nature (of having to be necessitated to that which reason prescribes through the law). For what one does not do with liking[f] he does in such a niggardly fashion – also probably with sophistical evasions from the command of duty – that the latter as an incentive, without the contribution of the former, is not very much to be counted on.

Now if to Christianity – in order to make good on it – one adds any sort of authority (even a divine one), even if one's intention in doing so is well-meaning and the end is actually just as good, then its worthiness to be loved has nevertheless disappeared: for it is a contradiction to *command* not only that someone should do something but that he should do it *with liking.*

Christianity has the intention of furthering love out of concern for the observance of duty in general; and it produces it too, because its founder speaks not in the quality of a commander demanding obedience to *his will*, but in that of a friend of humanity who appeals to the hearts of his fellow human beings on behalf of their own well-understood will, i.e. of the way they would of themselves voluntarily act if they examined themselves properly.

Thus it is from the *liberal* way of thinking – equally distant from a slavish cast of mind and from licentiousness – that Christianity expects the *effect* of its doctrine, through which it may win over the hearts of human beings when their understanding has already been illuminated by the representation of their duty's law. The feeling of freedom in the choice of the final end is what makes the legislation worthy of its love. – Thus although the teacher of this end also announces *punishments*, that is not to be understood – or at least it is not suited to the proper nature[u] of Christianity so to explain it – as though these should become the incentives for performing what follows from its commands; for to that extent it would cease to be worthy of love. Rather, one may interpret this only as a
8:339 loving warning, arising out of the beneficence of the lawgiver, of preventing the harm that would have to arise inevitably from the transgression of the law (for: *lex est res surda et inexorabilis.* Livy.);[v] because it is not

---

[f] *gern*

[u] *eigentümliche Beschaffenheit*

[v] "The law is deaf and inexorable"; the whole passage reads: *Leges rem surdam, inexorabilem esse, salubriorem, melioremque inopi quam potenti* ("The laws are deaf things, inexorable, more salutary and better to the powerless than to the powerful"); Livy, *History of Rome* 2.3.4.

Christianity *Christianity as human ideal — no authority but lesson or morals*

Christianity as a freely assumed maxim of life but the law which threatens
here; and the law, as an unchanging order lying in the nature of things, is
not to be left up to even the creator's arbitrary will[w] to decide its consequences thus or otherwise.

If Christianity promises *rewards* (e.g. "Be joyful and consoled, for everything will be repaid you in heaven"),[10] this must not be interpreted –
according to the liberal way of thinking – as if it were an offer, through
which the human being would be *hired*, as it were, to a good course of life;
for then Christianity would, once again, not be in itself[x] worthy of love.
Only the expectation[y] of such actions arising from unselfish motives can
inspire respect in the person toward the one who has the expectation; but
without respect there is no true love. Thus one must not take that promise *respect*
in this sense, as if the rewards are to be taken for the incentives of the
actions. Love, through which a liberal way of thinking is bound to the
benefactor, is not directed toward the good received by the needy person,
but instead merely to the benefactor's generosity of *will* which is inclined
to confer it, even if he does not have the resources or is prevented from
carrying it out by other motives which come from a regard for what is
universally best for the world.

That is the moral worthiness to be loved which Christianity carries
with it, which still glimmers through the many external constraints which
may be added to it by the frequent change of opinions; and it is this which
has preserved it in the face of the disinclination it would otherwise have
encountered, and (what is remarkable) this shows itself in all the brighter
light in an age of the greatest enlightenment that was ever yet among
human beings.

If Christianity should ever come to the point where it ceased to be
worthy of love (which could very well transpire if instead of its gentle spirit
it were armed with commanding authority), then, because there is no
neutrality in moral things (still less a coalition between opposed principles[z]), a disinclination and resistance to it would become the ruling mode
of thought among people; and the *Antichrist*, who is taken to be the
forerunner of the last day, would begin his – albeit short – regime (presumably based on fear and self-interest); but then, because Christianity,
though supposedly *destined* to be the world religion, would not be *favored*
by fate to become it, *the* (perverted) *end of all things*, in a moral respect,
would arrive.

[w] *Willkür*
[x] *für sich*
[y] *Ansinnen*
[z] *Principien*

Editorial notes

What does it mean to orient oneself in thinking?

1 Moses Mendelssohn, *Gesammelte Schriften* (Jubiläumsausgabe) (Stuttgart and Bad Cannstatt, 1929–) 3:2, 81–2, 198, 211.
2 The author of the *Results* was Thomas Wizenmann (1759–87). Cf. AK, 5:143.
3 See Jacobi, *On the Doctrine of Spinoza, Jacobis Werke* (Leipzig, 1812–25, reprint: Darmstadt, 1980) 4/1:176, 192.
4 Spinoza holds that thoughts are modes of God, considered as a thinking substance (*Ethics* IIP1 Proof), and that the human mind is the idea of an existing (extended) thing (viz. the human body), so that both minds and bodies are modes of the divine substance (*Ethics* IIP11, IIP13).
5 This may be a reference either to Spinoza's proof that there cannot be more than one substance with the same nature or attribute (*Ethics* IP5); or, more generally, to his argument that it is impossible for there to be more than one substance (*Ethics* IP10 Scholium); or, still more broadly, simply to Spinoza's willingness to infer real possibility from lack of contradiction.
6 This may be a reply to criticisms of Kant made by the popular Enlightenment philosophers J. G. Feder and G. A. Tittel. Or the target may be Christoph Meiners, *Outline of a Doctrine of the Soul* (Lemgo, 1786).
7 Cf. Ecclesiastes 1:1.
8 This became Jacobi's most prominent contention in the dispute with Mendelssohn, especially in *Reply to Mendelssohn's Imputations in His Writings to the Friends of Lessing, Werke* 4/2.

On the miscarriage of all philosophical trials in theodicy

1 "For my thoughts are not your thoughts, nor are your ways my ways, saith the Lord." Isaiah 55:8.
2 Count Pietro Verri (1728–97), economist, politician, moralist, and literary man. ("Verri" is the usual spelling of the name.) The reference is to *Sull'indole del piacere* (1773), which was translated into German by Christoph Meiners as *Gedanken über die Natur des Vergnügens* (Leipzig, 1777; *Thoughts Concerning the Nature of Pleasure*). Count Verri was a pioneer in the movement to abolish torture. For another reference to Verri, cf. AK 8:232. For a modern edition of *Sull'indole*, cf. *Sull'indole del piacere e del dolore, con altri scritti di filosofia e di economia*, ed. R. De Felice (Milan: Feltrinelli, 1964).
3 "But he is in one mind, and who can turn him? and what his soul desireth, even that he doeth."

4 "But ask now the beasts, and they shall teach thee: and the fowls of the air, and they shall tell thee: / Or speak to the earth, and it shall teach thee: and the fishes of the sea shall declare unto thee. / Who knoweth not in all these that the hand of the LORD hath wrought this? / In whose hand is the soul of every living thing, and the breath of all mankind. / Doth not the ear try words? and the mouth taste his meat?" "With him is strength and wisdom: the deceived and the deceiver are his."

5 The reference is to "the enlightened Berlin High Consistory which retained its liberal policies even under [the reactionary] King Friedrich Wilhelm II." AK 8:500. Cf. Wilhelm Dilthey, "Drittes Stück der Beiträge aus den Rostocker Kanthandschriften," *Archiv für Geschichte der Philosophie*, 3(1890) 418–50, reprinted as "Kant's Dispute with the Censors over the Right of Free Research in Religion," in *Wilhelm Dilthey: Gesammelte Schriften*, Vol. IV (Stuttgart and Göttingen: Teubner, Vandenhoech & Ruprecht, 2nd ed., 1959), pp. 285–309, cf. p. 288.

6 "God forbid that I should justify you: till I die I will not remove mine integrity from me. / My righteousness I hold fast, and will not let it go: my heart shall not reproach me so long as I live."

7 For Kant's claim that it is not legitimate to irrevocably bind oneself under oath to uphold a historical creed, since future progress in enlightenment might cast doubt on the reliability of the creed, see *Beantwortung der Frage: Was ist Aufklärung? (Answer to the Question: What Is Enlightenment?* 1784, AK 8:38–39).

8 Jean-André de Luc (1727–1817; Swiss scientist and moralist), *Lettres physiques et morales sur les Montagnes, et sur l'Histoire de la terre et de l'Homme* (La Haye, 1778–80, 6 vols).

9 Mountain range in Germany.

Religion within the boundaries of mere reason

1 Kant is reacting to H. A. Pistorius's review of his *Groundwork of a Metaphysics of Morals* (1785), in *Allgemeine Deutsche Bibliothek*, 66.2(1786): 447–63.

2 In what follows Kant is very likely reacting to August Wilhelm Rehberg's criticism of his moral theory – specifically to Rehberg's rejection of his claim that the law can be itself an effective principle of action, and to Rehberg's denial that the feeling of respect for the law can be more than just an empirical quantity. Rehberg developed his criticism in *Über das Verhältniß der Metaphysik zur Religion* (Berlin: Mylius, 1787; *Concerning the Relationship of Metaphysics to Religion*), and in his review of Kant's *Critique of Practical Reason*, in *Allgemeine Literatur-Zeitung*, Nr 188.a.b. (August 6, 1788): 345–60. Kant had already reacted to Rehberg in at least another place, namely the *Critique of Judgment*, AK 5:177, footnote.

3 Roman law, as distinguished from the common law of the Anglo-Saxon tradition, is the basis of the legal system in much of Europe. Roman civil law (*corpus juris civilis*), which governs the relations between citizens, was codified and published by the Emperor Justinian in A.D. 528–534.

4   The *Berlinische Monatsschrift* was an influential Berlin journal published un-
    der various titles from 1783 to 1811 under the editorship of Johann Erich
    Biester (1749–1816), who was at some time Frederick II's librarian. Frie-
    drich Gedike (1754–1803) was also its editor up to January 1792.

5   Johann David Michaelis (1717–91), orientalist, biblical scholar, and profes-
    sor of philosophy in Göttingen; the work *Moral* (in its German title) was
    posthumously edited and published by F. Stäudlin in 1792.

6   Gottlieb Christian Storr (1746–1805), dogmatic theologian, Tübingen pro-
    fessor of theology, and author of *Annotationes ad philosophicam Kantii de
    religione doctrinam*, (1793; *Observations Concerning Kant's Philosophical Doctrine
    of Religion*), in response to Kant. The book was translated into German by
    Storr's follower Johann Friedrich Flatt (1759–1821), as *D. Gottlob Christian
    Storr's Bemerkungen über Kant's philosophische Religionslehre. Aus dem Lateini-
    schem. Nebst einigen Bemerkungen des Übersetzers über den aus Prinzipien der
    praktischen Vernunft hergeleiteten Überzeugungsgrund von der Möglichkeit und
    Wirklichkeit einer Offenbarung in Beziehung auf Fichtes Versuch einer Kritik der
    Offenbarung* (Tübingen: Cotta, 1794).

7   *Neueste Kritische Nachrichten*, (1793) 225–9. This annual journal was pub-
    lished and edited from 1779–1807 by J. G. P. Möller (1729–1807), profes-
    sor of rhetoric and history at the University of Greifswald since 1765.

8   John 5:19: "*And* we know that we are of God, and the whole world lieth in
    wickedness."

9   According to Bohatec, Kant drew his information from Johann Ith,
    *Übersetzung und Kommentar über den Ezour-Vedam, oder die Geschichte, Religion
    und Philosophie der Indier* (*Translation and Commentary of the Ezour-Vedam, or
    the History, Religion and Philosophy of the Indians;* Bern, no date) pp. 10 ff., and
    from Pierre Sonnerat (French natural scientist and explorer, 1749–1814),
    Reise nach Ostindien und China auf Befehl des Königs unternommen (*Voyage to
    East-India and China, Undertaken at the King's Request;* 2 vols; Zürich, 1783),
    1, pp. 166, 249, both of which he had read. Cf. Bohatec, pp. 166–7, and AK
    8:505. The whole imagery of this passage, however, is drawn from the Chris-
    tian apocalyptic writers, notably Bengel, with whose work, *Ordo temporum*
    (*The Order of Time;* Tübingen, 1741), Kant was acquainted. Cf. *The Conflict of
    the Faculties*, AK 7:62, 80–81. J. A. Bengel (1687–1752) was a mystical
    theologian who predicted the end of the world for 1836.

10 Elsewhere, Kant speaks of a "heroic faith in virtue," AK 8:332.

11 Cf. J.-J. Rousseau (1712–1778), *Discours sur l'origine et les fondemens de
    l'inégalité* (*Discourses on the Origin and Grounds of Inequality*, 1755; German
    tr., 1756): "Men are evil. Grim and constant experience dispenses us from
    the effort of providing a proof of this. I have however proven, as I believe,
    that man is by nature good." Part I, Note IX (second paragraph).

12 The denominations "latitudinarian" and "indifferentist" come from J. F.
    Stapfter, *Institutiones theologiæ polemicæ universæ ordine scientifico dispositæ*, 5
    vols. (Zürich, 1743–47), 84 and 599 (cited after Bohatec, p. 176, footnote).
    Baumgarten refers to an *ethica rigida* as contrasted to a "lax one," in *Ethica
    philosophica* (eds. 1740, 1751, 1763), stating that "the more severe an ethics,
    the more perfect" (§ 4). Cf. also *Eine Vorlesung Kants über Ethik*, ed. Paul
    Menzer (Berlin: Heinse, 1924), p. 93; English trans. Infield/Macmurray,

Lectures on Ethics: "The man who conceives the moral law in such a [lax] way that it allows his feeble conduct to pass muster, who fashions lenient precepts for himself, we call a *latitudinarius*" (London: Methuen, 1930), p. 75. Many of Kant's theological notions and terms derive from the cited work of Stapfter, and from his *Grundlegung zur wahren christlichen Religion (Groundwork of the True Christian Religion)*, 12 Parts (Zürich, 1746–53).

13 Cf. *Metaphysics of Morals*, AK 6:384; also, *Reflexion* 7234, AK 19:291.

14 J. C. F. Schiller (1759–1805), *Über Anmut und Würde in der Moral.*

15 This was a basic principle of rigorist ethics. Kant could have found it stated in Heilmann's *Dogmatics*, a book which (according to Bohatec) he possessed and had certainly read. (Bohatec, p. 177, and footnotes.) J. D. Heilmann, *Compendium theologiæ dogmaticæ* (Göttingen, 1761), § 196.

16 "Only through this independent power of a self-determining will alone – a power which indeed cannot suppress the impulse of needs but can steer them according to its law and through its capacity – can we and must we, as rational beings which should not be looked at or used as *things*, think of ourselves as *persons*." Anonymous (but in fact, C. L. Reinhold), "Über die Grundwahrheit der Moralität und ihr Verhältnis zur Grundwahrheit der Religion" ("Concerning the Fundamental Truth of Morality and its Relation to the Fundamental Truth of Religion"), *Der neue Teutsche Merkur*, 2.3(1791): 225–80, 231. Reinhold further developed his distinction between "practical reason," as the law-giving faculty, and "will" understood as power of choice and as faculty of personality in volume two of his *Kantian Letters*, Nos. 7, 8, 9, 10: *Briefe über die Kantische Philosophie*, 2 vols. (Leipzig: Göschen, 1790 and 1792).

17 Cf. AK 8:19.

18 Cf. J.-J. Rousseau: "We have love *for oneself*, which is only concerned with ourselves, when our true needs are satisfied; self-love, however, which is an object of *comparison*, is never satisfied – nor can it be, because this sentiment, *in preferring ourselves to others*, also requires that others prefer us to themselves." *Émile ou de l'éducation*, (1762) Part 4, ed. John S. Spink, *Œuvres complètes* (Paris: Gallimard, 1969), Vol. 4, p. 493.

19 Romans 7:15: "For that which I do I allow not: for what I would, that I do not; but what I hate, that do I."

20 Romans 14:23: "And he that doubteth is damned if he eat, because *he eateth* not of faith: for whatsoever *is* not of faith is sin."

21 Sonnerat, *Reise nach Ostindien und China*, describes the customs of these places. Cf. AK 6:505.

22 Samuel Hearne (1745–1792), an English traveler at the service of the Hudson Bay Company. A brief account of Hearne's travels was to be found in Douglas's Introduction to *Cook's Third Voyage*, London, 1784. Cf. Wobbermin, AK 6:501. Perhaps Kant was familiar with Georg Förster, *Geschichte der Reisen die seit Cook an der Nordwest- und Nordöstküste von Amerika und in dem nördlichsten Amerika unternommen worden. ... (History of the Voyages Undertaken since Cook [...] in the Northwest and Northeast Coast of America and in Northmost America;* 3 vols; Berlin, 1792).

23 La Rochefoucauld, *Maximes* (1678), No. 583: "Dans l'adversité de nos

meilleurs amis, nous trouvons toujours quelque chose qui ne nous déplaît pas."

24 There is very likely a reference here to La Rochefoucauld. Cf. *Maximes* (1678), No. 207, "La folie nous suit dans tous les temps de la vie. Si quelqu'un paraît sage, c'est seulement parce que ses folies sont proportionnées à son âge et à sa fortune." ("Folly follows us throughout every stage of life. If someone appears wise, that's only because his follies are proportionate to his age and fortune.")

25 Kant repeats the same idea in *Toward Perpetual Peace* (*Zum ewigen Frieden*, 1795), where he attributes it to an ancient Greek; cf. AK 8:365. However, the identity of the author has not been established. Wobbermin, AK 6:502.

26 The saying is attributed to Sir Robert Walpole, referring to "certain patriots" and not to human beings in general: "All those men have their price."

27 Romans 3:9–10: "What then? are we better *than they*? No, in no wise: for we have before proved both Jews and Gentiles, that they are all under sin; As it is written, There is none righteous, no, not one."

28 "And the Lord God commanded the man, saying, Of every tree of the garden thou mayest freely eat: But of the tree of the knowledge of good and evil, thou shalt not eat of it: for on the day that thou eatest thereof thou shalt surely die."

29 "And when the woman saw that the tree was good for food, and that it was pleasant to the eyes, and a tree to be desired to make one wise, she took of the fruit thereof, and did eat, and gave also unto her husband with her; and he did eat."

30 Cf. Revelation 12:9: "Satan, which deceiveth the whole world . . ."

31 Romans 5:12: "Wherefore, as by one man sin entered into the world, and death by sin; and so death passed upon all men, for that all have sinned." That "in Adam we all sinned" is the Augustinian interpretation of this verse based on the Vulgate (Latin) translation. This interpretation was also common in the early Lutheran churches. Cf. Wobbermin, AK 6:502.

32 "How art thou fallen from heaven, O Lucifer, son of the morning! how art thou cut down to the ground, which didst weaken the nations!" Isaiah 14:12. Cf. Luke 10:18; Revelation 8:10. The church Fathers interpreted this fall of the morning star (*Luciferus*, in the Latin of the Vulgate) as the fall through sin of the prince of the angels.

33 Cf. Genesis 3:3–5, where the serpent tempts the woman to eat the fruit from the tree of knowledge of good and evil.

34 Cf. Martin Luther: "From the inception of sanctity up to its perfection there are infinite degrees." "Dictata super Psalterium: Psalmus LXXIV [LXXV]" *Kritische Gesammtausgabe* (Weimar, 1883–), Vol. 3, p. 512.

35 Colossians 3:9–10: "Lie not to one another, seeing that ye have put off the old man with his deeds; and have put on the new man, which is renewed in knowledge after the image of him that created him"; also Ephesians 4:22, 24.

36 "Verily, verily, I say unto thee, Except a man be born of water and of the Spirit, he cannot enter into the kingdom of God."

37 "And the earth was without form and void; and darkness was upon the face of the deep. And the spirit of God moved upon the face of the waters."

38 Colossians 3:9–10.

39 Cf. verse 15: "And it came to pass, that when [the nobleman] was returned, having received the kingdom, then he commanded these servants to be called unto him, to whom he had given the money, that he might know how much every man had gained by trading."

40 "Virtue (*virtus*) is named after man (*vir*); fortitude, however, pertains most to a man." Cicero, *Tusculanæ Disputationes*, II:18.43. *aner* ['ανήρ] in Greek means "man"; *andreios* ['ανδρείος] means both "male" and "valiant."

41 "They [the Stoics] say that the fountain-head of all disorders is intemperance, which is a desertion from all guide of the mind and right reason, so adverse to the precepts of reason that the cravings of the soul can in no way be reined or contained." Cicero, *Tusculanæ Disputationes*, 6:9.22.

42 Kant had been accused of not having been altogether fair to the Stoics in his *Critique of Practical Reason*. Cf. A. W. Rehberg's review of this work in *Allgemeine Literatur-Zeitung*, August 6, 1788, 188a and 188b, column 358 (last paragraph).

43 The saying *virtutes gentium, splendida vitia* (the virtues of the nations are splendid vices) has been traditionally attributed to Augustine and is consistent with the general tendency of his thought, even though it has never been found in any of his extant writings. Cf. Wobbermin, AK 6:502.

44 Cf. *Critique of Practical Reason*, AK 5:127, footnote.

45 Cf. Ephesians 6:12: "For we wrestle not against flesh and blood, but against principalities, against powers, against the rulers of the darkness of this world, against spiritual wickedness in high places."

46 Cf. A. G. Baumgarten (1714–1762), *Metaphysica*, 7th ed. (Halle, 1779), § 946: "God's end in creating the world was the perfection of creatures, so far as it is possible in the best world." However, Baumgarten's conclusion is that "therefore the ends of creation are the cult of God and religion," § 947. God's ultimate end in creating the universe was "his own glory," § 943.

47 John 1:1–2: "In the beginning was the Word, and the Word was with God, and the Word was God. The same was in the beginning with God."

48 John 1:3: "All things were made by him; and without him was not any thing made that was made."

49 Hebrews 1:3: "Who being the brightness of *his* glory, and the express image of his person, and upholding all things by the word of his power."

50 John 3:14: "For God so loved the world, that he gave his only begotten Son, that whosoever believeth in him should not perish, but have everlasting life." Cf. also I John 4:9–10: "In this was manifested the love of God toward us, because that God sent his only begotten Son into the world, so that we might live through him."

51 John 1:12: "But as many as received him, to them gave he power to become the sons of God, even to them that believe on his name."

52 Cf. Philippians 2:8.

53 Albrecht Haller (1708–1777), in his poem "Über den Ursprung des Übels" ("Concerning the Origin of Evil," 1734), 2:33–34. Kant alludes to the same line in his *Lectures on the Philosophical Doctrine of Religion*, 28:1077.

54 John 3:16: "For God so loved the world that he gave his only begotten Son, that whosoever believeth in him should not perish, but have everlasting life."

55 John 8:46: "Which of you convinceth me of sin? And if I say the truth, why do ye not believe me?"

56 Matthew 5:48: "Be ye therefore perfect, even as your Father which is in Heaven is perfect." Cf. Leviticus 11:44 and I Peter 1:16.

57 Matthew 6:33: "But seek ye first the kingdom of God, and his righteousness; and all these things shall be added unto you."

58 Romans 8:16: "The Spirit itself beareth witness with our spirit, that we are the children of God."

59 Philippians 2:12: "Wherefore, my beloved, as ye have always obeyed, not as in my presence only, but now much more in my absence, work out your own salvation with fear and trembling."

60 Francis Moore, *A New Collection of Voyages and Travels*, 1745; translated into German by G. J. Schwabe as *Allgemeine Historie der Reisen (A General History of Voyages)*, 3 vols. (1748). Cf. Wobbermin, AK 6:503.

61 Cf. Colossians 3:9–10.

62 Genesis 3:15–19.

63 Nicolas Malebranche (1638–1715), *De la recherche de la vérité* (*Concerning the Search of Truth*, 1674–75), Bk. IV, ch. 11.

64 Cf. Colossians 3:9–10.

65 Romans 6:6: "Knowing this, that our old man is crucified with *him*, that the body of sin might be destroyed, that henceforth we should not serve sin."

66 Galatians 5:24: "And they that are Christ's have crucified the flesh with the affections and lusts."

67 Romans 8:1: "There is therefore now no condemnation to them which are in Christ Jesus, who walk not after the flesh, but after the Spirit."

68 Matthew 5:25.

69 "And God blessed them, and said unto them, Be fruitful, and multiply, and replenish the earth, and subdue it: and have dominion over the fish of the sea, and over the fowl of the air, and over every living thing that moveth upon the earth."

70 Pierre-François Xavier de Charlevoix (1682–1761) wrote an account of his experiences as a Jesuit missionary in Canada entitled *Histoire et déscription générale de la Nouvelle-France (General History and Description of New France)*. Paris, 1744. Wobbermin, AK 6:503.

71 John 14:30: "... for the prince of the world cometh, and hath nothing in me."

72 Cf. Luke 4:5–7: "And the devil, taking him up into an high mountain, shewed him all the kingdoms of the world in a moment of time. And the devil said unto him, All this power will I give thee, and the glory of them: for that is delivered unto me: and to whomsoever I will give it. If thou therefore wilt worship me, all shall be thine."

73 Karl Friedrich Bahrdt (1741–92), a popular rationalist and voluminous writer. *System der moralischen Religion zur endlichen Beruhigung für Zweifler und Denker. Allen Christen und Nichtchristen lesbar.* (*System of Moral Religion for the Ultimate Pacification of Doubters and Thinkers. Readable by All Christians and Non-Christians*, Berlin, 1787; 3rd ed., 1791), cf. chapters 9 and 10. Cf. Wobbermin, AK 6:503.

74 The "fragmentarist" is the deist Hermann Samuel Reimarus (1694–1768),

sometime professor of oriental languages at Hamburg and popular author. Reimarus was the author of a stinging attack on the reliability of the biblical narratives conducted along the customary lines of rationalistic interpretation. The attack was so radical in tone that Reimarus himself had kept it secret during his lifetime. Fragments of it, however, were posthumously published by Lessing, without attribution, as part of his program of making public materials discovered at the Wolfenbüttel library, where he was then librarian. Lessing prefaced each fragment with a rebuttal of its attack on the reasonableness of Christian beliefs. These fragments (seven in number, 1774–8) eventually forced Lessing into a bitter dispute with the orthodox pastor Goeze. The "Fragment" at issue here is the seventh in the series.

75 Luke 22:19.

76 Cf. John 1:11–12.

77 Titus 2:14: ". . . that he might redeem us from all iniquity and purify unto himself a people for his own possession, zealous of good works."

78 Matthew 16:18: ". . . thou art Peter, and upon this rock I will build my church; and the gates of hell shall not prevail against it."

79 Mark 9:39–40: "But Jesus said, Forbid him not: for there is no man which shall do a miracle in my name, that can lightly speak evil of me. For he that is not against us is on our part."

80 John 4:48.

81 Johann Konrad Pfenniger (1747–92), pastor at Zürich; cf. his work, *Appellation an den Menschenverstand, gewisse Vorfälle, Schriften und Personen betreffend, (An Appeal to Common Sense, With Reference to Certain Events, Writings, and Persons;* Hamburg, 1776), especially No. 8. Wobbermin, AK 6:504.

82 Johann Kaspar Lavater (1741–1801), Swiss poet, physiognomist, and pietist theologian. He preached a religion of feeling and inner inspiration which brought God to the level of man. He advocated a literal reading of the Bible and was a great believer in the power of prayer, and in the possibility of miracles. He is notorious for his challenge to Moses Mendelssohn to convert to Chrisitanity. Lavater fitted Kant's image of the "enthusiast" perfectly. For Kant's correspondence with Lavater, see the Translator's Introduction above, pp. 49–50.

83 Cf. Genesis 22.

84 *Der höllische Proteus oder tausend-künstige Versteller (nebenst vorberichtlichen Grundbeweis der Gewissheit, daß es wirklich Gespester gebe),* abgebildet durch Erasmum Francisci, Nürnberg, 1708: *The Hellish Protheus, or the Deceiver of a Thousand Arts (Together with a preliminary justification of the certainty that ghosts truly exist),* depicted by Francis Erasmus. AK 6:504.

85 Romans 6:18: "Being then made free from sin, ye became the servants of righteousness."

86 Cf. Thomas Hobbes (1588–1679), *De cive* (1642) 1:12. Hobbes's full text reads: "Negari non potest, quin status hominum naturalis antequam in societatem coiretur, bellum fuerit; neque hoc simpliciter, sed bellum omnium in omnes." ("It cannot be denied that the natural state of men before they come together in society is war – not war in an ordinary sense but a war of all against all.")

87 *De cive,* 1:12.

88 Acts 5:29.

89 Acts 1:24: "Thou, Lord, which knowest the hearts of all men . . ."; Acts 15:8: "And God, which knoweth the hearts . . ."; Luke 16:5: ". . . but God knoweth your hearts."

90 I Peter 2:10: "Which in time past *were* not a people, but *are* now a people of God."

91 Titus 2:14: ". . . that he [Jesus Christ] might redeem us from all iniquity, and purify unto himself a peculiar people, zealous of good works."

92 Cf. "Idea for a Universal History," Prop. 6; AK 8:23.

93 Matthew 6:10: "Thy kingdom come. Thy will be done in earth, as it is in heaven." Luke 11:2: "Thy kingdom come. Thy will be done, as in heaven, so in earth."

94 Here Kant gives an interpretation of the traditional attributes of the Church: one, holy, catholic, apostolic. Cf. AK 6:504.

95 Matthew 7:21: "Not every one that saith unto me, Lord, Lord, shall enter into the kingdom of heaven; but he that doeth the will of my Father which is in heaven."

96 *Alphabetum Tibetanum missionum apostolicarum commodo editum . . .* , studio et labore Fr. Augustini Antonii Georgii emeritae Augustinui (Romae, 1762). Cf. AK 6:504.

97 According to Wobbermin, this etymological explanation is certainly erroneous. *Ketzer* is more likely to derive from *Kathari*, i.e., the "Catharans" or "pure ones," the most significant heretical sect in Medieval Europe in the twelfth and thirteenth century. The presence in the movement of an ancient manichean element is unmistakable. AK 6:504.

98 Here Kant is dealing with a problem to which Lessing had given the classical formulation: "Accidental truths of history can never become a proof of necessary truths of reason"; and again, "But to jump over from that historical truth [of the gospel] into a totally different class of truths; and to demand that I should construct all my metaphysical and moral concepts accordingly. . . . That, that is the broad and terrible ditch that I cannot overcome, however often and earnestly I have tried to make the jump." *"On The Proof of the Spirit and the Power" (Über den Beweis des Geistes und der Kraft, 1777), Gotthold Ephraim Lessing: Sämmtliche Werke,* ed. K. Lachmann and F. Muncker (Stuttgart/Leipzig/Berlin: Göschen, 1886–1924), Vol. 13, pp. 5, 7.

99 Cf. verse 13: "Consume them in wrath, consume them, that they may not be: and let them know that God ruleth in Jacob unto the ends of the earth."

100 Cf. Preface to the Second Edition, pp. 64–65 above, and the reference there.

101 Matthew 5:21ff., 44ff.

102 Romans 12:19; cf. Deuteronomy 32:35: "To me belongeth vengeance, and recompense."

103 Adrian Reland (1676–1718), a Dutch Orientalist, wrote *De religione mohammedica libri duo,* 2nd ed. (Trajecti ad Rhenum: 1717). Cf. II, Paragraph xvii. AK 6:504.

104 Hindu, or orthodox, sacred scriptural texts. They originated in the north of India around 1500 B.C.

105 Kant is very likely relying on Ith, *Übersetzung und Kommentar über den Ezour-*

Vedam, oder die Geschichte, Religion und Philosophie der Indier (Translation and Commentary of the Ezour-Veda, or the History, Religion, and Philosophy of the Hindus): "*Shasta* truly means science or cognition, *explanation*, clarification. According to this derivation, the *Shastri* cannot be anything but explanations, clarifications, of the Veda. We believe we can say that the intention of their authors was to present the Hindu religion from a rational perspective, to convince that its fables were all philosophical allegories."; pp. 87 ff. Cited after Bohatec, p. 431.

106 James 2:17: "Even so faith, if it hath not works, is dead, being alone."

107 II Timothy 3:16: "All scripture is given by inspiration of God, and is profitable for doctrine, for reproof, for correction, for instruction in righteousness."

108 John 16:13: "Howbeit when he, the Spirit of truth, is come, he will guide you into all truth."

109 John 5:39: "Search the scriptures; for in them ye think ye have eternal life: and they are they which testify of me."

110 Cf. *Die Metaphysik der Sitten (The Metaphysics of Morals)*, AK 6:327.

111 John 7:17: "If any man will do his will, he shall know of the doctrine, whether it be of God. . ."

112 *fides mercenaria, servilis, ingenua:* apparently these are terms coined by Kant. Cf. Bohatec, p. 440, note.

113 Cf. G. Achenwall, *Prolegomena iuris naturalis*, 5th ed. (Göttingen: 1781), § 85. Cited after Bohatec, p. 442, note.

114 Colossians 3:9–10.

115 Colossians 3:9–10; Ephesians 4:22,24.

116 Romans 9:18: "Therefore hath he mercy on whom he will have mercy, and whom he will he hardeneth."

117 *Salto mortale*, i.e. an upward leap accompanied by a rotation of the body that brings the head below the feet. Jacobi had recommended such a leap to Lessing, in order to gain the freedom of faith and thereby escape the determinism which – as Jacobi thought – is the inevitable consequence of a philosophy based on reason alone. In direct opposition to Jacobi, Kant here claims that faith (not reason) leads to a deterministic view of human destiny. Cf. F. H. Jacobi, *Concerning the Doctrine of Spinoza in Letters to Herr Moses Mendelssohn (Über die Lehre des Spinoza in Briefen an. Herrn Moses Mendelssohn;* Breslau: Löwe, 1785), pp. 32–3.

118 I Corinthians 15:28: "And when all things shall be subdued unto him, then shall the Son also himself be subject unto him that put all things under him, that God may be all in all."

119 Cf. I Corinthians 13:11: "When I was a child, I spake as a child, I understood as a child, I thought as a child: but when I became a man, I put away childish things."

120 I Corinthians 13:11.

121 Matthew 12:28: "But if I cast out devils by the Spirit of God, then the kingdom of God is come unto you."

122 Cf. Jewish religion is "a public national religion, which was always implicated with *civil society*, and always had a political purpose." J. S. Semler (died 1791; the major exponent of Enlightenment theology), *Letztes Glaubensbekenntnis*

über natürlicher und christlicher Religion, (A Recent Profession of Faith Regarding Natural and Christian Religion; Königsberg, 1792), p. 10. Cited after Bohatec, p. 461.

123 Cf. Semler, *Letztes Glaubensbekenntnis über natürliche und christliche Religion,* pp. 116, 126, where Semler sharply divides Christianity from Judaism. (Cited after Bohatec, p. 460.) Semler's book was a reply to one of Dr. Bahrdt's many books (cf. above, Part II, Kant's note on p. 96).

124 Cf. Matthew 5:48: "Be ye therefore perfect, even as your Father which is in heaven is perfect"; I Peter 1:16: "Because it is written, Be ye holy; for I am holy."

125 Cf. Matthew 28:20: "Teaching them to observe all things whatsoever I have commanded you: and, lo, I am with you always, even unto the end of the world."

126 The Sibylline books were a body of prophetic literature accumulated, according to tradition, by female seers (the first of whom, Sibyl, gave her name to her descendants) under the influence of a deity, usually Apollo. These books in Greek hexameter, which disappeared in A.D. 83, exerted a strong influence on Roman religion.

127 Revelation 12:9: "And the great dragon was cast out, that old serpent, called the Devil, and Satan, which deceiveth the whole world: he was cast out into the earth, and his angels were cast out with him."

128 Matthew 5:12. Greene and Hudson note that Kant uses *vergolten* (repaid) as opposed to the *belohnet* (rewarded) in Luther's Bible. Greene/Hudson, p. 125, note.

129 Cf. I Corinthians 15:26: "The last enemy that shall be destroyed is death."

130 I Corinthians 15:28. Cf. above, p. 151, note 118.

131 Cf. Matthew 26:64: "Jesus saith unto him. . . . Hereafter shall ye see the Son of man sitting on the right hand of power, and coming in the clouds of heaven."

132 Kant apparently derived his information on Zoroaster from Sonnerat, *Reise,* to which he explicitly refers in *The End of All Things,* AK 8:328–9, footnote.

133 Cf. above, Part I, editorial note 9, p. 208.

134 Ith, *Übersetzung und Kommentar,* Introduction, pp. 6 ff., 58, 88. Bohatec, p. 167, note 10.

135 Cf. Matthew 26:61–5.

136 Mark 3:28: "Verily I say unto you, All sins shall be forgiven unto the sons of men, and blasphemies wherewith soever they shall blaspheme"; also Ephesians 3:5.

137 I John 4:8: "He that loveth not knoweth not God; for God is love"; I John 4:16: "And we have known and believed the love that God hath to us. God is love; and he that dwelleth in love dwelleth in God, and God in him."

138 This is the Western (Augustinian) formula of the dogma of the Trinity. Cf. Wobbermin, AK 6:505. Cf. John 15:26: "But when the Comforter is come, whom I will send unto you from the Father, even the Spirit of truth, which proceedeth from the Father, he shall testify of me."

139 John 16:13: "Howbeit when he, the Spirit of truth, is come, he will guide you into all truth."

140 II Timothy 4:1: "I charge thee therefore before God, and the Lord Jesus Christ, who shall judge the quick and the dead at his appearing and his kingdom."

141 John 16:8: "And when he is come, he will reprove the world of sin, and of righteousness, and of judgment."

142 On Kant's interpretation of the Trinity, cf. *Reflexionen* 6092, 6093, AK 18:448–9.

143 "In those days came John the Baptist, preaching in the wilderness of Judæa, And saying, Repent ye: for the kingdom of heaven is at hand." Matthew 3:1–2.

144 "But I say unto you, That whoever looketh on a woman to lust after her hath committed adultery with her already in his heart."

145 "Be ye therefore perfect, even as your Father which is in heaven is perfect."

146 "But I say unto you, That whoever is angry with his brother without a cause shall be in danger of the judgement: and whosoever shall say to his brother, Raca, shall be in danger of the council: but whosoever shall say, Thou fool, shall be in danger of hell fire."

147 "Leave there thy gift before the altar, and go thy way: first be reconciled to thy brother, and then come and offer thy gift."

148 "But I say unto you, Swear not at all. . . . But let your communication be, Yea, yea; Nay, nay: for whatsoever is more than these cometh of evil."

149 "But I say unto you, That ye resist not evil; but whosoever shall smite thee on the right cheek, turn to him the other also. And if any man will sue thee at the law, and take away thy coat, let him have thy cloak also."

150 "But I say unto you, Love your enemies, bless them that curse you, do good to them that hate you, and pray for them that despitefully use you, and persecute you."

151 "Think not that I have come to destroy the law, or the prophets . . ."

152 "Enter ye in at the strait gate: for wide is the gate, and broad is the way, that leads to destruction, and many there be that go in thereat."

153 Cf.: "Strive to enter in at the narrow gate; for many, I say unto you, will seek to enter in, and shall not be able." Luke 13:24.

154 "Ye shall know them by their fruits. Do men gather grapes of thorns, or figs of thistles?"

155 "Not everyone that saith unto me, Lord, Lord, shall enter into the kingdom of heaven; but he that doeth the will of my Father which is in heaven."

156 "Let your light so shine before men, that they may see your good works, and glorify your Father which is in heaven."

157 "Moreover when ye fast, be not, as the hypocrites, of a sad countenance: for they disfigure their faces, that they may appear unto men to fast. Verily I say unto you. They have their reward."

158 "The kingdom of heaven is like a grain of mustard seed, which a man took, and sowed in his field: Which indeed is the least of all seeds: but when it is grown, it is the greatest of all herbs, and becometh a tree, so that the birds of the air come and lodge in the branches thereof. . . . The kingdom of heaven is like unto leaven, which a woman took, and hid in three measures of meal, till the whole was leavened."

159 "For unto every one that hath shall be given, and shall have abundance: but from him that hath not shall be taken away even that which he hath."

160 "Blessed are ye, when men shall revile you, and persecute you, and shall say all manner of evil against you falsely, for my sake. Rejoice, and be exceeding glad: for great is your reward in heaven."

161 "Then the steward said within himself . . . I am resolved what to do, that, when I am put out of the stewardship, they may receive me into their houses. So he called every one of his lord's debtors unto him, and said unto the first, How much owest thou my lord? And he said, a hundred measures of oil. And he said unto him, Take thy bill, and sit down quickly, and write fifty. . . . And the lord commended the unjust steward, because he had done wisely: for the children of this world are in their generation wiser than the children of light."

162 "For I was hungered, and ye gave me meat: I was thirsty, and ye gave me drink: I was a stranger, and ye took me in. . . . Then shall the righteous answer him, saying: Lord, when saw we hungered, and fed thee? or thirsty, and gave thee drink? When saw we thee a stranger, and took thee in? . . . And the King shall answer and say unto them, Verily I say unto you, Inasmuch as ye have done it unto one of the least of these my brethren, ye have done it unto me."

163 Cf. Ephesians 2:15–21.

164 The source of this citation is unknown.

165 Moses Mendelssohn (1729–86), renowned Enlightenment philosopher and a close friend of G. E. Lessing. With Lessing and C. F. Nicolai he contributed to *Briefe, die neueste Literatur betreffend (Letters Concerning the Most Recent Literature)*, one of the most important catalysts in the formation of the German Enlightenment. In 1763 his essay, *Abhandlung über die Evidenz in den metaphysischen Wissenschaften (Essay on Evidence in the Metaphysical Sciences)*, won first prize from the Berlin Academy. Kant's submission in the same competition, *Untersuchung über die Deutlichkeit der Grundsätze der natürlichen Theologie und der Moral (Inquiry Concerning the Clarity of the Principles of Natural Theology and Morality*, AK 2:273 ff.), was only awarded an honorable mention. In *Phädon oder über die Unsterblichkeit der Seele*, 1767 *("Phaedo," or on the Immortality of the Soul)*, Mendelssohn set out his argument for the immortality of the soul which Kant sought to refute in the second edition of the *Critique of Pure Reason* (B 395 ff.). In *Morgenstunden, oder Vorlesungen über das Dasein Gottes*, 1785 *(Morning Hours, or Lectures on the Existence of God)*, Mendelssohn elaborated once more the Cartesian argument for the existence of God and the argument from design. From 1783 until his death in 1786 he became involved in a correspondence with F. H. Jacobi on the question whether Lessing (who had died in 1781) had been a Spinozist. The correspondence eventually deteriorated into an open and bitter dispute in which reason itself, and its relation to faith, became the central issue. Kant's 1786 essay, *Was heißt: Sich im Denken orientiren? (What Does it Mean to Orient Oneself in Thinking?* pp. 1–14 above), is his contribution to the dispute.

The reference in the present note is to Mendelssohn's 1783 political treatise *Jerusalem oder über religiöse Macht und Judentum (Jerusalem, or on Religious Power and Judaism*, cf. *Gesammelte Schriften, Jubiläumausgabe*, Vol. 8 [Stuttgart-Bad Cannstatt: Fromann, 1983], p. 145). A similar comment by Kant concerning Mendelssohn can be found in *Der Streit der Fakultäten*, 1798 (*The Conflict of the Faculties*, AK 7:52, note). Section III of Kant's *Über den Gemeinspruch: Das mag in der Theorie richtig sein, taugt aber nicht in die Praxis*, 1793 (*On the Common Saying: That may be Correct in Theory, but it is no Use in Practice*, AK 8:307 ff.) is dedicated to a criticism of one of the theses defended by Mendelssohn against Lessing in the treatise *Jerusalem*.

166 Cf. *What Does it Mean to Orient Oneself in Thinking?* AK 8:142.

167 Kant is very likely referring here to August Willhelm Rehberg (political man in Hanover and writer, 1757–1836) who reviewed Kant's *Critique of Practical Reason* in the *Allgemeine Literatur-Zeitung*, August 6–7, 1788, Nos. 188a–188b, columns 345–60. Rehberg accused Kant of falling victim to the same amphiboly of reason of which he had accused the Leibnizians in his first *Critique* (columns 353–4). Specifically, Rehberg argued that pure Critique reason can indeed be the formal principle for morality but not the efficient cause of the actions that occur in the sensible world in accordance with it; hence some other motive must be sought for such actions than the law itself as formally stipulated by pure reason. Kant had tried to give evidence for the efficacy of pure reason in the sensible world by pointing to the feeling of respect for the law which he assumed every moral subject to have, and which he took to be the fundamental temporal determination of that subject attributable to the law itself. Rehberg argued that, on the contrary, that feeling could not be an effect of pure reason without the latter being thereby subjected to the conditions of space and time. To the extent that this supposed "respect" is a genuine feeling, it must be sensible and hence not the product of reason, i.e. either it is not a feeling at all or it must be a case of self-love (354). Just as the concept of creation can meaningfully apply only to a causal relation holding between two beings, one infinite and the other finite yet both equally noumenal, so too any moral efficacy of pure reason would have to be conceived as devolving into an effect just as noumenal as its cause. The concept of a sensible event brought about by pure reason would on the contrary entail just as much of an illicit transition from one level of categorization to another as the concept of a created appearance (356–7). Rehberg also accused Kant of courting enthusiasm. "The thought," he argued, "that the law itself must be the incentive of morality is itself enthusiasm *(Schwärmerei)*. For what else can it possibly be but enthusiasm (which consists in the fabrication of supersensible objects) if respect for the law is to be a feeling yet not a sensible feeling *(sinnliche Empfindung)*? And this enthusiasm immediately leads to another kind of enthusiasm, the worst of them all – the deadening of the senses" (355). The fundamental problem bedeviling Kant's position according to Rehberg is that whatever self-consciousness we can have of the law as effective in the sensible world would have to be empirical, hence not fit to detect a moral object. To claim any other self-consciousness would be to project into a supersensible world a consciousness which in fact can only be sensible. For Rehberg's review, cf. Christian Gottfried Schütz's letter to Kant of June 23,

1788 (Schütz, professor of rhetoric at Jena, was the founder of the *Jena Literaturzeitung*).

Also intended might be Johann August Heinrich Ulrich (1744–1807; professor of philosophy at Jena), whose book *Eleutheriologie oder über Freyheit und Nothwendigkeit* (Jena: Cröker, 1788) attacked Kant's attempt at reconciling causality through freedom and natural causality. Christian Jakob Kraus (1753–1807; professor of moral and political philosophy at Königsberg, sometime student of Kant and close friend) reviewed the book anonymously in the *Allgemeine Literatur-Zeitung*, April 25, 1788, No. 100, columns 177–84. For how much Kant might have had a hand in this review, cf. AK 8:524. For Ulrich's campaign against Kant, cf. Carl Leonhard Reinhold's letter to Kant of March 1, 1788, and Kant's reply of March 7, 1788.

168 *Fables*, 2:5,1–3:

Est ardelionum quædam Romæ natio,
Trepide concursans, occupata in otio
Gratis anhelans, multa agendo nil agens.

"There is a class of busybodies at Rome, hurriedly running in concourse, employed in idleness, out of breath for no reason, doing nothing while doing many things."

169 These practices were reported by Lepechin, *Tagebuch der Reise durch verschiedene Provinzen des Russischen Reiches*, 1776, 1, p. 280 *(Diary of a Voyage through Various Provinces of the Russian Empire)*, and by P. S. Pallas, *Reise durch verschiedenen Provinzen des Russischen Reiches*, 1771, 1, p. 354 *(A Voyage through Various Provinces of the Russian Empire)*. Cited after Bohatec, p. 510, note 6a.

170 "The wind bloweth where it listeth, and thou hearest the sound thereof, but canst not tell whence it cometh, and whither it goeth: so is every one that is born of the Spirit." John 3:8.

171 The Tunguses were a people of Siberia; the Wogulites, a Finnish people living in the Urals. According to Bohatec (p. 516, notes 24–25), Kant derived his knowledge of shamanism, and of the customs of such peoples as the Tunguses and the Wogulites (including their cult of the bear), from the works of J. G. Georgi, *Bemerkung einer Reise im Russischen Reich*, 1775 *(Report of a Voyage in the Russian Empire)*, *Beschreibung aller Nationen des Russischen Reiches*, 1776 *(Description of All the Nations of the Russian Empire)*, and from J. G. Gmelin, *Reisen durch Sibirien*, 1751 *(Voyages through Siberia)*.

172 The "Independents" were a Christian sect founded by John Robinson in 1610.

173 "For my yoke is easy, and my burden is light." Matthew 11:30.

174 "For this is the love of God, that we keep his commandments: and his commandments are not grievous." I John 5:3.

175 "For ye see your calling, brethren, how that not many wise men after the flesh, not many mighty, not many noble, are called." I Corinthians 1:26.

176 "But God hath chosen the foolish things of the world to confound the wise; and God hath chosen the weak things of the world to confound the things which are mighty." I Corinthians 1:27.

177 *Epistles*, 1:18. The saying is cited totally out of context. Pliny is writing to a client who wishes to postpone a court hearing because of a menacing

dream. After encouraging him to give the dream a good interpretation, as he had once done himself to a dream that had frightened him, Pliny goes on: "See then if you can follow my example, and give a happy interpretation to your dream; but if you still think there is more safety in the warning given by all cautious folk, 'When in doubt do nothing,' you can write and tell me." Tr. Betty Radice (Cambridge: Harvard, 1969), p. 55.

178   The thesis of probabilism was defined in 1577 by the Salamancan Dominican Bartolomeo de Medina with the now classical formula: "Si est opinio probabilis, licitum est eam sequi, licet opposita est probabilior." ("It is legitimate to follow a probable opinion even if there is an opposite and more probable one.") Cf. AK 6:506. The original intention of this moral doctrine was to prevent the proliferation of obligations by limiting their basis to laws of undoubted authority. The doctrine was especially favored by the Jesuit moralists but bitterly opposed by the Jansenists. Pascal satirized its abuses in *Lettres provinciales*, § 5 ff. Cf. *Œuvres complètes*, ed. Louis Lafuma (Paris: Aux editions du seuil, 1963), pp. 387 ff.

179   "And the Lord said unto the servant, Go out into the highways and hedges, and compel them to come in, that my house may be filled." Luke 14:23. The Gospel injunction, "compel them to come in," was used by Augustine as proof of the state's obligation to use force agains idolaters, heretics, and schismatics. Cf. *Epistles* Nos. 93 and 95. AK 6:506.

180   Genesis 22.

181   Cf. above, p. 6:173 (of Kant's text) and Kant's note.

182   A "hadji" is one who has undertaken the pilgrimage to Mecca (the "hadj"). Bohatec tried in vain to locate Kant's source for this proverb (p. 519, note 35a).

183   "And straightway the father of the child cried out, and said with tears, Lord, I believe, help thou mine unbelief." Mark 9:24.

184   Cf. Ovid, *Metamorphoses*, I, 128–55:
Last came the race of iron. In that hard age
Of baser vein all evil straight broke out . . .
Honour and love lay vanquished, and from earth,
With slaughter soaked, Justice, virgin divine,
The last of the immortals, fled away.
   Tr. A. D. Melville (Oxford: Oxford University Press, 1986), p. 5.
Astræa, daughter of Jupiter, was often considered the goddess of justice like her mother Themis.

185   "Pray without ceasing." I Thessalonians 5:17.

186   Ephesians 2:15–21.

187   "And Jesus said unto them. . . . If ye have faith as a grain of mustard seed, ye shall say unto this mountain, Remove hence to yonder place; and it shall remove; and nothing shall be impossible unto you." Matthew 17:20; cf. Luke 17:6.

188   The authorship of many psalms is traditionally attributed to King David.

189   "Having abolished in his flesh the enmity . . . to make in himself of twain one new man, so making peace. . . . Now therefore ye are no more strangers and foreigners, but fellow citizens with the saints, and of the household of God; And are built upon the foundation of the apostles and prophets,

Jesus Christ himself being the chief corner stone; In whom all the building fitly framed together groweth unto an holy temple in the Lord." Ephesians 2:15–21.

190   The reference is probably to the story of Amphion and Zethus, twin sons of Zeus by Antiope. The two brothers slew Lycus, the commander in chief of the Theban army who had maltreated their mother, and thereupon gained sovereignty over the city. They then began to fortify it. According to the story, Amphion walked around the city playing his lyre, and at its sound stones began to gather on their own accord until a wall rose. Cf. Apollodorus, *The Library*, 3.5.

191   Exodus 20:4.

192   "Not every one that saith unto me, Lord, Lord, shall enter into the kingdom of heaven; but he that doeth the will of my Father which is in heaven." Matthew 7:21.

193   "Neither do men light a candle, and put it under a bushel, but on a candlestick; and it giveth light unto all that are in the house." Matthew 5:15.

The end of all things

1   Victor Albrecht von Haller, *Imperfect Poem on Eternity* (1736). See *Hallers Gedichte*, edited by Ludwig Hirzel (Bibliothek alterer Schriftwerke der deutschen Schweitz, 1882), Volume 3, p. 151. cf. *Critique of Pure Reason* A613/B641 and AK 2:40.

2   "And the stars of heaven fell to earth, as a fig tree drops its late figs when it is shaken by a mighty wind. Then the sky receded, as a scroll when it is rolled up" (Rev. 6:13–14).

3   "Then death and Hades were cast into a lake of fire. This is the second death. And anyone not found written in the Book of Life was cast into the lake of fire. And I saw a new heaven and a new earth, for the first heaven and the first earth had passed away" (Rev. 20:14–21:1).

4   Pierre Sonnerat (1749–1814), French naturalist and traveler. Kant is referring to the German edition of his *Travels to East-India and China Undertaken by Royal Command from 1774 to 1781* (Zurich, 1783), in two volumes. In Volume 2, pp. 38ff., "Godeman" is mentioned as one of the gods of the Papuans and Burmese.

5   Cf. 2 Kings 2:11: "Then it happened, as they [Elijah and Elisha] continued on and talked, that suddenly a chariot of fire appeared with horses of fire, and separated the two of them; and Elijah went up by a whirlwind into heaven."

6   Cf. Numbers 16:32: "And the earth opened its mouth and swallowed them up, with their households and all the men with Korah, with all their goods."

7   The King James version reads: "And the angel whom I saw standing on the sea and on the land lifted up his hand to heaven and swore by him who lives forever and ever, who created heaven and the things that are in it, the earth and the things that are in it, and the sea and the things that are in it, that there should be delay no longer" (Rev. 10:5–6).

8　Presumably a reference to the Chinese philosopher Lao-Tsu (c. 600–531 B.C.), founder of Taoism, to whom the *Tao Te Ching* is attributed.

9　This paragraph alludes to a German translation of writings by the French Jesuit Gabriel F. Coyer (1707–82), *Moralische Kleinigkeiten* (Berlin, 1761). Cf. AK 7:83.

10　Matthew 5:12.

Index

Index

Galileo, 37
Gedike, F., 208
Genghis Khan, 21
Georgius, A. A., 117, 214, 220
Gmelin, J. G., 220
God: adoration of, 176, 189; author of
    the world, 17–20, 26; benevolence,
    19, 205; cause of the world, 153;
    concept of, 8–13, 18, 19, 24, 110,
    155, 165, 176, 178, 186; creator of
    the world, 17–21, 24, 26, 30;
    existence of, vii–viii, 35–6;
    experience of, x; fear of, 176;
    goodness, xxx, 19, 20–1; governor
    of the world, 18, 23, 94–5, 111,
    128, 137, 142; holiness, 19–20,
    infinity, 11; judge, 28, 45, 85, 87,
    93, 90–1, 94, 127, 142, 147, 159,
    187; justice of, 19, 21–3, 25, 26,
    89–93, 144, 190, 196–201, kingdom
    of, 85, 89, 105, 106, 111, 122, 128,
    135, 137, 139, 151, 158, 172, 184,
    186, 187, 189; love, 80, 126, 146;
    moral predicates, 19, 141–2;
    people of, 109–11; pleasing to, 68,
    72, 80–9, 91–2, 96, 99, 114–15,
    122–6, 133, 136, 143–4, 157,
    166–73, 179, 187–8; reverence for,
    176; servile worship of, 171; union
    with, 202; will, 19, 24–5, 111–14,
    126, 131, 143, 145, 172, 179;
    wisdom, 18, 23, 26, 187, 200, 202–3
God, Son of, 80, 84, 90–1, 144, 146–7,
    211
God, Trinity, 143–5, 217
God-man, 125
Goeze, J. M., 213
good, highest, viii, xxxviii
good principle, 79–81; victory of, 105–29
Gospel, 132, 137, 159, 186, 191
grace, xxi–xxv, 72–3, 88–93, 125, 144,
    169; effects of, 65–73; means of,
    182–91
Greece, 146, 189
Green, R. M., xxxvii
Greene, T. M., xxxvi, 38
guilt, xii, xv–xvii, 22, 60, 88–93; see also
    accountability; evil

hadji, 182, 221
Haller, V. A., 195, 211, 222
happiness (Glückseligkeit), viii, xvi,
    21–2, 34–6, 45, 59, 66–7, 71, 78,
    80, 85, 87, 91, 122, 137–8, 141,
    159; moral and physical, 85

Harz Mountains, 30
Hearne, S., 56, 209
Heilmann, J. D., 209
Hercules, 48
heretic, 117
hierarchy, 112
highest good, 14, 201
Hinduism, 90, 139, 142, 177
history, xxv–xxvi, xxxvii, 214
Hobbes, T., 108, 213
holiness, xxiv, 19, 36, 67–9, 80, 83–4,
    97, 126, 135, 137, 143–4, 145,
    157–8, 177–8, 183, 189–90; see also
    God, holiness
hope, xxv–xxvii, 64, 68, 71, 80, 86–8,
    91–2, 96, 106, 112, 122–6, 137,
    145, 151, 158–60, 167, 169, 173,
    176, 178, 189–90
Horace, 45, 55, 64, 199
Hudson, H. H., 38
humanity: predisposition, 48, 97,
    153–4, 168, 176–7; prototype of,
    80–1, 146; well-pleasing to God,
    80, 84, 125, 133

idolatry, 165, 178, 188–9
ill (Übel), 18–20, 22, 25, 90–1
illumination, 72, 98, 113
immortality, viii, xviii, xxv–xxvii, 28,
    86, 93, 131, 138, 155
impurity, of will, 53–4
incentive (Triebfeder), 33, 35–6, 47–55,
    59–60, 77–8, 81, 86, 95, 102, 112,
    118, 120, 125, 158–60, 187
incongruous counterparts, 5–6
Independents, the, 220
India, 45, 90, 119, 139, 142, 177, 198,
    214–15
indifferentists, 48, 208
innocence, 62–4, 70, 95
inquisitor, 179–80
inspiration, 112, 115, 119, 145
instinct, 54–5, 95
Islam, 177, 185, 221
Ith, J. 208, 214

Jachmann, R. B., xxxv
Jacobi, F. H., xxxiii, xxxviii, 4, 11, 206,
    215, 217–19
Jansenism, 221
Jesuits, 221
Jesus Christ, xxiii–xxiv, 79–84, 96,
    125–6, 132–3, 137–8, 142,
    203–4
Job, 25–7

226

Cambridge texts in the history of philosophy

Titles published in the series thus far

Antoine Arnauld and Pierre Nicole *Logic or the Art of Thinking* (edited by Jill Vance Buroker)

Boyle *A Free Enquiry into the Vulgarly Received Notion of Nature* (edited by Edward B. Davis and Michael Hunter)

Bruno *Cause, Principle and Unity* and *Essays on Magic* (edited by Richard Blackwell and Robert de Lucca with an introduction by Alfonso Ingegno)

Clarke *A Demonstration of the Being and Attributes of God and Other Writings* (edited by Ezio Vailati)

Conway *The Principles of the Most Ancient and Modern Philosophy* (edited by Allison P. Coudert and Taylor Corse)

Cudworth *A Treatise Concerning Eternal and Immutable Morality* with *A Treatise of Freewill* (edited by Sarah Hutton)

Descartes *Meditations on First Philosophy*, with selections from the *Objections and Replies* (edited with an introduction by John Cottingham)

Descartes *The World and Other Writings* (edited by Stephen Gaukroger)

Kant *Critique of Practical Reason* (edited by Mary Gregor with an introduction by Andrews Reath)

Kant *Groundwork of the Metaphysics of Morals* (edited by Mary Gregor with an introduction by Christine M. Korsgaard)

Kant *The Metaphysics of Morals* (edited by Mary Gregor with an introduction by Roger Sullivan)

Kant *Prolegomena to any Future Metaphysics* (edited by Gary Hatfield)

Kant *Religion within the Boundaries of Mere Reason and Other Writings* (edited by Allen Wood and George di Giovanni with an introduction by Robert Merrihew Adams)

La Mettrie *Machine Man and Other Writings* (edited by Ann Thomson)

Leibniz *New Essays on Human Understanding* (edited by Peter Remnant and Jonathan Bennett)

Malebranche *Dialogues on Metaphysics and on Religion* (edited by Nicholas Jolley and David Scott)

Malebranche *The Search after Truth* (edited by Thomas M. Lennon and Paul J. Olscamp)

Mendelssohn *Philosophical Writings* (edited by Daniel O. Dahlstrom)

Nietzsche *Daybreak* (edited by Maudemarie Clark and Brian Leiter, translated by R. J. Hollingdale)

Nietzsche *Human, all too Human* (translated by R. J. Hollingdale with an introduction by Richard Schacht)

Nietzsche *Untimely Meditations* (edited by Daniel Breazeale, translated by R. J. Hollingdale)

Schleiermacher *Hermeneutics and Criticism* (edited by Andrew Bowie)

Schleiermacher *On Religion: Speeches to its Cultured Despisers* (edited by Richard Crouter)